Blockchain for Financial Governance in Malaysia and Singapore

Ming Sen Thong

Blockchain for Financial Governance in Malaysia and Singapore

Transforming Regulatory and Shariah Compliance to Drive Financial Inclusion

palgrave
macmillan

Ming Sen Thong
Faculty of Law
Universiti Malaya
Kuala Lumpur, Malaysia

ISBN 978-981-96-1283-3 ISBN 978-981-96-1281-9 (eBook)
https://doi.org/10.1007/978-981-96-1281-9

This Palgrave Macmillan imprint is published by the registered company Springer Nature Singapore Pte Ltd.
The registered company address is: 152 Beach Road, #21-01/04 Gateway East, Singapore 189721, Singapore

Contents

About the Author

Dr. Ming Sen Thong is an Advocate and Solicitor of the High Court of Malaya who was called to the Malaysian Bar in 2014. As a corporate legal practitioner during his tenure with a top-tier law firm in Malaysia, he worked on a wide range of legal matters including corporate restructuring, capital markets regulatory compliance, and stock market listings. Besides corporate law, his expertise also includes blockchain technology and FinTech regulation.

As an ex-Legal500 rising star–turned-Web3 aficionado, Dr. Thong was part of a team of researchers who were the first to report on regulatory issues in the blockchain space in Malaysia. Since then, he has been using his blockchain knowledge to assist a string of leading Web3 companies with their content strategization for Web3 education and mass adoption.

Dr. Thong holds an LLB (Hons) from the University of London, a Master of Laws (LLM) (Distinction), and a Doctor of Philosophy (PhD) in law from Universiti Malaya.

Abbreviations

AML	Anti-money Laundering
BNM	Bank Negara Malaysia
CBDC	Central Bank Digital Currency
CDD	Customer Due Diligence
CEX	Centralized Exchanges
DAICO	Decentralized Autonomous Initial Coin Offering
DAO	Decentralized Autonomous Organization
DEX	Decentralized Exchange
DEFI	Decentralized Finance
DPOS	Delegated Proof of Stake
E2EE	End-to-End Encryption
EKYC	Electronic Know-Your-Customer
ERC	Ethereum Request for Comment
HDD	Hard Disk Drive
HSM	Hardware Security Module
HTTPS	Hypertext Transfer Protocol Secure
IAS	International Accounting Standards
ICO	Initial Coin Offering
IDO	Initial Decentralized Offering
IEO	Initial Exchange Offering
IFRS	International Financial Reporting Standards
IIMM	Islamic Interbank Money Market
ISF	Islamic Social Finance
KYC	Know-Your-Customer
M-CBDC	Multi-Central Bank Digital Currency
MAS	Monetary Authority of Singapore
MBS	Mortgage-Backed Securities

MIFID	Markets in Financial Instruments Directive
P2P	Peer-to-Peer
PBFT	Practical Byzantine Fault Tolerance
POA	Proof of Authority
POACT	Proof of Action
POB	Proof of Burn
POC	Proof of Concept
POET	Proof of Elapsed Time
POI	Proof of Importance
POS	Proof of Stake
POW	Proof of Work
RTXP	Ripple Transaction Protocol
SEA	South East Asia
SHA	Secure Hashing Algorithm
SPOF	Single Point of Failure
SROI	Social Return on Investment
SSE	Social Solidarity Economy
SSF	Social Solidarity Finance
STO	Security Token Offering
STR	Secure Transaction Reporting
TTP	Trusted Third Party
ZK-SNARK	Zero-Knowledge Succinct Non-interactive Argument of Knowledge

CHAPTER 1

To Know Blockchain Is to Know Web3

Abstract Blockchain is a distributed digital ledger system that has evolved through first- and second-generation networks, leading to the rise of cryptocurrency and smart contracts. Cryptocurrency has enabled fundraising mechanisms like initial coin offerings (ICOs) and security token offerings (STOs) whereas smart contracts offer the potential to transform traditional legal frameworks. Blockchain networks are customizable, allowing operators to choose privacy and accessibility levels. Consensus mechanisms allow users to commit to networks, with different models suited to various blockchain features. The trustless nature of blockchain makes it an ideal technology for fostering public trust in financial institutions. The socio-economic benefits of blockchain include enhancing social solidarity through decentralization, as advocated by Adam Smith, and reducing transaction costs by curbing opportunistic behaviors in contracts. However, for blockchain to realize its full potential, it must challenge existing systemic forces through Schumpeter's concept of creative destruction, reaching a tipping point for mass adoption and promoting financial inclusion.

M. S. Thong, *Blockchain for Financial Governance in Malaysia and Singapore*,
https://doi.org/10.1007/978-981-96-1281-9_1

1.1 Understanding the Technological Roots of Web3 by Tracing the Genesis of Blockchain

Blockchain is the technology that powers Web3, the iteration of the decentralized Internet that has already made its mark through decentralized applications (dApps) and decentralized finance (DeFi). Safe to say, Web3 is the key to unlocking the future of the Internet but as George Orwell once said, "he who controls the past controls the future." Hence, to understand Web3 as the future of the Internet, we are going back to the start by tracing the genesis of the technology that powers Web3, blockchain. In a way, blockchain is a technological reinvention of an old system, i.e., that of ledger records which have been in use since the times of the Venetian Republic back in the fifteenth century (Davidson et al., 2016).

Although digital ledgers were already in use by the late twentieth century, their use in a centralized manner resulted in issues of high costs in addition to the risks of misuse and abuse. These risks arose due to a lack of transparency common to centralized systems. In essence, the issues arose due to trust deficits whereby blockchain comes in to offer its decentralization solution to transform ledger records systems into what is colloquially known as "trust machines" that can remedy the existing systemic trust deficits by warranting the accuracy and integrity of information in the distributed ledger records by ensuring that the maintenance of the records, as well as the operations of the underlying networks, are not dependent on any centralized authority (De Fillipi et al., 2020).

The developmental roots of blockchain can be traced back to 1991 when Stuart Haber and Scott Stornetta laid down the foundations for cryptography by devising the concept of timestamping to prevent unauthorized tampering of documents (Haber & Stornetta, 1991). The following year they upgraded their cryptographic system by incorporating the use of the Merkle tree to enhance the efficiency of the system by utilizing the branching factor of two to summarize and verify large amounts of data efficiently through the use of progressive calculations that were computed in reliance on data stored in other hashes (Bayer et al., 1992). Six years later, Leslie Lamport, in his paper titled "The Part-Time Parliament," espoused the Paxos protocol which sets out the foundations for the consensus mechanisms of blockchain networks through the establishment of a consensus model that would facilitate a network of computers to reach an agreement where the circumstances are such that the network is unreliable or the computers are not infallible (Lamport, 1998).

Fast-forward to 2008, Satoshi Nakamoto, in a whitepaper titled "Bitcoin: A Peer-to-Peer Electronic Cash System," combined the concept of cryptographic timestamping with the use of the Paxos protocol to support the operations of electronic cash payment networks (Nakamoto, 2008). In this regard, it is notable that there were electronic cash payment systems that preceded the Bitcoin network, albeit Bitcoin is a pioneer as it is the first to utilize blockchain as the underlying technology. The use of blockchain enabled Bitcoin to break new grounds and venture into uncharted territories as the first decentralized and automated payment network which is equipped with self-policing features in the form of its in-built consensus mechanisms. Additionally, Bitcoin is also the first pseudo-anonymous payment system whereby the use of blockchain-based networks enables Bitcoin users to hide their identities from public view through the use of a pseudonym as their digital wallet identifier, though it should be noted that the identifier does not warrant total anonymity as it can be traced to the identity of the wallet holder.

1.1.1 Blockchain, the Technological Enabler that Makes Web3 Possible

Without blockchain, Web3 would have been a mere pipe dream. As blockchain is the technological enabler of Web3, it would not be possible to understand how Web3 operates without an understanding of blockchain. From a technological architectural perspective, blockchain is a network of data structures comprising blocks of information that are chained together by hashes which grant the feature of immutability to blockchain records by rendering it impossible for these records to be tampered with without invalidating the connecting hashes (Efanov & Roschin, 2018). The first generation of blockchain networks supported the functions of Bitcoin by facilitating the storage of cryptographically secured data of transactions in public ledgers which are accessible by the nodes of the network (Anwar et al., 2020).

Subsequently, the use of the blockchain-based distributed ledger records for the verification of information was expanded to cover their use as a trustless mechanism to facilitate the making of transactions, particularly financial ones between different parties. In this regard, it is notable that, unlike conventional networks, there is no central authority imbued with controlling powers under blockchain networks but instead the trustless mechanism of these networks is warranted by the use of cryptography to secure the integrity of transactions as validated by cryptographic keys of the transacting parties.

After the cryptographic validation of a proposed transaction by the initiating party, a smart contract is created and the data concerning the transaction would be sent to the designated node on the blockchain network which will verify the transaction. A verified transaction would then be forwarded to every participating node in the network under a process known as flooding which functions as a core tenet that supports the use of blockchain networks as trustless mechanisms. Following thereon, the block containing the information of the verified transaction will be added to the chain upon the reaching of a consensus among the participating nodes for the acceptance of the transaction as being valid in principle.

Two major limitations of the first generation of blockchain networks are their limited programming flexibility and data storage capacity. With the advent of second-generation blockchain networks, the limitations of first-generation networks were addressed through the inclusion in the technological architecture of a programmable infrastructure supported by public ledgers which can support the storage of vast amounts of cryptographic data (Fernandez-Caramez & Fragas-Lamas, 2018). The introduction of a programmable infrastructure that can accommodate the use of blockchain for a myriad of applications beyond the realm of the financial domain opens the door for the use of smart contracts that rely on computer programming logic for the execution of non-financial transactions with Ethereum standing out for its functions as a general purpose open-source programmable smart contract platform.

1.1.2 Blockchain, the Technological Ancestor of Crypto's Grandfather, Bitcoin

Blockchain is the foundational technology behind cryptocurrencies, serving as a decentralized and transparent ledger that records all transactions across a network. Each transaction is grouped into a "block," which is then linked to the previous one, forming a continuous "chain." This structure ensures that once a transaction is recorded, it cannot be altered or deleted, providing security and trust. For cryptocurrencies, blockchain plays a crucial role in ensuring that transactions are transparent, verifiable, and resistant to fraud. Since the blockchain is maintained by a network of nodes (computers) rather than a single central authority, it supports the decentralized nature of cryptocurrencies, allowing peer-to-peer transactions without intermediaries like banks. This decentralization also means that the blockchain is resilient to attacks or failures, as there is no single point of vulnerability. Additionally, blockchain's transparency allows anyone in the network to verify transactions, fostering a high level of trust and reliability in the system.

Thanks to blockchain, cryptocurrency was developed as a subset of digital currency under the concept of electronic money which dates to the late 1980s (Grinberg, 2012). Nonetheless, contrary to popular belief Bitcoin was not the first cryptocurrency as this honor belongs to eCash, which though employed cryptographic protocols did not employ the use of blockchain, i.e., it operated using a centralized system, albeit one which warranted anonymity to its users through the use of blind signatures that renders transactions to be untraceable (Tewari & Hughes, 2016). Although the company failed to take off, eCash's operational framework laid down the building blocks which were eventually built upon by the highly mysterious Satoshi Nakamoto to devise the Bitcoin payment model which gave rise to the cryptocurrency revolution. Notwithstanding the existence of eCash as the pioneer cryptocurrency, Bitcoin is arguably the first when it comes to the use of blockchain to support the operational framework of a cryptocurrency.

While Bitcoin may not have been pioneering cryptocurrency, the cryptocurrency revolution did stem from the launch of Bitcoin in 2009 whereby this timing could not have been better as it followed the implosion of the 2008 global financial crisis which was caused by the deregulation of the financial market which led to excessive risk-taking by banks. It was in this context that Bitcoin came in to offer a peer-to-peer (P2P) payment network through which transactions can be undertaken without the need for an intermediary, thereby providing an alternative for those who find it difficult to repose trust in conventional financial institutions such as banks.

Operating using a blockchain-based network, Bitcoin leverages decentralization by distributing the responsibility for the verification of transactions undertaken through its network to the nodes of the network. Firstly, transactions that are proposed to be undertaken are recorded in public ledgers before they are verified by the selected nodes of the network. Thereafter the relevant payment transfer will be executed under the transactions after which it will be broadcasted to all the nodes of the network before the block of information containing the details of the transaction is committed to the chain of the network. The rise of Bitcoin is illustrated by the astronomical increase in its market value which traded below USD1 per coin on the date of its launch, i.e., 3 January 2009, but has since multiplied by tens of thousands of times.

Given the astronomical price rise of Bitcoin, it is unsurprising to note that countless other cryptocurrencies have tried to follow the revolutionary path chartered by the legendary cryptocurrency leading to the birth of the term "altcoin" which refers to a group constituted by all cryptocurrencies except Bitcoin itself. In a way, the increasing number of altcoins serves to illustrate that there is room for improvements in the operations of Bitcoin as altcoins endeavor to fill the gaps in the cryptocurrency market that are left uncovered by Bitcoin. The growth of the cryptocurrency market driven by altcoins as well as Bitcoin itself is supported by the fact that Bitcoin's code is an open source, i.e., the code is accessible from the public repository GitHub and therefore available for public use (Gervais & Karame, 2014).

In this regard, it is notable that Bitcoin belongs to the category of fungible tokens, particularly the sub-category of payment tokens which can be exchanged for goods and services whereby there are two other subcategories of fungible tokens, namely, utility and security tokens (Luis et al., 2018). Utility tokens are somewhat similar to payment tokens in that they are exchangeable for goods and services, albeit subject to the limitation that the exchanged goods and services are provided by the issuer in contrast with payment tokens whereby the exchanged goods and services are generally provided by third parties. As for security tokens, they constitute investment instruments that can be traded for profits in an open market. In addition to fungible tokens, there are also non-fungible tokens which consist of tokens with unique features that allow them to be used for the certification of instruments or verification of identities. The use of fungible tokens to identify objects renders these tokens to be particularly suited to be deployed in connection with the Internet of Things (IoT)-related functionalities.

A particular phenomenon that has been driven by the rise of Bitcoin is that of crypto offerings which are public fundraising projects undertaken through the issuance of cryptocurrencies. Crypto offering started with ICO (initial coin offering), which involves the proprietors of projects publishing whitepapers that set out the blueprint for their projects before proceeding to issue cryptocurrencies that can be purchased by investors whereby the funds will be used for implementing the underlying project (Investopedia, 2020). However, the popularity of ICO resulted in it being hijacked by fraudsters, resulting in a situation whereby an estimated 80% of ICO launches were fraudulent scams (CoinTelegraph, 2018). It was against this contextual background that the crypto industry devised a solution in the form of initial exchange offering (IEO) which involves cryptocurrency exchanges undertaking the role of monitoring watchdogs by screening proposed ICOs for their authenticity and legitimacy before hosting such offerings on their exchanges.

Besides ICO and IEO, there is also STO which is essentially an ICO involving the issuance of security tokens, i.e., cryptocurrencies that fulfill the generally established criteria for securities, i.e., entails the investment of money under a common enterprise where there is an expectation of profits derived solely from the efforts of the promoter or a third party (SEC v. W. J. Howey Co, 1946). In this regard, it is notable that each form of crypto offering has its disadvantages. For ICO, there is the issue of risks arising from the high prevalence of fraud and vagueness as discussed above. As for IEO, there is the obstacle of high listing fees charged by hosting exchanges, particularly for well-known and reputable exchanges which can charge up to 20 BTC in addition to commission (CryptoPotato, 2020). As for STO, the fact that cryptocurrencies issued under this form of offering have the features of securities renders them subject to capital market regulations under most jurisdictions (Mendelson, 2019).

1.1.3 Making the Internet Smart Through the Decentralized Automation of Smart Contracts

Smart contracts are self-executing contracts with the terms of the agreement directly written into code. In the context of Web3, smart contracts play a critical role as self-executing contracts with the terms of the agreement directly written into codes to enable dApps to operate autonomously without the need for intermediaries. Smart contracts automatically enforce rules, trigger actions, and manage the exchange of assets, such as cryptocurrency or digital tokens, based on predefined conditions. Once deployed on a blockchain, smart contracts execute transparently and are immutable, meaning they cannot be altered, ensuring trust and reducing the risk of fraud. This automation enhances efficiency and lowers costs, as processes like payments, voting, and data exchange are conducted without human intervention. Additionally, smart contracts contribute to the decentralized nature of Web3 by allowing users to interact directly with protocols, creating a more secure and user-driven internet.

Analogically, smart contracts are akin to computer programs that can be used to execute the terms of a contract in an automated manner. Conceptually, the idea of smart contracts is similar to that of vending machines whose earliest documented use arose from the work of Hero of Alexandria, who was a Greek engineer-cum-mathematician who lived sometime around 215 BC. Alexandria's invention took the form of a machine that dispensed holy water derived from Egyptian temples in return for the insertion of coins into the machine whereby this machine was the first documented use of the concept of vending machine (Lan, 2015). In his seminal paper titled "The Idea of Smart Contracts," which was published in 1997, Nick Szabo, who was an American computer scientist, took the concept of vending machines to a whole new level by using it as the framework for the idea of smart contracts which aim to facilitate the transfer of proprietary ownership in an automated manner upon the fulfillment of the prescribed conditions, though the level of technological infrastructure development back then rendered Szabo's conception of smart contracts to be very much a utopian dream (Szabo, 1997).

Fast-forward to 2024 however, the level of technological development renders Szabo's conception of smart contracts to be plausible in reality with the idea of smart contracts gaining traction through the promise of cost-efficient transactions that can be undertaken without the need for any intermediary. However, at this juncture of its development the mainstream use of smart contracts would need to overcome a host of issues not least of which are those on the legal recognition of such contracts whereby addressing this issue would be crucial if smart contracts are to fulfill its promise of paving the way for the wide use of cross-border digital contracts (Herian, 2018). Besides that, given the fact that the operations of smart contracts are intrinsically tied to empirical conditions and real-life events another issue that stands in the way of the mainstream use of these contracts is that of a lack of reliable off-chain data feeds, i.e., oracles (Al-Breiki et al., 2020).

The issue in this regard relates to the critical need for smart contracts for reliable and trustworthy oracles to support its autonomous protocols which are tasked with monitoring and enforcing contractual obligations. In other words, the automated feature of smart contracts relies heavily on there being reliable and trustworthy oracles failing which these contracts would not be able to enforce themselves in a proper and timely manner. The general industry practice of relying on HTTPS connections to access data sourced from trustworthy websites operated by reputable parties does not fit the needs of smart contracts which may lack network access (Muhlberger et al., 2020). In any event, digital signatures are not available under HTTPS connections, thereby rendering the data sourced from these connections to be unable to fulfill the requirements of smart contracts.

The operational frameworks of smart contracts are such that they are built on top of blockchain platforms with Ethereum being the most popular choice, though there are other options available such as NEM and IBM's Hyperledger Fabric. Ethereum-based smart contracts have greater programming flexibilities when it comes to leveraging cryptocurrencies to facilitate the enforcement of contractual terms as these contracts facilitate the execution of the necessary payments as per the contractual terms in an automated manner upon the occurrence of the specified events or fulfillment of the prescribed conditions.

Nonetheless, the role of cryptography in smart contract systems goes further than cryptocurrencies as transactions undertaken through smart contracts are screened using cryptographic techniques to warrant their authenticity and legitimacy. After the cryptographic validation of the underlying transactions through the relevant consensus mechanism of the network, the details of the transactions are encoded into algorithms before the block of relevant information is added to the chain before being timestamped to warrant their accuracy and immutability (Allam, 2018). In terms of the critical element of finality, which is a highly valued feature of commercial transactions, smart contracts certainly come in handy as they provide the element of absolute finality.

This is because once the details of the underlying transactions connected to a particular smart contract have been encoded and committed to the blockchain network, it would be undertaken in fulfillment of the programmed instructions in an automated manner, i.e., without the need for any intervention. It would not be possible to interrupt the operations of the smart contract whether by making any changes to it or to stop it altogether. The element of absolute finality warranted by smart contracts renders them to be particularly suited to be used for speculative transactions, i.e., under circumstances where the contractual outcome would be dependent on external conditions such as market developments etc. Given the absolute finality of smart contracts, it is imperative that the contracting parties thoroughly discuss and properly consider their options and decisions before encoding their transaction in the form of a smart contract as there is no way back once this is done.

1.2 Making Web3 Possible with Blockchain

Web3 leverages the features of decentralization, accuracy, and immutability provided by blockchain technology to create a more secure, transparent, and user-centric internet. Decentralization in Web3 means that control is distributed across a network of nodes rather than being concentrated in a single entity, empowering users with greater control over their data, identity, and digital assets. This shift reduces the risk of censorship, data breaches, and monopolistic control, as no single party has overarching authority. The resulting data transparency and immutability foster trust among users, as they can be confident that the information and transactions, they engage with are accurate and free from manipulation.

Zooming into the decentralized features of blockchain which supports Web3 as a decentralized Internet, a blockchain network is a decentralized system that leverages cryptography for the recording and storage of information in shared ledger records whereby the nodes of the network would validate the information stored in the blocks which are added to the network's chain in a linear and chronological order (Sultan et al., 2018). As every node of the network, i.e., the computers through which participants access the network, would have a copy of the whole set of blockchain records, this warrants the trustless nature of blockchain. The self-verifying nature of the information stored on blockchain-based shared ledger records renders the technology particularly suited for use in the context of financial transactions whereby parties generally have to resort to the services of intermediaries to procure the requisite degree of trust before entering into a transaction. Conceptually, the decentralized feature of blockchain allows it to function as an application layer on top of existing internet protocols thereby opening up a whole new dimension of possibilities for digital transactions by remedying the issue of trust deficits which stands in the way of the full-scale use of digital transactions.

Regarding the accuracy of blockchain networks which supports the transparency of Web3, the information that is added to the blocks of a chain is validated through the cryptographic hashing mechanism that utilizes the concept of timestamping to warrant that the information has not been improperly altered (Gao & Nobuhara, 2017). As for immutability, this is warranted by the fact that information stored in blockchain-based ledger records is shared with all the nodes of the network whereby this effectively protects the information against unauthorized alterations. This is because any unauthorized alteration of information would need to replicate across every copy of the information held by the nodes of the network whereby this would be a practical impossibility, particularly in the context of public blockchains.

How the immutability of blockchain networks supports the user-centricity of Web3 is warranted by the fact that the information stored in blockchain-based ledger records is validated by the cryptographic hashing mechanism whereby the use of timestamping would result in any unauthorized alteration, however small, to bring about a ripple effect across the network, eventually culminating in a major change which would be manifested under the avalanche or butterfly effect (Harish & Devi, 2018). The operator of the network would then be aware of this development and can proceed to trace the source of the effect, i.e., the source of the unauthorized alteration, before taking the necessary actions based on the network's protocols.

1.2.1 Bulldozing the Walled Gardens of Web2 with Blockchain

The centralized structure of Web2 has led to the creation of walled gardens by allowing a few major companies to dominate the internet, controlling vast amounts of data, resources, and services. In Web2, platforms such as Facebook, Google, and Amazon have centralized power by becoming the primary gateways for users to access information, communicate, and transact online. These Big Tech companies create walled gardens by locking users into their ecosystems, where data, content, and services are tightly controlled and often not interoperable with other platforms. This means that users must rely on these centralized entities for most of their online activities, from social networking to shopping, while these companies dictate the terms of service, monetize user data, and limit cross-platform functionality.

Web2's walled gardens stifle competition, reduce user freedom, and create environments where the controlling companies can prioritize their interests over those of the users. As a result, while Web2 has enabled significant growth and innovation, its centralized nature has also led to the concentration of power and control, creating barriers that prevent a truly open and interconnected Internet. All this is set to change with the dawn of Web3 which would be using blockchain-based decentralization to break down the walled gardens of Web2. The main difference between Web2 and Web3 lies in the differences between conventional centralized databases and blockchain-based decentralized databases that enable participants to independently verify information stored on the database without having to rely on a centralized authority (Mattila, 2016).

Unlike conventional centralized databases which store their records in one place, the ledger records of blockchain databases are distributed across the nodes of the network thereby ensuring that the records stored by each of the participants would be the same as those stored by the rest. While the use of other distributed ledgers that involve the duplication of records could break down the walled gardens of Web2, the use of non-blockchain-based distributed ledgers leads to a potential problem in the form of double spending, which involves the improper repetitive use of the same parcel of digital assets through the unauthorized replication of the relevant set of digital information that are copied and pasted before being sent to multiple recipients (Chohan, 2021).

Through the use of blockchain-based decentralized databases, double spending would be virtually impossible as thanks to the cryptographic encryptions of these databases, any unauthorized duplication of the digital information for a parcel of digital assets would be immediately apparent. This is because the duplicated information would be incoherent with the other information in the shared ledger records, thereby allowing any unauthorized duplication to be easily detected by the users of the network who each have a full set of information recorded in the network's distributed ledger records precisely to enable these participants to independently and effectively verify the integrity of any digital information received by them.

Additionally, the decentralized mode of information distribution under blockchain-based databases also effectively addresses the risks associated with conventional centralized databases particularly those concerning single point of failure (SPOF) whereby the risks arising from SPOF may result in the breach of the security framework of a conventional centralized database bringing about catastrophic consequences due to the massive data leak of the information stored in the database (Bodkhe et al., 2020).

1.2.2 Choosing the Right Blockchain Network for Web3 DApps

In general, blockchain networks can be categorized into public and private as well as permissioned and permissionless. Public blockchains are those which allow anyone to access the information stored in the network without having to undergo any identity verification procedure or meet any stipulated requirements whereas private blockchains are those which require users to have their identities verified or properly fulfill the prescribed criteria before being allowed to access the information stored in the network (Guegan, 2017). On the other hand, permissioned and permissionless blockchain networks are distinguished based on the extent to which they allow users to execute, write, and commit operations under the network. Permissionless blockchains are those that allow any user to execute write and commit operations under the network whereas permissioned blockchains are those that only allow authorized users to execute such operations (Helliar et al., 2020).

Given the fact that blockchain has been much touted for its transparency feature, the use of public permissionless blockchains (examples of which include Bitcoin and Ethereum) is the perfect embodiment of this feature of the technology as these blockchains allow anyone to access the information on its network as well as execute write and commit operations thereunder (Farah, 2018). Going down a step in the degree of transparency is public permissioned blockchains (an example of which is that of Sovrin's digital identity platform) which, though allows anyone to access the information on its network, only allows authorized users to execute write and commit operations under its network. At the bottom rung of the transparency ladder are private permissioned blockchains which can be categorized into consortium and enterprise blockchains based on the authorization levels required to access the information of the network as well as to execute write and commit operations under the network.

Whereas consortium blockchains (examples of which include Corda and Hyperledger) only allow authorized users to access the information of the network as well as to execute write and commit operations under the network, enterprise blockchains (an example of which is that of the IBM Food Trust supply chain tracking platform) go even further by allowing only the operator of the network to execute write and commit operations whereby access to the network's information may be allowed for authorized users, though it may also be fully private, i.e., only accessible to the network's operator (Dib et al., 2018).

Generally, the risk of malicious actors in the context of permissioned blockchains is considerably less than that in permissionless blockchains because participation in permissioned blockchains requires users to verify their identities before qualifying as an authorized user of the network (Tsai et al., 2017). In the event of any breach of the rules of the network, this may result in the revocation of authorization which may result in the non-compliant user losing the eligibility to execute write and commit operations under the network. Notwithstanding the reduced risks of malicious actors in the context of permissioned blockchains, some have questioned the departure of these blockchains particularly private ones, i.e., enterprise and consortium blockchains from the decentralization ideals of blockchain.

Nonetheless, permissioned blockchains do have a certain degree of utility, particularly in the context of the sharing of verified information in a selective manner between a group of participants. In this regard, it is notable that network operators of permissioned blockchains can configure the accessibility of information in its ledger records based on the credentials of its users thereby rendering these blockchains to be particularly useful for sharing verified information in an across-the-board manner with the level of disclosure being determined by the credentials of the user. This effectively allows organizations such as financial institutions that deal with sensitive personal information to leverage blockchain for other advantages besides those arising from decentralization without sacrificing the privacy of such information which is shared through their networks.

1.2.3 *Choosing the Right Consensus Mechanism for Web3 DApps*

Choosing the right type of decentralized consensus mechanism for Web3 functions is a critical decision that involves balancing several key considerations to ensure the security, efficiency, and scalability of a blockchain network. One of the primary considerations is the level of security needed, as consensus mechanisms like Proof of Work (PoW) and Proof of Stake (PoS) offer different levels of protection against attacks. PoW, used by Bitcoin, is highly secure but energy-intensive, while PoS, used by Ethereum 2.0, is more energy-efficient but relies on the economic stake of participants to secure the network.

Another important factor is scalability, especially as Web3 applications grow and demand higher transaction throughput. Mechanisms like Delegated Proof of Stake (DPoS) or newer alternatives like Proof of Authority (PoA) can offer faster transaction processing but may involve trade-offs in decentralization or security. Additionally, the degree of decentralization is crucial, as more decentralized mechanisms tend to be more resistant to censorship and collusion but may also be slower or less efficient. Finally, considerations around community governance, environmental impact, and long-term sustainability also play significant roles. For instance, networks focused on environmental sustainability might prioritize mechanisms with lower energy consumption, while those aiming for broad participation may favor more inclusive or democratic models. While PoW, PoS, DPoS, and PoA are the relatively more common types of consensus mechanisms, there are a few others that come with their respective pros and cons.

(a) **Proof of Activity (PoAct)**

PoAct is a consensus mechanism proposed by four persons one of which was Charlee Lee (who was the founder of Litecoin). PoA combines PoW and PoS to create a hybrid approach that aims to leverage the strong points of PoW and PoS to create a foolproof mechanism (Bentov et al., 2014). On the one hand, PoW was devised to provide safeguards against the problem of tragedy of commons which involve miners acting solely to further their self-interests whereby this issue is likely to be particularly pertinent after the 21 million issuance limit of Bitcoin has been reached. On the other hand, PoS was devised to mitigate the risks of a 51% attack by requiring potential hijackers who intend to take control of the network to expend sufficient resources to hold at least 51% of the cryptocurrency volume processed by the network whereby this is practically impossible, though anyone who can do so would be rightfully entitled to take control of the network.

PoAct first requires miners to solve cryptographic equations like PoW, albeit for a critical difference in that unlike PoW whereby the mining blocks contain transactions, the mining blocks of PoA are devoid of any transaction but merely consist of templates containing header information and reward addresses. Once the blocks are mined, the PoA consensus mechanism switches to the PoS operating model whereby the header information in the block would determine the chosen miners based on their staked amount of cryptocurrency holdings whereby a higher amount of such holdings would translate into a higher chance of being chosen. In this manner, PoA effectively combines the use of both the PoW and PoS consensus mechanisms to address the problem of the tragedy of commons and the risks of a 51% attack.

(b) **Proof of Authority (PoA)**

PoA was proposed in 2017 by Gavin Wood (who was the former Chief Technical Officer (CTO) and co-founder of Ethereum) as a consensus mechanism that allocates mining rights based on the reputation of nodes whereby the reputation levels of the nodes are ascertained based on the extent to which the legal identity of the person operating the nodes has been validated (Avasthi & Saxena, 2018). In other words, nodes that are operated by persons whose legal identities have been properly validated would have a high level of reputation and be deemed trustworthy by the network, thereby securing a greater entitlement to mining rights that correspond to their reputation levels and vice versa for nodes which are operated by persons whose legal identities have not been properly validated. In terms of its utility value,

PoA is best suited for use by companies that aim to maintain their privacy while leveraging the benefits of blockchain whereby an example of a platform that uses PoA for its operations is Microsoft Azure which provides blockchain-based solutions for private networks. Conceptually, PoA is similar to PoS whereby under a network that operates using the PoA consensus mechanism the worthiness of nodes is ascertained based on their reputation levels whereas under a network that operates using the PoS consensus mechanism the worthiness of nodes is determined by their staked cryptocurrency holdings.

(c) **Proof of Burn (PoB)**

PoB was a concept created by Iain Stewart (who is Professor of Mathematics at the University of Warwick) as a more environmentally sustainable option to PoW which consumes a high amount of electricity (Karantias et al., 2020). In contrast with PoW which requires miners to have extensive computing powers supplied by complex hardware such as application-specific integrated circuits (ASICs), PoB entails the burning of cryptocurrencies as a way of demonstrating a commitment to the network whereby this commitment is rewarded with the right to mine. In this regard, the higher the number of cryptocurrencies burnt by a miner, the greater would be the extent of the miner's commitment to the network which in turn would translate into a better chance of being selected to be the next block validator. The cryptocurrency burning process involves the sending of the cryptocurrencies to be burnt to publicly verifiable addresses that do not have private keys (i.e., eater addresses), thereby rendering the sent cryptocurrencies to be inaccessible and thereby unusable.

From a market perspective, the burning of cryptocurrencies reduces their availability, which under the economic theory of supply and demand would enhance their market value. Conceptually, PoB is similar to PoS, albeit for the fact that whereas PoS requires miners to stake their cryptocurrency holdings to demonstrate their commitment to the network, PoB goes further by requiring miners to burn their cryptocurrencies thereby enabling miners to not only show their commitment to the network but also help increase the market value of the network's cryptocurrencies as well.

(d) **Proof of Capacity (PoC)**

PoC (which is also referred to as Proof of Space [PoSpace]) was formulated by Stefan Dziembowski (who is a professor of computer science at the University of Warsaw) in 2015 as a consensus mechanism that allocates mining rights based on the extent to which miners has shown a legitimate interest in providing service to the network (Hattab & Alyaseen, 2019). Under the PoC consensus mechanism, the winning nodes are those which allocate the most substantial amount of memory or disk space to be used for operations of the network. Conceptually, PoC is similar to PoW, albeit for the fact that instead of the contribution of processing power under PoW, PoC entails the contribution of digital storage space.

(e) **Proof of Elapsed time (PoET)**

PoET, which was developed by Intel, allocates mining rights using a lottery system under which each node has equal winning chances (Chen et al., 2017). In terms of its operations, the PoET algorithm would randomly generate a wait time for each node in the network whereby every node would have to be in sleep mode for the duration of the wait time allotted to it. The winning node is the node that has been allocated with the shortest wait time as it would be the first to wake from its sleep mode and proceed to verify the transaction before adding the block of information to the chain. Conceptually, PoET is similar to PoW, albeit for the former's energy-saving features which compel participating nodes to go into sleep mode for a specified period in contrast with PoW whereby the nodes are working all the time.

(f) **Proof of Importance (PoI)**

PoI was first introduced by NEM as a consensus mechanism that allots mining rights (or as NEM calls it harvesting rights) based on the importance score of a user (He et al., 2018). Conceptually PoI aims to address the limitation of PoS which encourages users to hoard cryptocurrencies to have better chances of securing mining rights. The novelty of PoI lies in the fact that it is the first consensus mechanism that aims to grant harvesting rights based on the overall support of the user to the network whereby the calculation of importance score is based on four factors, i.e., vesting, transaction partners as well as the number and size of transactions. The vesting process is similar to PoS whereby users are required to hold a minimum of 10,000 XEM tokens (i.e., the native cryptocurrency of NEM's blockchain platform) to be eligible for consideration for the allotment of harvesting rights.

A higher volume of XEM holdings would equate to a higher importance score which in turn translates into better chances of securing harvesting rights. It is through the second, third, and fourth factors that PoI distinguishes itself from PoS and other consensus mechanisms. The second factor that is taken into consideration for the calculation of the importance score, i.e., that of transaction partners involves an assessment of the parties which users of the NEM blockchain platform are transacting with whereby transactions involving other users on the platform (i.e., intra-platform transactions) would be rewarded with higher importance score. As for the third and fourth factors of the number and size of transactions, the increase in the importance score of users of the NEM blockchain platform would be greater if they undertake more frequent and larger transactions.

(g) **Delegated Proof of Stake (DPoS)**

DPoS was developed in 2014 by Daniel Larimer (who is the co-founder of the Steem platform) as a more democratic alternative to PoS through the insertion of the additional element of voting power which is granted in proportion to the amount of cryptocurrency held by a miner (Yang et al., 2019). Although the precise mechanism of the voting system may differ for different projects, the general idea is that each user gets to put forward their proposed miners during the voting process and upon the completion of the mining process the rewards collected by the user would be shared proportionally between the user and the miners who worked on the project. In short, DPoS strives to improve upon the PoS framework by adding a layer of reputational filter in the form of a voting system that ensures that miners who can participate in the network are those who have a sufficient reputation as evidenced by the votes received by them.

(h) **Practical Byzantine Fault Tolerance (pBFT)**

pBFT was devised to address the Byzantine Generals' Problem that was conceived in 1982 as a logical dilemma to illustrate how a group of Byzantine generals may face communication issues when making decisions as to how to proceed (Chondros et al., 2012). Under the dilemma, each general supposedly has their army located in different locations around the targeted city whereby the generals need to come to a consensus for their decision as to what should be done. In other words, the Byzantine Generals' Problem refers to the problem faced by the generals in reaching a consensus as to how to proceed irrespective of whether the consensus decision is to attack, retreat, or otherwise. The generals must agree to proceed in the same way as they are required to act in unison by executing their decisions in a synchronized manner.

The key challenge of the Byzantine Generals' Problem lies in ensuring that the communication messages between the generals are effectively transmitted as this is critical to ensuring that the consensus decision is made with the participation of all the generals who would be agreeable to executing the decision. Given the distributed decision-making process of blockchain networks, the Byzantine Generals' Problem is a pertinent one as malicious nodes may stand in the way of the operations of a network by refusing to concur with the majority of the nodes. The pBFT consensus mechanism addresses the risks posed by malicious nodes in this regard by assuming the presence of such nodes in a network whereby so long as the number of these nodes does not exceed two-thirds of the total number of nodes in the network the operations of the network would not be thwarted by the malicious nodes as the support of two-thirds of nodes is sufficient to amount to consensus for the decision-making process of the network.

1.3 Laws from Selected Jurisdictions: Malaysia and Singapore

In Malaysia, the use of private keys is governed by the Digital Signature Act 1997, section 2 of which defines "digital signature" as "a transformation of a message using an asymmetric cryptosystem such that a person having the initial message and the signer's public key can accurately determine whether the transformation was created using the private key that corresponds to the signer's public key; regardless of whether the message has been altered since the transformation was made." The hacking of private keys would amount to forging a digital signature which is defined in the Digital Signature Act 1997 as "(a) to create a digital signature without the authorization of the rightful holder of the private key; or (b) to create a digital signature verifiable by a certificate listing as subscriber a person who either does not exist or does not hold the private key corresponding to the public key listed in the certificate."

As for blockchain networks, they would be regulated under the Computer Crimes Act 1997, section 2(1) which defines a "computer network" as "an interconnection of communication lines and circuits with a computer or a complex consisting of two or more interconnected computers." The carrying out of a 51% attack on a blockchain network would amount to the offence under section 4(1) of the Computer Crimes Act 1997, i.e., securing unauthorized access to a computer network to cause an event "which impairs the normal operations" of the network.

In Singapore, the use of private keys falls under section 18(1) of the Electronic Transactions Act 2010 which defines "secure electronic signature" as being "(a) unique to the person using it (b) capable of identifying such person (c) created in a manner or using a means under the sole control of the person using it, and (d) linked to the electronic record to which it relates in a manner such that if the record was changed the electronic signature would be invalidated." Section 19(2) the Electronic Transactions Act 2010 sets out the presumptions of validity of signature of private keys as it provides that "it is presumed, unless evidence to the contrary is adduced, that (a) the secure electronic signature is the signature of the person to whom it correlates, and the secure electronic signature was affixed by that person with the intention of signing or approving the electronic record."

As for blockchain networks, they would be regulated under section 2(1) of the Computer Misuse Act 1993 which defines "computer networks" as "an electronic, magnetic, optical, electrochemical, or other data

Table 1.1 Blockchain risks and cybersecurity laws in Malaysia and Singapore

Blockchain risks	*Malaysia Cybersecurity Laws*	*Singapore Cybersecurity Laws*
Hacking of private keys	Digital Signature Act 1997	Electronic Transactions Act 2010
51% attack	Computer Crimes Act 1997	Computer Misuse Act 1993

Source: Author's Own

processing device, or a group of such interconnected or related devices, performing logical, arithmetic, or storage functions, and includes any data storage facility or communications facility directly related to or operating in conjunction with such device or group of such interconnected or related devices." The carrying out of a 51% attack on a blockchain network would amount to the offense under section 6(1)(a) of the Computer Misuse Act 1993 of unauthorized use or interception of computer service by securing "access without authority to any computer to obtain, directly or indirectly, any computer service." (Table 1.1)

1.3.1 *Challenges to Blockchain Adoption in Malaysia*

According to Malaysia's National Blockchain Roadmap 2021–2025, the key main challenge to blockchain adoption in the country is a lack of regulatory certainty with 57% of organizations choosing it as a barrier to adoption. Malaysia lacks comprehensive and clear regulations specifically tailored to blockchain and cryptocurrencies. This regulatory uncertainty makes it difficult for Malaysian organizations to navigate the legal landscape and can discourage investment in blockchain projects.

The second main challenge to blockchain adoption in Malaysia is a lack of in-house capabilities, with 56% of organizations choosing it as a barrier to adoption. Blockchain technology requires a combination of skills from various fields, including computer science, cryptography, finance, and law. The tech support staff of Malaysian organizations lack the requisite cross-disciplinary skill set to use and apply blockchain technology for the operations of the organizations.

The third main challenge to blockchain adoption in Malaysia is financial challenges or inadequate funding, with 52% of organizations choosing it as a barrier to adoption. Implementing blockchain technology often requires a significant upfront investment in infrastructure, software development, and talent acquisition. The high costs required to deploy and maintain blockchain networks present a barrier for smaller businesses and startups in Malaysia who are looking to adopt blockchain.

The fourth main challenge to blockchain adoption in Malaysia is the existing legacy systems, with 50% of organizations choosing it as a barrier to adoption. Blockchain networks may lack the protocols to communicate effectively with the existing legacy systems in use by businesses. The removal of this barrier to adoption for Malaysian organizations requires blockchain networks to be interoperable with existing legacy systems to enable the integration of these networks with legacy systems.

The fifth main challenge to blockchain adoption in Malaysia is potential security threats, with 29% of organizations choosing it as a barrier to adoption. While blockchain is touted for its security features, it is not immune to vulnerabilities, especially in the smart contracts and code used in decentralized applications. The removal of this barrier to adoption for Malaysian organizations requires ensuring the security of blockchain networks.

1.4 Is Blockchain Ready for Mass Adoption?

At this point of its development, a fair assessment of blockchain would be that it is still in a relatively nascent stage whereby the potential for its uses and the possible areas in which the uses can be deployed are still very much in a search and exploration phase. A crucial step in this regard is to understand the functions, features as well as limitations, and risks associated with blockchain which will help ascertain the actual potential of the technology in terms of the fulfillment of the expectations engendered by it. In this regard, it may be worthwhile to assess some popular claims about blockchain and assess their accuracy or lack thereof.

(a) **The Myth of Blockchain as a Trustless System**

Any reference to blockchains as being trustless is more of a term of convenience as the notion that blockchains are trustless should not be taken literally as the operations of blockchains do require a certain degree of trust, albeit much less than those of conventional networks. For permissioned blockchain networks, there is a need for participants to repose trust in the operators and validators who are tasked with managing the operations of the network. As for permissionless networks, the absence of operators and validators results in a lower trust requirement for these networks, though there is still a basic level of trust requirement as the participants would need to repose trust in the cryptographic framework which governs the hashing mechanism of the network.

The need for trust is because the verification of information stored in the ledger records of the network is done in reliance on the cryptographic hashes that chain together the blocks of information stored under the network. In short, as the levels of trust required to support the operations of blockchain networks are considerably less than those required for conventional networks it can be said that blockchain minimizes trust requirements whereby, although it is not entirely accurate to denote blockchain networks as trustless, they are generally referred to as such for simplicity reasons.

(b) **The Myth of Blockchain as a Truth Machine**

Linked to the notion of blockchain as a trustless mechanism is the notion that blockchain is a truth machine that can decipher the truth by distinguishing between facts and falsehoods. The notion that blockchain is a truth machine is very much inaccurate, particularly for blockchain networks that deal with non-native digital assets and thereby must rely on external data input for their operations. In essence, blockchain is not able to assess the truth value or falsity degree of the information submitted as its data input but instead would take any information that fulfills the parameters as set out in its consensus mechanism framework as being valid (Meva, 2018). In other words, blockchain has no way of discerning between truth and falsehoods about the information constituting the data input submitted into the network's ledger records but instead relies on the verification process as undertaken through the consensus mechanism whereby so long as a set of information is not incompatible with the pre-existing information in the ledger records the set of information would be deemed as true and processed as such by the network.

In the context of blockchain networks which deal solely with native digital assets, the risks of false information are negligible as the operations of these networks do not rely much on external data input. On the other hand, the risks of false information are greater for blockchain networks that deal with non-native digital assets as the operations of these networks are dependent on external data input wherefore these networks would generally require the services of a trusted third party to help warrant the accuracy of external data input by verifying the nature of the information constituting the input (Yaga et al., 2018).

(c) **The Myth of Blockchain Records Having Absolute Immutability**

Although blockchain-based ledger records are generally referred to as being immutable, this should not be taken to mean that the immutability of these records is absolute. The notion that blockchain-based ledger records have absolute immutability arose from the fact that only additions but not deletions can be made to the information stored in these records (Puthal et al., 2018). Nonetheless, this does not mean that there is no way in which the information stored in blockchain-based ledger records can be altered. This is because theoretically this information can be altered if there are sufficient participants under the network who consent to the alteration under the consensus mechanism of the network. The risks of collusion between the network participants to initiate an improper alteration of the information in the network's ledger records are greater for public blockchains where the colluding participants would simply need to garner sufficient computing powers where the consensus mechanism in use is PoW, or hold the requisite volume of cryptocurrency where the consensus mechanism in use is PoS, to prompt the network to approve the said alteration (Tasatanattakool and Techapanupreeda, 2018).

In contrast, the risks of collusion are lower in the context of private blockchains where the network participants would usually be legally prohibited from undertaking any collusion or improper actions to subvert the operations of the network whereby these prohibitions would be set out in an agreement to which the network participants are required to signify their assent before being allowed to join the network. In short, blockchain-based ledger records can be said to be immutable, though this is not absolute as it is subject to the condition that there is no collusion between the network participants to subvert the operations of the network by manipulating the underlying consensus mechanism whereby the risks of such collusion are greater in the context of public blockchains as compared to private ones.

(d) **The Myth of Blockchain as Being Ready for Mass Adoption**

At this stage of its development, blockchain is still very much facing a host of challenges that stand in the way of its wide use whereby the key challenges are the technology's lack of scalability and interoperability. With regard to blockchain's lack of scalability which stems from the limited transaction processing speeds of blockchain networks, the addressing of this challenge is critical to render the technology ready for mass adoption. From an on-chain perspective, the solutions for blockchain's lack of scalability involve increasing blockchain networks' block sizes and reducing the byte size of the information stored in each block of these networks (Kohad et al., 2020).

From an off-chain perspective, one of the solutions for blockchain's lack of scalability is the sharding mechanism which involves the grouping together of a subset of nodes into smaller networks, i.e., shards whereby these nodes would then be responsible for validating the transactions allocated to their respective shards. Besides that, other off-chain solutions involve the use of a second layer of blockchain network on top of the pre-existing one as exemplified by Bitcoin's Lightning Network.

As for blockchain's lack of interoperability, this is due to the absence of a standardized protocol that can be used to facilitate communications between different blockchain networks whereby this results in the incompatibility of the operational functions of these networks (Pang, 2020). If blockchain is to be ready for mass adoption, the operational functions of blockchain networks must be of such nature to allow their integration with existing systems used by business organizations which are unlikely to throw out these systems due to cost considerations.

Nonetheless, at this juncture, blockchain has quite a long way to go before the technology can reach its tipping point for mass adoption because, in addition to the key challenges of lack of scalability and interoperability, there are also other challenges in the form of security and privacy issues, regulatory uncertainties as well as talent development and environmental considerations. As for the question of whether if or when blockchain will be able to transcend these challenges to reach its tipping point of mass adoption, only time can tell.

No doubt, blockchain has laid a strong foundation and shown its potential to revolutionize Web3, but it still has a long way to go before it can be considered fully ready for widespread adoption. The technology is still a work in progress that requires further development, standardization, and problem-solving to overcome the numerous challenges it currently faces. Based on the current state of blockchain technology, it is evident that while blockchain holds significant promise for Web3, it may yet be fully ready to meet the demands and expectations associated with this new phase of the Internet.

1.4.1 *Alternative Decentralized Ledger Technologies to Blockchain*

Some alternative decentralized ledger technologies (DLTs) to blockchain include:

(a) **Directed Acyclic Graphs (DAGs)**

DAGs are a type of data structure where transactions are represented as nodes, and each transaction can be directly connected to multiple previous transactions (Kahmann et al., 2023). DAGs aim to achieve scalability and eliminate the need for miners, potentially offering faster transaction speeds and lower fees.

While both DAGs and blockchain are distributed ledger technologies, DAGs utilize concurrent consensus algorithms that allow for the simultaneous validation of transactions and the formation of a partial order of transactions. On the other hand, blockchain typically relies on linear consensus mechanisms such as PoWor PoS, or variations thereof to validate and agree on the sequential order of transactions added to the ledger.

(b) **Distributed Hash Table (DHT)**

DHT is a network in which each node stores a subset of the key-value pairs based on a consistent hashing algorithm which ensures that each key is assigned to a specific node, typically based on its hash value (Sit, 2008). This assignment distributes the keys evenly across the nodes in the network, helping to balance the load and ensure scalability.

While both DHT and blockchain are distributed ledger technologies, DHT's decentralized data system organizes data as key-value pairs, and each node in the network stores a subset of the data based on a consistent hashing algorithm. On the other hand, blockchain's decentralized data storage organizes data as blocks linked together in a chronological chain that is cryptographically linked to form a tamper-evident and immutable ledger.

(c) **Hashgraph**

Hashgraph is a distributed consensus algorithm and data structure that aims to achieve high throughput, fast finality, fairness, and security in distributed systems (Bech, 2021). The algorithm uses a gossip protocol for information dissemination and a voting-based consensus algorithm.

While both Hashgraph and blockchain are distributed ledger technologies, Hashgraph achieves decentralization through an algorithm protocol through which nodes in the network gossip with each other, and consensus is reached through virtual voting, which is designed to be Byzantine fault-tolerant (BFT). On the other hand, blockchain achieves decentralization by distributing transaction validation across a network of nodes.

Advantages of blockchain over these alternative decentralized ledger technologies include:

(a) **Security**

Blockchain's consensus mechanisms, cryptographic techniques, and decentralized nature make it inherently secure against tampering and fraud. Its immutability ensures that once data is recorded, it cannot be easily altered without consensus from the network.

(b) **Interoperability**

Many blockchain platforms and protocols support interoperability, allowing different blockchain networks to communicate and interact with each other. This interoperability facilitates the exchange of assets and data across different blockchain ecosystems.

(c) **Infrastructure**

Blockchain has seen significant adoption across various industries, including finance, supply chain, healthcare, and more. This widespread adoption has led to the infrastructural development that supports the use of blockchain.

While some of the alternative decentralized ledger technologies may offer certain advantages such as scalability or faster transaction speeds in specific use cases, blockchain's security, interoperability, and widespread adoption make it a preferred choice for the financial domain which involves trustless transactions and immutable records.

1.5 Appraising the Socio-economic Sense of Blockchain Use

As with other forms of technological changes, there are two general approaches in which the changes brought about using blockchain can be classified from a socio-economic perspective. On the one hand, there is the neoclassical approach which views blockchain-enabled changes as improvements to the production process whereas on the other hand, there is the alternative institutional approach which views blockchain-enabled changes as having deep-rooted evolutionary effects that transcend the production process by improving the efficiency of the macro socio-economic framework (Davidson et al., 2018). The neoclassical approach postulates that blockchain-enabled changes occur within the limited domain of technical efficiency through the lowering of production costs whereas the institutional approach postulates that blockchain-enabled changes reach deep into the socio-economic governance frameworks by enhancing the operational efficiencies of these frameworks on a general scale and all-encompassing scope.

To put it simply, the neoclassical approach puts forth the proposition that blockchain-enabled changes pave the way for the growth of marginal profits by enhancing the efficiency of the production process by lowering the relevant cost factors. An example of this is the use of blockchain for the KYC verification process, thereby lowering the regulatory compliance costs of financial institutions which in turn raises the marginal profits of these institutions. Concerning the institutional approach, however, a deeper level of discussion is required to elucidate the matter as it involves the role of blockchain-enabled changes in enhancing the efficiency of socio-economic governance frameworks by lowering transaction costs, i.e., the costs of coordinating transactions under these frameworks.

1.5.1 The Dollars and Cents of Blockchain Use

In his article "The Problem of Social Cost," Ronald Coase laid down his theory of transaction costs which postulates that firms seeking to acquire goods or services from external providers inevitably end up incurring transaction costs concerning the information search, bargaining, decision-making as well as monitoring and enforcement processes. Two decades earlier, Coase, in his article "The Nature of the Firm," laid down the theory of the firm which postulates that relationships between firms are governed by profit maximization considerations whereas intra-firm decisions are undertaken based on entrepreneurial coordination (Coase, 1937).

Under Coase's theory of the firm, the higher transaction costs of contracts with external parties result in long-term contracts being deemed as being more cost-effective due to the reduced transaction costs of such contracts as opposed to short-term ones. This led to internal pricing systems being devised to reproduce the conditions of an external competitive market, albeit within the boundaries of a firm, to help reduce the costs of production of goods and services within the firm to render internal production a viable alternative to the sourcing of such goods and services from external parties.

To put it simply, the Coase Theorem postulates that transaction costs arise due to externalities of the formation of contractual relationships with outsiders. In the financial domain, for example, the externalities resulting in the incurrence of transaction costs arise mainly from the on-boarding verification process which can be intricately complex, particularly in the context of new customers. In this regard, transaction costs in the financial domain manifest primarily in the form of intermediary fees concerning the verification of identities and credentials of the users of financial services as part of the onboarding process.

As blockchain comprises a chain of transaction blocks which theoretically can extend in an ad infinitum manner, blockchain networks have virtually limitless storage capacities whereby this wealth of readily accessible and cryptographically secure information renders the use of these networks to be very much a boon for the remedying of transaction costs for the information search process in addition to facilitating the bargaining process. This is because the availability of the wealth of verified information under the data repository stored in the shared ledger records of blockchain networks enables the contracting parties to easily access information of similar transactions, thereby enabling the parties to be more certain of their respective bargaining positions which in turn results in a smoother bargaining process.

As for the transaction costs that arise from the monitoring and enforcement processes, the automated feature of smart contracts which allows them to operate in a self-executing manner renders them ideal for use to monitor the degree of compliance by contracting parties with their respective obligations (Savelyev, 2016). Additionally, the parameters of a contractual transaction can be encoded as part of the algorithm of smart contracts, thereby enabling the automatic triggering of the predetermined consequences in the event of any breach by the parties of their contractual obligations resulting whereby the consequences would depend on the nature and extent of the breach. Nonetheless, on the other hand, there are the costs associated with the devising of smart contracts as well as those related to the inflexibilities of these contracts due to their nature of absolute finality (Szczerbowski, 2018). All in all, the extent to which smart contracts can reduce transaction costs would depend on the nature of the underlying transaction whereby the use of smart contracts would come in handy concerning transactions under which there is a high risk of opportunistic behaviors on the part of the contracting parties.

1.5.2 *The Opportunities and Risks of Blockchain Use*

The role of blockchain-enabled changes in reducing transaction costs is best explained using Williamson's theory of the role of opportunism as applied to the incurrence of transaction costs whereby controlling opportunistic behaviors can lead to a reduction in transaction costs. In line with Williamson's theory, the increased transparency brought about by the use of blockchain-based shared ledger records coupled with the enhancement of contractual security brought about by the use of cryptographic techniques for the processing of transactions can reduce the risks of opportunistic behaviors on the part of the contracting parties and thereby reduce transaction costs (Berg et al., 2019). In this regard, it is notable that how blockchain-enabled changes bring about a reduction in transaction costs by internalizing the costs of opportunistic behaviors as part of the contracting mechanism is not unlike how hierarchies and relational contracting reduce transaction costs as postulated by Williamson.

A deeper assessment of transaction costs reveals that they arise from factors such as the possibility of unexpected events that may affect the performance of contractual obligations as well as the costs associated with the formation and enforcement of contracts. In this regard, two key issues which arise from these factors are firstly that of information asymmetry leading to adverse selection and secondly the issue of moral hazard which entails risky behaviors on the part of the contracting parties. An example of how blockchain can address these issues is illustrated by the use of smart contracts that lower the effects of the possible contingencies under the contextual circumstances of a transaction by taking into account the probabilities of the execution and enforcement of transactions as part of its programming algorithm.

With the possibility of unexpected events being catered for through the algorithm of smart contracts, this would presumably reduce the risks of opportunistic behaviors on the part of the contracting parties (Cong & He, 2018). In other words, smart contracts can help reduce the ex post contractual transaction costs associated with the renegotiation of contractual terms in the event of the occurrence of unexpected events. As for the ex ante contractual transaction costs, i.e., the costs associated with information search, bargaining and decision-making processes, these costs could be reduced through the use of blockchain-based shared ledger records whereby the information therein serves as a repository of verified information that is readily accessible by the contracting parties. Not only would this reduce the costs associated with information search but it would also facilitate the bargaining process by enabling the parties to have a better understanding of the market conditions whereby this would in turn improve the decision-making process of the parties. In short, blockchain can be said to be the technological embodiment which can be used to implement Williamson's vision of the way in which limiting the extent of opportunistic behaviors can translate into a reduction in transaction costs.

Security is a fundamental consideration in the use of blockchain for Web3, as the decentralized and transparent nature of blockchain technology introduces both opportunities and challenges. Having assessed the opportunities arising from the use of blockchain for Web3, we also need to consider the challenges of balancing the two sides of the coin. The notion that blockchain networks offer foolproof security due to the use by these networks of cryptographic encryption techniques for their identity verification and information validation processes is not entirely accurate because, as with any other digital technological systems, blockchain networks do face security risks, though these risks are substantially reduced through the use of cryptographic encryption techniques. Notwithstanding the use of cryptographic encryption techniques which render the information stored in blockchain networks to have better security protection against unauthorized access and undue tampering, the network participants still face a certain degree of risks, particularly concerning the management of their private keys which serve as the gateway to access the network (Madnick, 2019).

The critical role of private keys as an access point to blockchain networks renders them prime targets for hackers as the obtaining of the private keys would enable the hacker to gain entry into the network which would recognize the hacker as a legitimate user of the network, i.e., as the true owner of the keys. Consequently, the security of blockchain networks is very much dependent on the proper management by the participants of their private keys. Nonetheless, the security risks arising from the management of private keys of users are limited by the extent of the control of the user over the network, i.e., the extent of computational power where the consensus mechanism in use is PoW and the level of cryptocurrency holdings where the consensus mechanism in use is PoS.

An even greater security risk for blockchain networks is the occurrence of a 51% attack whereby malicious nodes take control of the operations of the network to initiate unauthorized transactions and to cause damage to the network (Sayeed & Marco-Gisbert, 2019). Although conceptually the risks of a 51% attack are similar to the risks of collusion as discussed in the context of the immutability of the information stored in blockchain-based ledger records, there is a crucial difference between the two in that the latter involves the making of improper alteration to information stored in the network whereas the former involves the illegal hijacking of the operational framework of the network which poses a critical risk to the systemic integrity of the network.

1.5.3 *Is Blockchain Use Socio-economically Sound?*

No doubt the popularity of blockchain has been driven by the fame of the legendary cryptocurrency Bitcoin, though from a conceptual point of view it is important to note that blockchain is the underlying technology of Bitcoin but that blockchain is not synonymous with Bitcoin. On the one hand, blockchain has been touted as the technology that will lead humanity toward the Industrial Revolution (IR 4.0), whereas, on the other hand, there are concerns that blockchain may fail to live up to its expectations much like the bubble memory technology, which started as a promising technology back in the 1980s as a magnetic data storage, and which was touted as a possible replacement for hard disk drives (HDD), but ended up falling into oblivion (Kubitz, 1979). Nonetheless from a socio-economic perspective, the central feature of blockchain, i.e., that of decentralization, renders it to be particularly useful when it comes to remedying the trust deficits in the corporate and financial domains through the use of blockchain-based networks to facilitate the carrying out of trust-free transactions.

From a macro perspective, standing in the way of blockchain reaching its tipping point to pave the way for the mass adoption and use of the technology are the existing systemic forces that very much prefer to retain the current status quo of centralized frameworks. Applying the Schumpeterian growth theory which posits that old technologies will be replaced by innovations brought about by entrepreneurial investments, blockchain would have to leverage the innovation brought about by technological entrepreneurs to boost the productive forces underlying the technology and through this process overcome the "facts of social organization" which tend to be resistant to changes by affirming the status quo. In the context of blockchain, these "facts of social organization" which take the form of centralized authorities and institutions would have an ingrained tendency to be averse to the decentralization feature of blockchain as this would render them practically redundant.

Under the Schumpeterian growth theory, blockchain would be the technological tool that catalyzes an industrial revolution under which the existing economic and financial operational frameworks would be replaced with new ones through a process known as creative destruction. In this connection, the use of blockchain has already heralded the rise of a decentralized digital economy under which the provision of services and trading of goods are governed by cryptography leading to the birth of a discipline involving the study of the decentralized digital economy, i.e., the field of crypto-economics which constitute as a branch of microeconomics (Voshmgir & Zargham, 2020). Nonetheless, only time will tell as to the extent to which the revolutionary potential of blockchain would translate into real-world reality.

1.6 Exploring the Social Facets of Blockchain

From a macro societal perspective, the decentralized feature of blockchain-based systems renders them to be properly aligned to the much-touted modern-day ideals of democracy as decision-making powers under these systems are distributed among the users straddling all levels of the system (Wright & De Filippi, 2015). Additionally, the use of blockchain-based decentralized systems also serves as an effective manner in which the principle of the wisdom of the crowd can be harnessed to improve decision-making processes by relying on the collective opinion of the masses to enhance the prospects of making the right decisions. In any event, even if the decisions made turn out to be wrong, blockchain-based decentralized systems would still fare better than conventional ones as decentralization facilitates the diffusion of the consequences of the mistake by leveraging the ripple effect to disperse the consequences across the multiple decision-making centers in the system.

1.6.1 Blockchain for Social Stability and Public Trust

The promise of decentralized systems is illustrated by the belief of Adam Smith that the use of decentralized systems for the making of decisions can grant the critical element of stability to social order (Smith, 1776). Smith reasoned that since humans are imperfect and imperfectible, the wide-ranging and permanently lasting human imperfections that exist at both the individual and group levels render it foolhardy for decision-making autonomy to be reposed in the hands of a select few as is the case under a centralized system. Smith posited that given the imperfections of humans, our decision-making process tends to be clouded by biases and prejudices which prompt him to put forth his support for the use of polycentric decision-making models such as those used under decentralized systems. Smith believed that the diffusion of decision-making powers across the network of stakeholders would dilute the effects of our personal biases and prejudices thereby allowing us to have better chances of making the right decisions.

In other words, Smith believed that as polycentrism allows more parties to contribute to the decision-making process, we would have better chances of reaching the correct decision using decentralized systems. Further supporting his case for the use of decentralized systems, Smith disagreed with the notion that certain individuals are better placed to make decisions than others as he believed that well-renowned individuals such as political and industry leaders as well as academicians and even philosophers are just as subjected to limitations and affected by imperfections as everyone else and therefore are just as likely to make decisions which turn out to be wrong. In this regard, Smith was particularly critical of political leaders whom he perceived as easily corruptible and have a high tendency to fall victim to the flattery of their surrounding cogs, thereby rendering these leaders to be prone to misusing or even abusing their powers to establish socially dysfunctional monopolies to further their interests and agendas at the expense of the general public.

The essence of Smith's case for the use of decentralized systems was that the imperfect decision-making skills of humans coupled with the flawed characteristics of human nature render the making of mistakes to be inevitable whereby the use of centralized systems would exacerbate the consequences of these mistakes due the use of a central decision-making point. In contrast, decentralized systems which entail the distribution of decision-making powers across all levels of the system would effectively enable the diffusion of the consequences of any mistake, thereby minimizing the effects of these consequences. Accordingly, Smith has long propounded the use of decentralized systems for the establishment of stable social orders whereby if he had lived in our modern times, he would most certainly have given his approval to the use of blockchain which has the core feature of decentralization as its main tenet.

The concept of trust is invariably tied to the element of reliability which is a prerequisite for a relationship of dependency. In the context of financial services, the customers rely on financial institutions for the provision of these services whereas these institutions rely on their customers for their business reputation which is, whether directly or indirectly, correlated to their revenue. Hence, the importance of public trust in financial institutions is two-fold, i.e., for customers to be able to rely on the financial services offered by financial institutions and for these institutions to be able to rely on their customers for the building of their business reputation, and to one extent or another, even the generation of revenue. The core tenet of public trust is trust which is defined by Strawson as a form of reactive attitude which is formed based on emotions stemming from moral judgments of specific action descriptions to events that have come to their knowledge (Strawson, 1949).

In the context of the financial services domain, the relevant events that dampened public trust would be financial scandals which may cause the public to have unfavorable moral judgments about the integrity and accountability of financial institutions. The harboring of these judgments could result in the public forming a reactive negative attitude to financial institutions which in turn could result in them shying away from engaging the services of these institutions. In a way, the occurrence of financial scandals is a betrayal of public trust by the implicated financial institutions which, in the words of Jones, have departed from a fundamental trait of one trust, i.e., the trait of being trusting (Jones, 1996). This trait is all the more important in the context of the financial services domain given the depositing of money by the public in financial institutions.

1.6.2 *Blockchain for Social Solidarity and Power Distribution*

The origins of the concept of social solidarity can be traced back to the Rochdale Principles devised by the Rochdale Society of Equitable Pioneers which was established in 1844 whereby the Principles laid down the foundation for the social cooperatives movement (Poirier, 2014). In more modern times, the concept of social solidarity has manifested in the form of social solidarity economy (SSE) developed by the Intercontinental Network for the Promotion of the Social Solidarity Economy (RIPESS) which was established during the second Conference on Social Economy in the North and the South held in Quebec, Canada, in 2001.

In essence, SSE aims to establish ethical relationships based on care and cooperation as their foundations to remedy the effects of unbridled capitalism ravaging the modern-day economic system in a departure from the originating ideals and fundamental principles of the system as envisaged by Adam Smith (Kawano et al., 2009). In contrast with the unbridled capitalism prevalent in the conventional economic framework, SSE supports the undertaking of a bottom-up development approach whereby the collective vision of the community together with their active participation would serve as the operating model of the economy as reflected through its inclusive notion that no one should be left behind. In the financial domain, the concept of SSE is manifested in the form of social and solidarity finance (SSF). SSF principles were developed by the microfinance industry to support the needs of SSE (i.e., in response to the relationships of interdependence between the social and financing institutions comprising the SSE framework) whereby the objective of the SSF domain is to facilitate the implementation of its principles to address the long-term needs of the collective enterprises constituted by these institutions. If these principles are properly implemented with the support of technologies such as blockchain, SSF principles could go a long way toward supporting SSE specifically for remedying the effects of unbridled capitalism particularly that of financial exclusion.

The existing centralized frameworks of economic and financial systems are rooted in the need for efficiency as centralized systems help establish clear knowledge structures by minimizing repetition and duplication of information whereby the efficiency arising from the resulting certainty is much needed when the global economic and financial systems were at the early stages of their development (Dewatripont & Maskin, 1995). However, the efficiency brought about by the use of centralized frameworks comes at the cost of accumulation of powers which renders the operations of these frameworks vulnerable to misuse and abuse because as the saying goes, "power tends to corrupt, and absolute power corrupts absolutely." In other words, centralization gives rise to a distinct hierarchical structure which brings about efficiency to the system and precisely because of the existence of such a hierarchy, those who govern the system are at liberty to manipulate the system for their benefit.

Additionally, decentralized systems reduce the risks of catastrophic failures to which centralized systems are subject. This is because as decisions under a decentralized system are made at the local level, any error or mistake in the decision-making process whether due to inaccurate information, judgmental errors, or otherwise, would only affect the relevant locality (Angelis & Da Silva, 2019). In contrast, under a centralized system, the decision-making process is undertaken almost exclusively by those who sit at the apex of the hierarchy whereby the effects of wrong decisions would affect not only the decision-makers who got it wrong but also the other stakeholders under the system. Cases in point are the collapses of national financial systems such as that of Iceland (2008) with a debt of USD85 billion (Farmbrough, 2019), and Greece (2015) with a debt of USD 323 billion (CNN, 2015), whereby the consequences of these collapses affected not only the institutions themselves but also the local population and the regional economy.

1.6.3 Blockchain for Social Finance and Financial Inclusion

From a *Shariah* perspective, the concept of social finance takes the form of Islamic social finance which is rooted in the Quranic call for the establishment of a sustainable economy based on the teachings of Islam that man is a *khalifah* (vicegerent) and *abd* (servant) who is commanded by God to use the faculties endowed upon him and the resources bestowed to him to help develop the world around him in a just and fair manner for the betterment of the general society (Zain et al., 2017). Islamic social finance requires the application of *Shariah* principles in the context of Islamic financial services in a manner that is based on the concepts of risk-sharing, profit-sharing, and fixed-repayment rates imbued with the elements of accountability and transparency to ensure that the transactions would further the objectives of Islamic social finance which is for the promotion of social welfare and justice. Traditionally, Islamic social finance has relied on the mechanisms of *zakat*, *waqf*, and *sadaqah* to further its objectives, though in recent times these traditional channels have been plagued by issues affecting their respective collection frameworks and distribution models.

The growing awareness of Islamic social finance is very much in line with the shift in the conventional financial system toward newfound ideological approaches such as Ethical, Social, and Governance (ESG) investment and Socially Responsible Investment (SRI). In this day and age of ours in which humanity is becoming increasingly conscious of the impact of our consumption of natural resources and the sacrifice of long-term global health for short-term profits, Islamic social finance has much to contribute in terms of showing the way forward toward the establishment of a more sustainable financial ecosystem supported by the twin pillars of ethical capital investment and value-based financial banking (Jouti, 2019). *Zakat* as the core mechanism of Islamic social finance would have a central role to play in the journey toward the establishment of a global financial ecosystem in which there is better socio-economic balancing coupled with less income inequalities.

In Malaysia, Islamic social financing forms a key component in the development of the country's Islamic financial services domain as strategy 5C of BNM's Financial Sector Blueprint 2022–2026 provides for the elevation of social finance as an integral part of the country's Islamic finance ecosystem. Under strategy 5C, BNM would be facilitating the use of a wide range of financing models including blended finance models and funding escalator models to promote the achievement of impactful social outcomes. As for Singapore, although the government has not established any official Islamic social financing policy, it has put into practice the spirit of Islamic social financing by making available channels for Muslims in the country to spend their *zakat*, *infaq*, and *sadaqah* as well as through the establishment of programs to support the needs of the less fortunate in the Muslim community through the provision of funds for the building of mosque (*masjid*), school (*madrasah*) as well as for scholarships and funerals of needy Muslims in the country (Riyanto et al., 2021).

The concept of financial inclusion originated from the antonym of the term "financial exclusion" which was devised by Leyshon and Thrift back in 1993 to refer to processes that hinder those who come from poor and disadvantaged social groups from being able to have access to financial services (Packman, 2014). Building on the term financial exclusion, Sarma defined the concept of financial inclusion as comprising three aspects about the relationship between the financial system with members of the public, i.e., accessibility, suitability, as well as affordability (Sarma, 2008). The World Bank further expanded on this concept when it included the sub-concept of voluntary exclusion which refers to the conscious choice of a segment of the unbanked who opt not to use financial services for one reason or another such as individual, cultural, or religious reasons, whereby it is imperative to distinguish the segment of the unbanked who voluntarily exclude themselves from those who were involuntarily excused as the latter group is the target of financial inclusion–related policy intervention (The World Bank, 2014).

The effects of financial exclusion are particularly hampering for the poor as access to financial services is a critical element for the poor to escape from the cycle of poverty (Chibba, 2009). The importance of financial inclusion is reflected in the United Nations Capital Development Fund's (UNCDF) view that financial inclusion is a prime enabler for 8 of the 17 SDGs including SDG1 on eradicating poverty. As for the World Bank, it also holds the opinion that "financial inclusion is a key enabler to reducing poverty and boosting prosperity," yet it is precisely those who are poor who have to bear the brunt of the consequences of being unbanked (The World Bank, 2018). This is because although access to financial services may be taken for granted by the ordinary men on the street particularly those who are living in urban areas where there is a plethora of financial services on offer and which are available at their choosing, financial services are a luxury that those who are less fortunate can ill-afford. Inevitably, the lack of access to financial services results in the poor being caught up in the vicious cycle of poverty as without access to such services the poor are unable to have their savings, get a job, start a business, or even to obtain any credit services for their business or personal needs such as for their children's education or health.

References

Al-Breiki, H., Ur Rehman, M. H., Salah, K., & Svetinovic, D. (2020). Trustworthy blockchain oracles: Review, comparison, and open research challenges. *IEEE Open Access, 8*, 85675–85685. https://ieeexplore.ieee.org/stamp/stamp.jsp?arnumber=9086815

Allam, Z. (2018). On smart contracts and organisational performance: A review of smart contracts through the blockchain technology. *Review of Economics and Business Studies, 11*(2), 137–156. https://content.sciendo.com/download-pdf/journals/rebs/11/2/article-p137.xml

Angelis, J., & Da Silva, E. R. (2019). Blockchain adoption: A value driver perspective. *Business Horizons, 62*(3), 307–314.

Anwar, S., Anayat, S., Butt, S., & Saad, M. (2020). Generation analysis of blockchain technology: Bitcoin and Ethereum. *International Journal of Information Engineering and Electronic Business, 12*(4), 30–39. http://www.mecs-press.org/ijieeb/ijieeb-v12-n4/IJIEEB-V12-N4-4.pdf

Avasthi, A. A., & Saxena, A. (2018). Two hop blockchain model: Resonating between proof of work (PoW) and proof of authority (PoA). *International Journal of Information Systems & Management Science, 1*(1), 128–131. https://papers.ssrn.com/sol3/papers.cfm?abstract_id=3363575

Bayer, D., Haber, S., & Stornetta, W. S. (1992). Improving the efficiency and reliability of digital time-stamping. In R. Capocelli, A. De Santis, & U. Vaccaro (Eds.), *Sequences II: Methods in communication, security and computer science* (pp. 329–334). Springer. http://citeseerx.ist.psu.edu/viewdoc/download?doi=10.1.1.46.5923&rep=rep1&type=pdf

Bech, J. (2021). Hashgraph: Modelling and review (Master's thesis). University of Surrey, Faculty of Engineering and Physical Sciences.

Bentov, I., Lee, C., Mizrahi, A., & Rosenfield, M. (2014). Proof of activity: Extending Bitcoin's proof of work via proof of stake. Cryptology ePrint Archive (No. 452). https://eprint.iacr.org/2014/452.pdf

Berg, C., Davidson, S., & Potts, J. (2019). Blockchain technology as economic infrastructure: Revisiting the electronic markets hypothesis. *Frontiers in Blockchain, 2*, 22. https://www.frontiersin.org/articles/10.3389/fbloc.2019.00022/full

Bodkhe, U., Tanwar, S., Parekh, K., Khanpara, P., Tyagi, S., Kumar, N., & Alazab, M. (2020). Blockchain for industry 4.0: A comprehensive review. *IEEE Access, 8*, 79764–79800. https://ieeexplore.ieee.org/stamp/stamp.jsp?arnumber=9069885

Chen, L., Xu, L., Shah, N., Gao, Z., Lu, Y., & Shi, W. (2017). On security analysis of proof-of-elapsed-time (PoET). In *Stabilization, safety, and security of distributed system* (Lecture Notes in Computer Science, Vol. 10616), 282–297. https://www.researchgate.net/profile/Lin_Chen34/publication/320246838_On_Security_Analysis_of_Proof-of-Elapsed-Time_PoET/links/5cd74989299bf14d958df857/On-Security-Analysis-of-Proof-of-Elapsed-Time-PoET.pdf

Chibba, M. (2009). Financial inclusion, poverty reduction, and the Millennium Development Goals. *The European Journal of Development Research, 21*(2), 213–230. https://www.researchgate.net/publication/46526321_Financial_Inclusion_Poverty_Reduction_and_the_Millennium_Development_Goals

Chohan, U. W. (2021). The double spending problem and cryptocurrencies. *SSRN Electronic Journal*. https://doi.org/10.2139/ssrn.3090174

Chondros, N., Kokordelis, K., & Roussopoulos, M. (2012). On the practicality of 'practical' byzantine fault tolerance. In *Middleware 2012* (Lecture Notes in Computer Science, Vol. 7662), 436–455. https://arxiv.org/pdf/1110.4854.pdf

CNN. (2015, February 2). Greek debt crisis: Who has most to lose? https://money.cnn.com/2015/01/28/investing/greek-debt-who-has-most-to-lose/

Coase, R. H. (1937). The nature of the firm. *Economica, 4*(16), 386–405. https://onlinelibrary.wiley.com/doi/full/10.1111/j.1468-0335.1937.tb00002.x

CoinTelegraph. (2018, July 13). New study says 80 percent of ICOs conducted in 2017 were scams. https://cointelegraph.com/news/new-study-says-80-percent-of-icos-conducted-in-2017-were-scams

Cong, L. W., & He, Z. (2018). Blockchain disruption and smart contracts. *The Review of Financial Studies, 32*(5), 1754–1797. https://academic.oup.com/rfs/article/32/5/1754/5427778

Crypto Potato. (2020, June 24). What is an initial exchange offering (IEO) and how it differs from ICO? https://cryptopotato.com/what-is-an-initial-exchange-offering-ieo-and-how-it-differs-from-ico/

Davidson, S., de Filippi, P., & Potts, J. (2016). Economics of blockchain. In *Public Choice Conference, Fort Lauderdale, United States*. https://papers.ssrn.com/sol3/papers.cfm?abstract_id=2744751

Davidson, S., de Filippi, P., & Potts, J. (2018). Blockchains and the economic institutions of capitalism. *Journal of Institutional Economics, 14*(4), 639–658. https://hal.archives-ouvertes.fr/hal-01850927/file/57%20-%20(2018)%20JoIE%20-%20Blockchain%20and%20Capitalism.pdf

De Filippi, P., Mannan, M., & Reijers, W. (2020). Blockchain as a confidence machine: The problem of trust and challenges of governance. *Technology in Society, 62*, 101284. https://www.sciencedirect.com/science/article/pii/S0160791X20303067

Dewatripont, M., & Maskin, E. (1995). Credit and efficiency in centralized and decentralized economies. *Journal of Review of Economic Studies, 62*, 541–555. https://scholar.harvard.edu/files/maskin/files/credit_and_efficiency_in_centralized_and_decentralized_economies.pdf

Dib, O., Brousmiche, K. L., Durand, A., Thea, E., & Hamida, E. B. (2018). Consortium blockchains: Overview, applications and challenges. *International Journal on Advances in Telecommunications, 11*(1–2), 51–64. https://www.researchgate.net/profile/Omar_Dib/publication/328887130_Consortium_Blockchains_Overview_Applications_and_Challenges/links/5be99602299bf1124fce0ab9/Consortium-Blockchains-Overview-Applications-and-Challenges.pdf

Efanov, D., & Roschin, P. (2018). The all-pervasiveness of the blockchain technology. *Procedia Computer Science, 123*, 116–121. https://www.researchgate.net/publication/322912211_The_All-Pervasiveness_of_the_Blockchain_Technology

Farah, N. R. A. (2018). Blockchain technology: Classification, opportunities, and challenges. *International Research Journal of Engineering and Technology, 5*(5), 3423–3426. https://www.irjet.net/archives/V5/i5/IRJET-V5I5659.pdf

Farmbrough, H. (2019, December 23). How Iceland's banking collapse created an opportunity. *Forbes*. https://www.forbes.com/sites/heatherfarmbrough/2019/12/23/how-icelands-banking-collapse-created-an-opportunity/

Fernandez-Carames, T. M., & Fraga-Lamas, P. (2018). A review on the use of blockchain for the Internet of Things. *IEEE Access, 6*, 32979–33001. https://ieeexplore.ieee.org/stamp/stamp.jsp?arnumber=8370027

Gao, Y., & Nobuhara, H. (2017). A decentralized trusted timestamping based on blockchains. *IEEJ Journal of Industry Applications, 6*(4), 252–257. https://www.jstage.jst.go.jp/article/ieejjia/6/4/6_252/_pdf

Gervais, A., & Karame, G. (2014). Is Bitcoin a decentralized currency? *IEEE Security and Privacy Magazine, 12*(3), 54–60. https://www.researchgate.net/publication/270802537_Is_Bitcoin_a_Decentralized_Currency

Grinberg, R. (2012). Bitcoin: An innovative alternative digital currency. *Hastings Science and Technology Law Journal, 4*(1), 159–208. https://repository.uchastings.edu/cgi/viewcontent.cgi?article=1063&context=hastings_science_technology_law_journal

Guegan, D. (2017). Public blockchain versus private blockchain. Documents de travail du Centre d'Economie de la Sorbonne (No. 17020). https://halshs.archives-ouvertes.fr/halshs-01524440/document

Haber, S., & Stornetta, W. S. (1991). How to time-stamp a digital document. *Journal of Cryptology, 3*(2), 99–111. https://link.springer.com/article/10.1007/BF00196791

Harish, V., & Sridevi, R. (2018). A brief survey on blockchain technology. *Advances in Intelligent Systems and Computing, 1090*, 249–258. https://www.researchgate.net/profile/Srujan_Raju/publication/339984737_Proceedings_of_the_Third_International_Conference_on_Computational_Intelligence_and_Informatics/links/5f2288e44585 15b729f338d4/Proceedings-of-the-Third-International-Conference-on-Computational-Intelligence-and-Informatics.pdf#page=253

Hattab, S., & Alyaseen, I. F. T. (2019). Consensus algorithms blockchain: A comparative study. *International Journal on Perceptive and Cognitive Computing, 5*(2), 66–71. https://journals.iium.edu.my/kict/index.php/IJPCC/article/download/103/75

He, Q., Guan, N., Lv, M., & Yi, W. (2018). On the consensus mechanism of blockchain/DLT for internet of things. In *IEEE 13th International Symposium on Industrial Embedded Systems* (pp. 1–10). http://user.it.uu.se/~yi/pdf-files/2018/sies18.pdf

Helliar, C. V., Crawford, L., Rocca, L., Teodori, C., & Veneziani, M. (2020). Permissionless and permissioned blockchain diffusion. *International Journal of Information Management, 54*, 102136. https://doi.org/10.1016/j.ijinfomgt.2020.102136

Herian, R. (2018). Legal recognition of blockchain registries and smart contracts. EU Blockchain Observatory and Forum. http://oro.open.ac.uk/59481/15/Legal%20Recognition%20of%20Blockchain%20Registries%20and%20Smart%20Contracts%20%28Final%20Draft%20Report%20%2B%20Appendix%29.pdf

Investopedia. (2020, September 26). Initial coin offering (ICO). https://www.investopedia.com/terms/i/initial-coin-offering-ico.asp

Jones, K. (1996). Trust as an affective attitude. *Chicago Journals, 107*(1), 4–25.

Jouti, A. T. (2019). An integrated approach for building sustainable Islamic social finance ecosystems. *ISRA International Journal of Islamic Finance, 11*(2), 246–266. https://www.emerald.com/insight/content/doi/10.1108/IJIF-10-2018-0118/full/pdf?title=an-integrated-approach-for-building-sustainable-islamic-social-finance-ecosystems

Kahmann, F., Honecker, F., Dreyer, J., Fischer, M., & Tonjes, R. (2023). Performance comparison of directed acyclic graph-based distributed ledgers and blockchain platforms. *Journal of Computers, 12*, 257.

Karantias, K., Kiayias, A., & Zindros, D. (2020). Proof of burn. *Journal of Financial Cryptography and Data Security* (Lecture Notes in Computer Science, Vol. 12059), 523–540. https://eprint.iacr.org/2019/1096

Kawano, E., Masterson, T. N., & Teller-Elsberg, J. (2009). Solidarity economy I: Building alternatives for people and planet (Papers and reports from the 2009 U.S. Forum on the Solidarity Economy). https://d1wqtxts1xzle7.cloudfront.net/31351729/fse.pdf

Kohad, H., Kumar, S., & Ambhaikar, A. (2020). Scalability issues of blockchain technology. *International Journal of Engineering and Advanced Technology, 9*(3) https://www.ijeat.org/wp-content/uploads/papers/v9i3/C5305029320.pdf

Kubitz, W. J. (1979). Computer technology: A forecast for the future. *Clinic on Library Applications of Data Processing, 16*, 135–161. https://www.ideals.illinois.edu/bitstream/handle/2142/1098/Kubitz.pdf?sequence=2

Lamport, L. (1998). The part-time parliament. *ACM Transactions on Computer Systems, 16*(2), 133–169. https://courses.cs.washington.edu/courses/csep590/04wi/papers/lamport-part-time-parliament.pdf

Lan, P. (2015). Using a new lens to examine the dynamics of typewriter and vending machine industries. *International Journal of Business and Social Science, 6*(3), 19–31. http://ijbssnet.com/journals/Vol_6_No_3_March_2015/3.pdf
Luis, O., Liudmila, Z., Ingrid, B., & Gerhard, S. (2018). To token or not to token: Tools for understanding blockchain tokens. In *International Conference of Information Systems, San Francisco, United States*. https://www.zora.uzh.ch/id/eprint/157908/1/To%20Token%20or%20not%20to%20Token_%20Tools%20for%20Understanding%20Blockchain%20Toke.pdf
Madnick, S. (2019). Blockchain isn't as unbreakable as you think. MIT Management Sloan School Working Paper CISL# 2019-21. http://web.mit.edu/smadnick/www/wp/2019-21.pdf
Mattila, J. (2016). The blockchain phenomenon – The disruptive potential of distributed consensus architectures (ETLA Working Papers, No. 38). https://www.econstor.eu/bitstream/10419/201253/1/ETLA-Working-Papers-38.pdf
Mendelson, M. (2019). From initial coin offerings to security tokens: A U.S. federal securities law analysis. *Stanford Technology Law Review, 22*(1), 52–103. https://www-cdn.law.stanford.edu/wp-content/uploads/2019/01/Mendelson_20180129.pdf
Meva, D. (2018). Issues and challenges with blockchain: A survey. *International Journal of Computer Sciences and Engineering, 6*(12), 488–491. https://www.researchgate.net/profile/Dr_Divyakant_Meva/publication/330384987_Issues_and_Challenges_with_Blockchain_A_Survey/links/5c3da807299bf12be3c8d2ca/Issues-and-Challenges-with-Blockchain-A-Survey.pdf
Muhlberger, R., Bachhofner, S., Ferrer, E. S., Di Ciccio, C., Weber, I., Wohrer, M., & Zdun, U. (2020). Foundational oracle patterns: Connecting blockchain to the off-chain world. Business Process Management: Blockchain and Robotic Process Automation Forum, 35–51. https://arxiv.org/pdf/2007.14946.pdf
Nakamoto, S. (2008). Bitcoin: A peer-to-peer electronic cash system. https://git.dhimmel.com/Bitcoin-whitepaper/
Oracle. What is the Internet of Things (IoT)? https://www.oracle.com/internet-of-things/what-is-iot/
Pang, Y. (2020). A new consensus protocol for blockchain interoperability architecture. *IEEE Access, 8*, 153719–153730. https://ieeexplore.ieee.org/stamp/stamp.jsp?arnumber=9170602
Poirier, Y. (2014). Social solidarity economy origins and definitions: An international perspective. In *Developments in solidarity economy in Asia* (pp. 71–89). Asia Solidarity Economy Council. http://www.ripess.org/wp-content/uploads/2017/09/Solidarity-Economy-and-other-Concepts-Poirier-July-2014.pdf

Puthal, D., Malik, N., Mohanty, S. P., Kougianos, E., & Das, G. (2018). Everything you wanted to know about the blockchain. *IEEE Consumer Electronics Magazine, 7*(4), 6–14. https://www.researchgate.net/publication/326102908_Everything_You_Wanted_to_Know_About_the_Blockchain_Its_Promise_Components_Processes_and_Problems

Riyanto, S., Nizar, M., & Herningtyas, R. (2021). *Muslim's philanthropy in Singapore and the role of government.* *Sociología y Tecnociencia.

Sarma, M. (2008). Index of financial inclusion (Working Paper No. 215). Indian Council for Research on International Economic Relations. http://www.icrier.org/pdf/Working_Paper_215.pdf

Savelyev, A. (2016). Contract law 2.0: Smart contracts as the beginning of the end of classic contract law. Working Paper of Basic Research Program No. 71. National Research University Higher School of Economics. https://wp.hse.ru/data/2016/12/14/1111743800/71LAW2016.pdf

Sayeed, S., & Marco-Gisbert, H. (2019). Assessing blockchain consensus and security mechanisms against the 51% attack. *Journal of Applied Sciences, 9*(9), 1788. https://www.mdpi.com/2076-3417/9/9/1788/pdf

Search IT Operations. GitHub. https://searchitoperations.techtarget.com/definition/GitHub

Securities and Exchange Commission v. W. J. Howey Co., 328 U.S. 293 (1946)

Sit, E. (2008). Storing and managing data in a distributed hash table (Doctoral dissertation). Massachusetts Institute of Technology, Department of Electrical Engineering and Computer Science.

Smith, A. (1776). *The wealth of nations.* W. Strahan and T. Cadell. https://www.ibiblio.org/ml/libri/s/SmithA_WealthNations_p.pdf

Strawson, P. F. (1949). Trust. *Analysis, 9*(6), 83–97.

Sultan, K., Ruhi, U., & Lakhani, R. (2018). Conceptualizing blockchains: Characteristics and applications. In *11th IADIS International Conference Information Systems 2018.* https://www.researchgate.net/publication/325464908_Conceptualizing_Blockchains_Characteristics_Applications

Szabo, N. (1997). The idea of smart contracts. Nick Szabo's Papers and Concise Tutorials. https://nakamotoinstitute.org/literature/the-idea-of-smart-contracts/

Szczerbowski, J. J. (2018). Transaction costs of blockchain smart contracts. *Journal of Law and Forensic Science, 6*(2) https://papers.ssrn.com/sol3/papers.cfm?abstract_id=3258285

Tasatanattakool, P., & Techapanupreeda, C. (2018). Blockchain: Challenges and applications. In *Proceedings of the International Conference on Information Networking* (pp. 473–475). https://www.researchgate.net/publication/324725048_Blockchain_Challenges_and_Applications

Tewari, H., & Hughes, A. (2016). Fully anonymous transferable ecash. Cryptology ePrint Archive: Report 2016/107. https://eprint.iacr.org/2016/107

The World Bank. (2014). Global financial development report 2014: Financial inclusion. https://openknowledge.worldbank.org/bitstream/handle/10986/16238/9780821399859.pdf

The World Bank. (2018). Financial inclusion. https://www.worldbank.org/en/topic/financialinclusion/overview

Tsai, W., Bai, B. X., & Yu, L. (2017). Design issues in permissioned blockchains for trusted computing. In *2017 IEEE Symposium on Service-Oriented System Engineering* (pp. 153–157). https://www.researchgate.net/profile/Wei-Tek_Tsai2/publication/317423084_Design_Issues_in_Permissioned_Blockchains_for_Trusted_Computing/links/5e835b0a4585150839b296fd/Design-Issues-in-Permissioned-Blockchains-for-Trusted-Computing.pdf

Voshmgir, S., & Zargham, M. (2020). Foundations of cryptoeconomic systems. *Interdisciplinary Research Institute for Cryptoeconomics.* https://epub.wu.ac.at/7782/1/Foundations%20of%20Cryptoeconomic%20Systems.pdf

Wright, A., & De Filippi, P. (2015). Decentralized blockchain technology and the rise of Lex Cryptographia. *SSRN Electronic Journal.* https://papers.ssrn.com/sol3/papers.cfm?abstract_id=2580664

Yaga, D., Mell, P., Roby, N., & Scarfone, K. (2018). Blockchain technology overview (National Institute of Standards and Technology Internal Report 8202). https://arxiv.org/ftp/arxiv/papers/1906/1906.11078.pdf

Yang, F., Zhou, W., Wu, Q., Long, R., Xiong, N. N., & Zhou, M. (2019). Delegated proof of stake with downgrade: A secure and efficient blockchain consensus algorithm with downgrade mechanism. *IEEE Access, 7*, 118541–118555. https://ieeexplore.ieee.org/stamp/stamp.jsp?arnumber=8798621

Zain, N. R., Rabiah, E., & Ali, A. E. (2017). An analysis on Islamic social finance for protection and preservation of Maqaṣid al-Sharīah. *Journal of Islamic Finance, Special Issue*, 133–141. https://iris.unito.it/bitstream/2318/1671714/2/2-Social-Finance-And-Unconventional-Financing-Alternatives-An-Overview.pdf

CHAPTER 2

Money Makes the World Go Round, Blockchain Makes Financial Regulatory Compliance Affordable

Abstract Regulatory technology (RegTech) refers to the use of technology for regulatory monitoring and compliance, while supervisory technology (SupTech) is a subset focused on regulators using technology to ensure compliance. Both Malaysia and Singapore have adopted these technologies, though risks remain, particularly with blockchain-based systems. Regulatory sandboxes are the preferred method to mitigate these risks. In the 1MDB case study, we examine the scandal's impact on public trust in financial institutions in Malaysia and Singapore. While public trust in financial institutions remains high in Singapore, the 1MDB scandal has damaged public trust in financial institutions in Malaysia. The case study explores how blockchain could serve as a technological safeguard to mitigate the risks of the recurrence of scandals such as 1MDB through document tamper-proofing, improving financial audits, strengthening anti–money laundering (AML)/know-your-customer (KYC) and customer due diligence (CDD) processes, and tracking beneficial ownership based on the Bank for International Settlements' (BIS) concept of embedded supervision.

M. S. Thong, *Blockchain for Financial Governance in Malaysia and Singapore*,
https://doi.org/10.1007/978-981-96-1281-9_2

2.1 The Big Mad World of Financial Regulations

In Europe and America, both of which lead the global financial network, financial institutions have to comply with a host of complex regulations, respectively, the European Union (EU) Markets in Financial Instruments Directive (MiFID II8) and the United States (US) Dodd-Frank Wall Street Reform, both of which were introduced following the 2008 global financial crisis and requires financial institutions to keep track of all interactions which are connected with each financial transaction processed by them (Butler & O'Brien (2019). In other parts of the world, every jurisdiction would generally impose its own set of financial monitoring and reporting requirements.

In general, like most corporations, financial institutions are also required to comply with the applicable financial reporting and auditing requirements notably the International Financial Reporting Standards (IFRS) and the International Accounting Standards (IAS). Collectively, these regulations impose a huge administrative burden on financial institutions which is reflected in the rising degree of the complexities of their financial monitoring and reporting obligations. IBM has estimated that globally regulators from around the world are producing an average of 20,000 financial regulations per year whereby in 2020 it was estimated that these regulations have exceeded the astounding benchmark of 300 million pages (Bektenova, 2018).

The specific areas of the financial industry that have witnessed a rise in the complexity of compliance standards are those of AML and KYC. In the United States which serves as the epitome and leader of the global financial industry, the introduction of AML and KYC policies started back in the late 1980s through the putting in place of policies that require banks to store information of their customers and to raise the alarm in the event of any suspicious transaction detected during the monitoring of the transactions carried out by these customers (Lootsma, 2017). It has been estimated that financial institutions incur an estimated USD60 million a year to ensure that their operations properly comply with AML and KYC policy requirements (RealWire, 2019).

In the particular context of client onboarding, it has been estimated that the process costs financial institutions an average of USD6,000 per customer (ABA, 2019). The importance of financial institutions putting in place a smooth customer onboarding process as part of their respective operations is highlighted by the fact that a survey by global accounting firm Deloitte found that 38% of prospective customers will abandon the onboarding process if they find that the process takes too long and 26% based their choice of financial institution on the whether it has an "easy enrolment and login" process (Kinyua, 2020).

2.1.1 *One Costly Scandal for Financial Institutions*

Inevitably the imposition of a more stringent regulatory compliance framework for financial institutions after the implosion of the 2008 financial crisis, coupled with the more recent 1 Malaysia Development Board (1MDB) scandal laid bare the fault lines in the financial regulatory compliance domain, led to an increase in financial costs expended by these institutions for regulatory compliance purposes whereby banks, in particular, were reported to be spending more than USD270 billion annually to ensure due compliance with their regulatory compliance obligations (International Banker, 2018). It is in this context that American and European banks are increasingly turning to technology for their regulatory compliance endeavors, spending up to USD20 billion every year for their RegTech initiatives (Bloomberg, 2017). The increased spending by financial institutions on RegTech initiatives has not gone unnoticed as investments in RegTech ventures recorded a Year-on-Year (YoY) increase of 244% to reach almost USD19 billion in 2021 (Capgemini, 2021).

In Malaysia which played host to the 1MDB scandal, the post-scandal data indicates that the regulatory compliance costs of financial institutions amounted to USD890 million in 2019 whereby although large financial institutions, i.e., those with more than USD10 billion assets spent more on regulatory compliance than smaller financial institutions, the latter spent a disproportionate amount relative to the size of their assets (LexisNexis, 2019a). Nonetheless, the regulatory compliance costs of financial institutions in Malaysia are dwarfed by those of financial institutions in Singapore which expended a total of USD3.13 billion of such costs in 2019, though the benefits of the use of compliance technologies are reflected in faster due diligence and alert clearances, thereby minimizing the negative impact of AML compliance issues on productivity and consumer acquisition (LexisNexis, 2019b).

2.2 Comply with RegTech and Monitor with SupTech

The regulatory complexity of the financial world which has resulted in the rising regulatory compliance costs in Malaysia, Singapore, and around the world has paved the way for the increasing use of RegTech which refers to a set of technologies that can be used by regulators to reduce their burden of monitoring and supervising the due compliance of financial institutions with the applicable regulations including the use of the technologies by these institutions themselves to reduce their cost expenditure to secure due compliance with the applicable regulations (Arner et al., 2017). The World Economic Forum (WEF) defines RegTech as "the application of various new technological solutions that assist highly regulated industry stakeholders, including regulators, in setting, effectuating and meeting regulatory governance, reporting, compliance and risk management obligations" (World Economic Forum, 2022). Artificial intelligence (AI), which "refers to the simulation of human intelligence in machines that are programmed to think like humans and mimic their actions," is one of the technologies which can be used to support RegTech frameworks. As the WEF notes, "AI can be used to monitor data for regulatory risks, natural-language processing can help organizations better understand regulatory requirements, and blockchain can help track and verify compliance data."

The roots of RegTech can be traced back to the financial crisis of 2008 when excessive risk-taking by banks eventually led to the subprime mortgage crisis whereby the deregulation of banks which preceded the crisis allowed them to engage in high-risk financial transactions. Other than the factor of excessive risk-taking by banks, the 2008 financial crisis was also caused by the transfer of risks brought about by the sale of subprime mortgages by banks and other lenders to bigger banks which then repackaged these mortgages in the form of mortgage-backed securities (MBS) and collateralized debt obligations (CDOs) (Investopedia, 2021). Similarly, the use of credit default swaps (CDS) which entailed the element of risk transfer by functioning as bets on securitized mortgage prices also contributed to the 2008 financial crisis (Finance and Economics Club IITG, 2018). With the use of MBS, CDOs, and CDS having created a high level of leverage in the mortgage market, the reduction in demand for housing in the US as a result of the collapse of bond funding of subprime mortgages which resulted in lenders ceasing to dish out loans for subprime and other risky mortgages led to a downward spiral in house prices which culminated in the 2008 financial crisis (Federal Reserve History, 2013). After the crisis, a host of regulations was introduced to reel in the activities of banks with the primary objective of ensuring that there are sufficient risk management frameworks that are put in place to govern their activities (Charles, 2008).

A sub concept of RegTech is that of SupTech. Unlike RegTech which encompasses the use of technology for regulatory supervision and monitoring by regulators as well as regulatory compliance by financial institutions, SupTech only entails the use of technology for regulatory monitoring and oversight by regulators. In essence, SupTech involves the incorporation as part of regulatory frameworks automatic monitoring components that exercise oversight over a market's ledger records to evaluate the degree of compliance by the financial institutions operating in the market whereby the practical implementation of this concept has been driven primarily by the developments of blockchain as the underlying technology (BIS, 2020). The current generation, i.e., the fourth generation of SupTech, adopts a prescriptive approach under which "data is collected through automated reporting/real-time monitoring and processed using robotic process automation (RPA)/artificial intelligence (AI)-based validation enabling prescriptive, analytics and action plans" (OECD, 2021). A notable example of SupTech application is the Central Bank of Brazil's (BCB) "SupTech - Natural Language Processing Applications for Supervision project (SupTech-NLP)" which was launched in 2020 to incorporate AI-based applications for the processing of documents using NLP techniques as part of the BCB's supervision processes.

2.2.1 Blockchain Boost for RegTech and SupTech in Singapore and Malaysia

As the saying goes, "In every crisis there is an opportunity" and so tech entrepreneurs began looking into ways in which they can capitalize on the regulatory compliance headache of financial institutions. From the outset, the origins of the idea underlying blockchain can be traced back to 1991 with the invention of a mechanism to prevent and detect unauthorized tampering with digital documents by timestamping them (Haber & Stornetta, 1991). Although they did patent their invention, it lapsed in 2004 and five years later the inventor of Bitcoin, who goes by the pseudonym Satoshi Nakamoto, took the idea to a whole new level by using blockchain as the basis for the development of a peer-to-peer (P2P) protocol for Bitcoin (Chohan, 2017).

In the context of RegTech, the advent of Bitcoin in 2009, which led to the emergence of blockchain, took place just a year after the 2008 financial crisis. In a way, industry experts have suggested that the timing of the emergence of blockchain is not so much due to mere fortuity but instead was more of a result of the banking and finance industry's response to the deficiencies of the then-existing technologies. These deficiencies led to a loss of the human element in exercising discretion, resulting in an unduly high degree of inflexibility due to over-reliance on procedural codes, eventually culminating in unsustainable levels of systemic risks for the entire operational framework (Jagannathan et al., 2016).

The decentralized recording features of blockchain coupled with the automated execution functions of smart contracts render these two technologies particularly suited for regulatory compliance (Chaisse & Kirkwood, 2022). For regulatory compliance purposes, blockchain-based ledger records can be used as a tool to monitor financial transactions to identify individuals or institutions that need to be red-flagged for suspicious activities such as money laundering and terrorism financing before analyzing the records for any regulatory non-compliance (Panisi, 2017). As for smart contracts, they can be used to codify the relevant regulations as part of the monitoring system to facilitate the red-flagging process before subsequently issuing automated reports to highlight the systemic risks posed by regulatory non-compliance (Mignolicio, 2020). In this manner, blockchain-based smart contracts can play a complementary role as part of the regulatory compliance framework.

Globally, because of the occurrence of a string of financial crises and scandals in recent times which have affected the reputation of financial institutions such as the 1MDB scandal involving Goldman Sachs and the oversight failure of Deutsche Bank in the Epstein saga, public trust in financial institutions has very much hit rock bottom whereby most would agree that financial institutions can no longer be considered as "honest institutions" (Thirkell-White, 2014). In this regard, the use of blockchain as part of the operations of financial institutions could be a way of improving the levels of public trust in these institutions as the trustless nature of blockchain brings about a high degree of transparency, particularly when used in tandem with public and permissionless decentralized ledgers (Hughes et al., 2019). Besides that, the use of blockchain would also dispense with the need for financial institutions to maintain centralized databases which entails human resource costs and the possibility of the making of errors as well as the risks of fraud whereby similar benefits arise from the disintermediation features of blockchain which dispense with the need for third-party intermediaries (Chang et al., 2020).

In the context of Asia Pacific (APAC), Singapore is leading the way for the regional RegTech domain through the establishment in April 2021 of a new RegTech grant scheme under which the Monetary Authority of Singapore (MAS) would be committing USD35 million to promote the adoption and integration of RegTech solutions as part of the risk management and compliance functions of financial institutions in Singapore (MAS, 2021). Over in Malaysia, Bank Negara Malaysia (BNM) has outlined in its Annual Report 2021 as one of its key strategies for promoting financial stability in the country through the adoption of "regulatory and supervisory technologies to enhance our efficiency and effectiveness" (BNM, 2021).

As for SupTech, Singapore is also leading the way for APAC as illustrated by its Suspicious Transaction Reports (STRs) network analytics tool which analyses the STRs submitted by financial institutions to improve supervisory levels, its text analysis tool which subjects financial audits submitted by financial institutions to qualitative analysis for potential red flags and its predictive modeling tool which utilizes a multi-factor logistic regression model that to predict the risk of misconduct of financial advisers in the country over two years based on factors such as their working history, track record, and history of misconduct, etc. (FSB, 2020).

In October 2021, Singapore upped its ante in the field of SupTech when the MAS collaborated with the Bank for International Settlements Innovation Hub (BISIH) through Project Ellipse which is a proof of concept (POC) to explore the use of data analytics to generate insights through the development of a platform that would enable regulatory to "digitally extract, query and analyse a large quantity of data from diverse sources" to identify and assess emerging risks in a real-time manner before taking the necessary supervisory and/or enforcement actions to mitigate or address the risks before they escalate (BIS, n.d.).

As for Malaysia, BNM has deployed SupTech for the monitoring of remittance transactions as the central bank thinks that the cash-intensive and cross-border nature of the remittance industry renders it particularly susceptible to money laundering and terrorism financing risks (BNM, 2019). Accordingly, BNM has deployed SupTech in the remittance industry through the use of predictive analysis of transactional data at the industry and sectoral levels, licensee levels, and at customer and transaction levels. This is very much in line with BNM's third strategic thrust to advance digitalization of the financial sector under its Financial Sector Blueprint 2022–2026 which envisages providing "support for the greater use of technology for regulation and supervision" (BNM, 2022).

2.3 One Big Trust Issue in Malaysia and Singapore

In general, the Singaporean population has a relatively high degree of trust in the country's financial institutions as reflected in the 2021 edition of the Banking Trust Index for Singapore (BTIS) published by the Association of Banks in Singapore (ABS). According to the Index which measures public trust of banks in Singapore, the country's banking industry is the only domain that has managed to increase its trust capital, i.e., by seven points, as the other domains, namely, NGOs, media, business, and the Government, recorded a reduction in their trust capital by four, three, three, and two points respectively (ABS, 2021). The increase in the country's banking industry is mainly due to the increased trust of the Singaporean public in the ability of the local banking industry to meet evolving expectations thanks to the use of technological innovation to promote greater accountability.

The situation is a bit different, however, in Malaysia as the 1MDB scandal has highlighted the fundamental issues concerning the auditing process of state funds. The chronology of events was such that Ernst and Young (EY) was dismissed by the 1MDB board for refusing to sign off the state fund's 2010 financial statement, after which KPMG was hired to replace EY but KPMG too was later dumped after it inquired into 1MDB's offshore assets in the Cayman Islands. Thereafter, Deloitte was engaged during the period from 2011 to 2015, but it eventually was ordered to pay USD80 million as settlement costs for its role in the 1MDB scandal. Other than auditing firms, the 1MDB scandal also implicated a local bank, i.e., AmBank, which has reached a settlement worth USD2.83 billion with Malaysia's Ministry of Finance for the bank's role in the scandal, including the issuance of bonds and conversion of funds.

Worse still is the fact that the 1MDB scandal implicated Tabung Haji, i.e., the Malaysian Haji Pilgrims Fund Board, whose role is to facilitate the management of the financial savings of Muslims in the country for their pilgrimage to Mecca. As Tabung Haji has previously bought a piece of land at the Tun Razak Exchange (TRX) from 1MDB for RM188.5 million

(The Edge, 2015), Transparency International-Malaysia (TI-M) has issued a public notice to urge the disclosure of all relevant financial information for the purchase in the spirit of public accountability (TI-M, n.d.). Back in the late 1980s and early 1990s, there was another major financial scandal involving Bank Bumiputera Malaysia Berhad (BBMB) which was established in 1965 as part of Malaysia's affirmative action policies aimed at promoting economic and social advancement among the Bumiputera population.

The scandal revolved around allegations of mismanagement, corruption, and financial irregularities within the bank, including bad loans, questionable lending practices, and embezzlement (Abdullah et al., 2014). The scandal highlighted several regulatory failings and weaknesses in the country's financial oversight and governance including a lack of effective supervision, inadequate risk management, weak enforcement of banking regulations, inadequate response to early warning signs, and ineffectiveness of risk-based supervision. As these scandals involve possible misuse of public funds meant for religious purposes, the possible impact on the levels of public trust in Malaysian financial institutions should not be underestimated notwithstanding the absence of publicly available data on the level of public trust in Malaysian financial institutions.

2.3.1 1MDB Counterfactual Case Study: A Theoretical Approach

The first part of our case study is a theoretical analysis aimed at exploring how the notorious scandal might have been prevented or mitigated using modern technologies like blockchain. The idea is to hypothesize an alternative reality (a "counterfactual") where these technologies were in place and examine their potential impact on the scandal's development. In this theoretical approach, the study would likely focus on how blockchain technology could have enhanced transparency, accountability, and traceability in the financial operations involved in the 1MDB scandal. The theoretical case study demonstrates how RegTech- and blockchain-based solutions might have changed the outcome of the 1MDB scandal, reducing corruption and restoring public trust in financial systems.

2.3.1.1 Blockchain as a Trustless Technology

The autonomous nature of blockchain means that it can operate in a disintermediated manner through the operations of distributed trust among the participants of the network (Chen & Bellavitis, 2020). This stands in contrast with the conventional mode of financial institutions which needs to be supported by a network of intermediaries who could be prone to undue influence, coercion, or duress or perhaps even the potential for bribery and corruption by powerful and greedy humans who are looking to misuse the financial system to perpetrate money laundering or other fraud. In contrast, the autonomous nature of blockchain which brings with it the element of disintermediation means that the risks associated with human vulnerabilities are reduced significantly.

The immutable nature of blockchain records means that it would not be possible to manipulate or modify the data in these records once they have been accepted by the network thereby rendering the records to be tamper-proof (Hofmann et al., 2017). This stands in contrast with the conventional mode of financial institutions which uses records that are not cryptographically secured, thereby rendering them to be prone to unauthorized tampering by greedy humans looking to cover up their misuse of the financial system to perpetrate money laundering or other fraud. In contrast, the cryptographic security of blockchain records using hashing and timestamping mechanisms means that it would be mathematically impossible for the data in these records to be tampered with.

2.3.1.2 Blockchain as a Technological Watchdog

The 1MDB scandal, like many instances of financial fraud, stems from the inherent greed in human nature, where individuals exploit weaknesses in the system for personal gain. While no technology can eliminate this risk, blockchain offers a powerful solution by acting as a technological watchdog that can significantly strengthen the integrity of financial systems. Blockchain's immutable ledger ensures that once a transaction or record is entered, it cannot be altered or tampered with. This feature provides a new level of transparency, where every action within the system is permanently recorded and available for review. In financial systems prone to fraud, this transparency makes it significantly harder for individuals to manipulate records, hide illicit activities, or divert funds without detection.

In addition to transparency, blockchain fosters accountability. By creating a traceable audit trail, it holds individuals and institutions responsible for their actions. Whether it's tracking the movement of funds, ensuring the authenticity of financial documents, or verifying the ownership of assets, blockchain ensures that fraudulent actions are more easily detectable and harder to conceal. This heightened accountability reduces the opportunities for money laundering, embezzlement, and other financial crimes. While blockchain cannot fully prevent misuse of the financial system, it can mitigate the risks associated with human greed. It enhances the ability of regulators and financial institutions to monitor activities in real time, reducing the likelihood of fraud going unnoticed for extended periods. Furthermore, by strengthening transparency and accountability, blockchain plays a vital role in restoring public trust—not just in the financial system, but also in public service delivery and government institutions. This trust is essential for the healthy functioning of society, as it encourages compliance, ethical behavior, and confidence in the overall governance framework.

2.3.1.3 Blockchain as an Anti-hijacking Technology

As with any technology, blockchain is not immune to the risk of being hijacked or misused by individuals in power seeking to exploit the financial system for money laundering, fraud, or other illegal activities. However, blockchain stands apart from conventional systems due to its decentralized, autonomous, and immutable nature, which makes it uniquely resistant to such manipulation. In traditional financial systems, centralized authorities such as banks or government institutions control the flow of information and decision-making. This concentration of power creates vulnerabilities that can be exploited by those with the right influence or intent. A single point of failure allows for easier manipulation, whether through falsification of records, suppression of information, or the exploitation of regulatory loopholes. Human greed, often at the root of financial scandals like 1MDB, can flourish in these centralized systems because individuals can leverage their power over the system without widespread scrutiny.

In contrast, blockchain's decentralized nature fundamentally changes the dynamics of control. Instead of relying on a single entity or authority, blockchain distributes the decision-making and verification processes across a network of participants. Every transaction or record added to the blockchain must be validated by a consensus of the network, making it extremely difficult for any single actor or even a group of actors to alter or manipulate the system without the majority's agreement. This feature is a powerful safeguard against centralized corruption. The decentralized nature of blockchain entails the distribution of the decision-making and verification process, thereby dispensing with the need for a centralized authority (Pereira et al., 2019). This stands in contrast with the centralized frameworks of conventional financial institutions which render them to be prone to be misused by greedy humans who are looking to perpetrate money laundering or other fraud. In contrast, the use of decentralized blockchain means that these greedy humans would have to extend the coverage of their hijacking to the whole network of participants which would be practically impossible.

2.3.1.4 Blockchain as a Democratic Booster

The fundamental premise is that of check and balance to maintain an optimum equilibrium for the role and powers of the various arms of public governance (Jett, 2001). Yet in the context of the 1MDB scandal, it has illustrated that there is a palpable lack of check and balance when it comes to mitigating the risks of the misuse of the financial system for money laundering or other fraud by those from the executive arm of public governance. The 1MDB scandal is unique as it involves the element of abuse of power which renders the political philosophy of democracy even more relevant because as the saying goes, "power corrupts, absolute power corrupts absolutely," hence the need for the use of blockchain as a technological watchdog to enhance the element of check and balance in the financial system to mitigate the risks of future misuse of the financial system for money laundering or other fraud by those from the executive arm of public governance.

The fact of the matter is that the conventional top-down approach to the regulation of the financial system in which the public is reduced to the role of a mere bystander is incompatible with the notion of people's power under the political philosophy of democracy. The use of blockchain which entails the bottom-up approach through its decentralized, autonomous, and immutable features could neutralize the effects of the conventional top-down approach particularly through the incorporation of public blockchains even if they may be permissioned for certain aspects. The use of blockchain with its trustless nature is very much in line with the true spirit of democracy whereby this would go a long way toward restoring public trust in the financial system in the aftermath of the 1MDB scandal.

2.3.2 1MDB Counterfactual Case Study: A Practical Approach

The second part of our case study explores how specific technologies, if implemented, could have practically prevented or mitigated the 1MDB scandal. Unlike the theoretical approach, which focuses on what could have happened, the practical approach analyzes real-world applications of technologies like blockchain and how they might have been used to address the exact problems that led to the scandal. In this practical counterfactual scenario, had these blockchain-based systems been implemented, the core mechanisms of fraud and money laundering within the 1MDB scandal could have been detected and prevented early. The approach demonstrates how existing technology can be used in real-world settings to improve financial integrity, transparency, and regulatory effectiveness.

2.3.2.1 Blockchain as a Trust Anchor

"Trust Takes Years to Build, Seconds to Break, and Forever to Repair." If only 1MDB transactions were governed using blockchain by leveraging the technology as a trust anchor, then most likely would not have ended up like the scandal that it is. For starters, every transaction of the 1MDB fund would have been recorded on a block before being inserted as part of the chain and is automatically validated by the cryptographic connections between each block forming the chain, i.e., through a process known as hashing.

The hashing process means that all transactions in 1MDB's blockchain-based ledger records can be taken at face value, i.e., as it is without the need for further verification since the cryptographic encryption which forms part of the hashing process makes it mathematically impossible for the records to be fraudulently altered as the effects of the tampering would be immediately evident (Halewi & Krawczyk, 1999). This is because the network functions of blockchain are such that when a transaction has been verified it is added to the ledger records which are accessible by all the participants of the network, thereby ensuring the provenance of the records as it would not be possible for any participant to unilaterally alter the records as theoretically, this would require the participant to have to alter the records held by every participant on the network which would be practically impossible (Chowdhury, 2019).

Leveraging the trustless nature of blockchain which allows the technology to function as a trust anchor, the provenance of 1MDB-s blockchain-based ledger records could potentially be boosted by the mathematical and practical impossibility of making unauthorized changes to these records, thereby allaying the risks of tampering with information which could have materialized in the scandal. To put it simply, it is mathematically and practically impossible to alter the information in blockchain-based ledger records except with the consensus of all the participants in the network; hence, blockchain records are designated as a single source of truth.

Nonetheless, there is still a plausibility that those in power could coerce the participants in the network to unanimously consent to such alterations to 1MDB's blockchain-based ledger records but the use of public permissioned blockchains could help address this plausibility whereby the use of public blockchains would be justified on the basis that it involves public funds with commercially sensitive information being subjected to permission clearances. In the financial world, where due to the powerful allure of money coupled with the intrinsic greed in human nature, trust is a precious commodity that once lost could take a long to restore, hence the critical role of blockchain with its trustless nature.

2.3.2.2 Blockchain for AML/KYC and CDD Verification

"Trust But Verify." In Malaysia, section 16(1)(a) of the Anti-Money Laundering, Anti-Terrorism Financing and Proceeds of Unlawful Activities Act 2001 as read together with section 16(1)(b) provides that "a reporting institution shall not open or operate any anonymous account or any account which is in a fictitious, false or incorrect name nor establish or conduct any business relationship, transaction or activity involving a fictitious, false or incorrect name." In Singapore, paragraph 7.1 of the Notice PSN01 Prevention of Money Laundering and Countering the Financing of Terrorism – Specified Payment Services as read together with paragraph 2 provides that "a payment service provider shall identify each customer through their full name, including any aliases unique identification number, address, date of birth and nationality."

The implementation of these CDD provisions in today's age of financial digitalization and globalization is such that the silo mode of operations of central banks is no longer tenable and the 1MDB scandal, whose web of money laundering activities span across at least ten countries, is a prime example of this (Bloomberg, 2018). In the particular context of the 1MDB scandal, the sheer scale of the web of money laundering activities reflects on the palpable failings of the first line of regulatory defense against money laundering, i.e., customer due diligence through KYC protocols.

In line with the BIS' agenda of facilitating dialogue and cooperation between central banks through the free exchange of information, forging a common understanding and making decisions of common actions between these banks, a good starting point to address the failings of existing KYC protocols as illustrated by the 1MDB scandal would be the use by central banks of the shared utility KYC model in the form of a blockchain-based e-KYC decentralized framework which for starters would help lower the costs for KYC verification by dispensing with the need for a trusted third party (TTP) because, in a blockchain-based KYC verification framework, a copy of the blockchain would be distributed to each of the participating nodes, thereby doing away with the need for a TTP and the associated costs (Sinba & Kaul, 2018).

In addition to reducing costs, the use of a blockchain-based KYC decentralized framework would also enhance the efficiency of the KYC verification process as it would reduce the time required to complete the process. This is because through the use of blockchain-based KYC frameworks central banks would have access to a self-verifying and trusted KYC credentials database, thereby dispensing with the need to engage intermediary third parties to verify the credentials of prospective customers. The validity of the information stored in the blockchain records is warranted through the use of a secure hash algorithm (SHA) which refers to a family of cryptographic hash functions published by the National Institute of Standards and Technology (NIST).

The use of SHA cryptographic hash for the processing of financial transactions would be a boost to the operations of the financial domain where there is a perennial risk of fraudulent tampering with information stored in a network. SHA leverages the challenge-and-authentication process to safeguard the integrity of data by ensuring that it would not be compromised during the transfer process by warranting that any tampering attempt would automatically invalidate the transaction (Maxim Integrated, 2019). Through the use of sequential storage, any unauthorized changes in one part of the ledger records can be automatically detected as the ledger record containing the information that has been tampered with would not match with the other ledger records that have been distributed to other participating nodes in the network. This allows any number of untrusted intermediaries to handle a set of data while still maintaining the integrity of the data up till the point it reaches its final destination.

For the use of blockchain for KYC verification to be feasible in practice, central banks would need to come together to form a network that would form the basis for the KYC verification process for customers of the central banks under the network. Upon the formation of such a network, blockchain can be deployed in the form of a digital identity management grid whereby the details and information which form part of the parameters of the screening and compliance framework would be recorded on a chain that is accessible by financial institutions (Nabi, 2017). The use of such a blockchain-based digital identity management grid could potentially transform the existing complicated and cumbersome KYC verification process into a simple checking procedure with the relevant details and information of a particular individual being automatically verified by a blockchain host network whereby these verified details and information would be accessible by the participants of the network (Singhal et al., 2020).

This operational mode of arrangement brings about much convenience for customers who would be spared the hassle of having to undergo KYC verification process every time they subscribe to the services of a different financial institution whereas for the financial institutions themselves, the use of a blockchain-based digital identity management grid would bring about much costs reduction and time savings as they no longer need to engage in the extensive process of gathering the relevant KYC credentials of their new customers before verifying these credentials with third-party intermediaries to ascertain as the degree of compliance with the applicable regulations. As for central banks, the use of a blockchain-based KYC verification process may help bolster their efforts to combat money laundering, particularly when it comes to the use of the international financial system to undertake cross-border money laundering activities such as in the case of the 1MDB scandal.

Nonetheless, for the wide use of the blockchain-based KYC verification process to be plausible in reality, financial institutions must be willing to share their customers' sensitive information whereby this would require the establishment of a new ecosystem in which trust is the norm. In this regard, it is notable that one of the hindrances highlighted by the MAS for its inability to detect the money laundering transactions under the 1MDB scandal in an earlier manner is that its regulatory policy is such that it "does not track the funds flowing into and out of banks in Singapore. To do so, in the absence of an investigation into a possible crime, would be a serious violation of privacy" (MAS, 2019). In other words, the constraints of privacy considerations compel the MAS to take a reactive, as opposed to a proactive, approach to its regulatory policy for the detection and investigation of money laundering activities.

Concerning the issue of finding the optimum balance between privacy and accessibility, some industry experts have proposed the development of a blockchain-based system which can process transactions using a real-time accounting mechanism that leverages on the technology's zk-SNARK protocol to ensure that notwithstanding the public accessibility of data which are recorded on distributed ledgers, the particulars of these data can only be accessed by authorized parties such as regulators and auditors, thereby harnessing the automatic recording features of blockchain and the transparency brought about by the immutability of public blockchain ledger records without compromising on the privacy of the data or the confidentiality of the customers of the relevant financial institutions (Wang & Kogan, 2018).

In the context of the blockchain-based KYC verification process, the use of zk-SNARK protocol for the distribution of data to the relevant stakeholders may be able to help satisfy due disclosure requirements for regulatory transparency purposes while potentially ensuring that the benefits of transparency would not come at the price of the privacy of the beneficial owners of financial funds. This is because the zk-SNARK mechanism can be used to validate the fact that the identity of the owners is in due compliance with the applicable regulations, thereby warranting the integrity of the shareholding framework without disclosing the identity of the owners or arrangement of the framework (Meralli, 2020). In this manner, central banks such as the BNM and MAS would no longer be hindered by the constraints of privacy considerations from taking a proactive approach to the undertaking of CDD as part of their AML/KYC regulatory policies for the detection and investigation of money laundering activities, thereby helping to reduce the risks of something similar to the 1MDB scandal from happening again in the future.

2.3.2.3 Blockchain for Triple-Entry Accounting

"The Numbers Don't Lie, But They Can Be Manipulated." In Malaysia, Section 67(1) of the Financial Services Act 2013 provides that "every institution shall appoint an auditor for each financial year who meets such requirements or has such qualifications set out in any standards as may be specified by the Bank." In Singapore, Section 37(1)(a) of the Payment Services Act 2019 as read together with section 37(4)(a) provides that "a licensee must, on an annual basis and at its own expense, appoint an auditor to carry out, for the year in respect of which the auditor is appointed, an audit of the accounts of the licensee." In many ways, the 1MDB scandal has highlighted the fault lines of existing audit procedures for financial institutions. In the aftermath of the 1MDB scandal, the MAS imposed a USD1 million fine on DBS Bank, a USD1.3 million fine on UBS Bank and shut down the local unit of Switzerland's Falcon Bank for regulatory breaches (Reuters, 2016). In Malaysia, KPMG, for its role in failing to red-flag suspicious transactions, agreed to a settlement with the government of Malaysia, whereby, according to the settlement, USD80 million was paid by KPMG to the Ministry of Finance in January 2022 (MOF, 2022).

How KPMG had failed to raise the red flag on suspicious transactions undertaken 1MDB board to the point of risking its independence and impartiality as an external auditor is worrying, to say the least as it highlights the extent to which the effectiveness of external financial audits is dependent on the accuracy of the information records submitted by the clients who are also the paymasters of the external financial auditors. It is in this context that the trustless and decentralized feature of blockchain may come in handy in the context of the use of triple-entry accounting to safeguard the integrity of the financial audit process.

The origins of triple-entry accounting date back to 1989 when Japanese academic Yuji Ijiri came up with the idea, which was subsequently improved upon by Ian Grigg, of cryptographically sealing financial accounting records before these records are coded into smart contracts and entered into a blockchain-based ledger records a copy of which is distributed to the parties, thereby adding a layer of integrity to the validity of financial accounting records (Ijiri, 1986). This extra copy of records, i.e., the third copy in addition to the debit and credit records, is referred to as trebit under Grigg's concept of "the receipt is the transaction" whereby the cryptographically and smart contract encoded digitally signed receipt would greatly reduce the risks of transaction fraud in addition to reducing the redundancies associated with internal recording (Cai, 2019).

In the context of triple entry accounting, the trustless nature of blockchain-based ledger records coupled with the cryptographic sealing and smart contract encoding may be able to help dispense with the need for after-the-fact verification, thereby saving much time for both the professional auditors who would be spared the tedious task of verifying the accounting records and the financial institutions themselves who would be spared the arduous obligations of supplying voluminous information to substantiate their accounting records (Supriadi, 2020). If 1MDB had used triple entry accounting for its internal bookkeeping, the decentralized feature of blockchain means that the ledger records of the branches or departments of the various financial institutions could be automatically recorded in the same database in a customized manner, although these branches and departments may be using different computer systems (Guo & Liang, 2016).

Accordingly, KPMG may have been able to have access to these blockchain-based ledger records which, thanks to their cryptographic sealing and smart contract encoding, can be taken at face value, thereby dispensing with the requirement of after-the-fact verification with the 1MDB board which would have been a big boost to transparency and accountability. Upon inspection of these ledger records using the principles of momentum accounting which is commonly associated with triple entry accounting, KPMG could have been able to identify the unusually high rate of change in income and capital outflow whereby this can be immediately red-flagged as indicating the possibility of suspicious transactions.

Had 1MDB been properly administered for its avowed purposes, the fund may have been able to benefit from the use of triple entry accounting as the real-time tracking and recording functions of blockchain-based ledger records can speed up the payment settlement process, thereby improving the capital flows of the fund, which in turn allows it to keep less capital in its reserves.

2.3.2.4 Blockchain for Beneficial Interest Tracking

"Tracking is Not Just About Monitoring, It's About Understanding." In Malaysia, section 13(1) of the Anti-Money Laundering, Anti-Terrorism Financing and Proceeds of Unlawful Activities Act 2001 as read together with section 13(3)(b) provides that "a reporting institution shall keep a record of any transaction involving the domestic currency or any foreign currency exceeding such amount as the competent authority may specify whereby the record shall include the identity and address of the beneficiary or the person on whose behalf the transaction is conducted, where applicable." In Singapore, paragraph 7.13 of the Notice PSN01 Prevention of Money Laundering and Countering the Financing of Terrorism – Specified Payment Services provides that "a payment service provider shall inquire if there exists any beneficial owner in relation to a customer" except where the customer falls under the list of entities set out in paragraph 7.16.

The issue of beneficial interest is a pertinent one in the 1MDB scandal because according to the facts of the legal case in the US courts, between 2009 and 2011 more than USD1 billion were transferred from 1MDB to a Swiss bank account held in the name of Good Star Limited due to the false representations by 1MDB officials that the account belonged to PetroSaudi. According to the Federal Court judgment in *Dato' Sri Mohd Najib bin Hj Abd Razak vs PP*, the account was beneficially owned by Low Taek Jho aka Jho Low, who then laundered more than USD400 million of the funds for his gratification as well as for that of his associates (Dato' Sri Mohd Najib bin Hj Abd Razak v. Public Prosecutor, 2021).

From the perspective of the regulators, blockchain's automated recording features could enable the beneficial ownership of bank accounts to be tracked and updated in a real-time manner whereby this could lead to greater transparency before the undertaking of any financial transaction (Jarwal, 2019). Additionally, the use of blockchain-based tracking of the beneficial ownership of bank accounts in tandem with smart contracts can facilitate the automation of the process for the transfer of funds whereby the identity of the beneficial owners can be confirmed automatically using DIDs which are encoded into the parameters of smart contracts (Li et al., 2019). The use of DIDs and smart contracts in this regard could potentially help deter opportunistic behavior by those who may engage in fraudulent activities without compromising the privacy of the personal information of the beneficial owners.

If the transfer of the USD1 billion to the Good Star Limited Swiss account beneficially owned by Jho Low was subjected to identity confirmation using DIDs which are encoded into smart contracts equipped with blockchain-based beneficial ownership tracking mechanisms, the relevant financial institutions and regulators, namely, BNM could have been able to see through the ruse of the misrepresentations of the 1MDB officials whereby the execution of the transaction could have been prevented which in turn could have averted the misappropriation by Jho Low of more than USD400 million. As the guardian of Malaysia's financial system, BNM's approval for the outgoing transfer of USD1 billion is necessary under the central bank's exchange control policies whereby the central bank could have exercised its authoritative discretion to suspend the transfer had it been aware of the details of beneficial ownership of the recipient if a blockchain-based beneficial ownership tracking mechanism was in place and used by the central bank.

2.4 A Realistic Perspective on the Prospects of Blockchain Use for Restoring Public Trust in Financial Institutions

The potential revolutionary role of blockchain and how this may upset the existing status quo in terms of the hierarchical structure and balance of power of government administrators as well as financial regulators and institutions may result in the adoption and use of blockchain being dictated by considerations which are outside the scope of the operations of the technology. In other words, the adoption and use of blockchain may be dictated by non-technological factors such as the systemic factors which are prevalent in the established political and financial hegemony, particularly the political will of the government and the degree of concession of market-leading financial institutions.

How this plays out in reality is reflected by the fact that governments tend to hide behind the veil of official secrecy whereas most of the financial institutions which have ventured into the blockchain domain are those who are deemed to have sufficient industry reputation to be part of blockchain-related consortiums in the banking and finance industry or those who have the financial resources to undertake experiments to explore the possible use of blockchain for their operations (Prewett & Prescott, 2019). In short, the adoption and use of blockchain for restoring public trust in financial institutions would depend on the commitment of the government of the day and the concession willingness of financial institutions whereby those who have firm industry reputations and strong financial reserves would be those which are most likely to be able to embrace the use of blockchain as part of their operations.

From a technological perspective, the discussions have set out how the use of blockchain could mitigate the risks of a similar scandal as that of 1MDB. If Malaysia is to restore public trust in its financial institutions including both state-owned and private ones, the role of blockchain as a trust anchor renders the technology ideal for the Malaysian government's agenda in this regard, though this would be dependent on the political will to commit to mitigating the risk of a repeat of a similar scandal as that of 1MDB. As for Singapore, it too could do with the use of blockchain to further boost the trust levels of its population in the country's financial institutions in line with the government's commitment to the use of digital technologies to drive the innovation of its financial system.

2.4.1 *Lending the Regulators an Embedded Blockchain Hand*

The challenges facing financial regulators are set to increase in time to come whereby a notable development in this regard is the rise of decentralized finance (DeFi) which in 2021 recorded a 30% year-on-year (YoY) increase in money laundering activities involving about USD8.6 billion in cryptocurrencies (Chainalysis, 2022). In light of the increasing propensity for the use of the DeFi domain for money laundering purposes, it may not be too far-fetched to suggest that the next 1MDB scandal could take place through the DeFi domain as opposed to the conventional financial system whereby this is because the domain operates using cryptocurrencies which operate in a pseudo-anonymous manner or even total anonymity for some cryptocurrencies such as privacy coins. As the Chainalysis 2022 Crypto Crime Report ("Chainalysis Report") explains, "Cybercriminals dealing in cryptocurrency share one common goal: Move their ill-gotten funds to a service where they can be kept safe from the authorities and eventually converted to cash. That's why money laundering underpins all other forms of cryptocurrency-based crime."

Notwithstanding the propensity for the domain DeFi to be a hotbed for money laundering activities, the use of blockchain could help regulators trace the proceeds of such activities more effectively as compared to the conventional fiat-based financial system. This is because although the ownership of cryptocurrencies may be pseudo-anonymous or anonymous, transactions involving the proceeds of money laundering activities in the form of cryptocurrencies can be tracked on the relevant blockchain network when these proceeds are transferred to other wallets or converted into fiat money. As the Chainalysis Report explains, "The biggest difference between fiat and cryptocurrency-based money laundering is that, due to the inherent transparency of blockchains, we can more easily trace how criminals move cryptocurrency between wallets and services in their efforts to convert their funds into cash." Nonetheless, the decentralized nature of the DeFi domain would bring newfound challenges to regulators whereby it would be even more imperative that central banks form close collaboration with each other as a silo approach would have little efficacy in regulating the DeFi domain with its decentralized, i.e., cross-border mode of operations.

It was against this context that the concept of embedded supervision has come to the fore in recent times to advocate the use of blockchain as a tool to facilitate the monitoring and supervision of financial regulators. In its report titled "Embedded Supervision: How to Build Regulation into Blockchain Finance," the BIS evaluated the emergence of the DeFi domain as a shadow financial system and explored how regulators can harness the use of blockchain through the concept of embedded supervision as part of their regulatory frameworks for the automatic monitoring of the compliance of decentralized markets through the replacement of the existing intermediary-based data verification with blockchain-enabled data credibility verification which operates through economic consensus (BIS,

2020). Although the BIS stated in the report that regulations should not be written in such a manner as to purposely accommodate the use of technology in the financial sector, it does concede that regulations should be flexible enough to evolve following the prevalent technologies used in the sector.

The main objective of the concept of embedded supervision is to reduce the administrative burden of regulators through the establishment of trust-creating mechanisms for the regulation of decentralized markets in contrast with conventional data verification frameworks which rely heavily on laws and the threat of legal penalties, data credibility frameworks under the concept of embedded supervision would be warranted by the underlying economic conditions. Accordingly, the role of the regulators in this regard is greatly reduced as they would be freed from the existing burden to which they are subject under conventional data verification frameworks of having to constantly manage the conflicting parameters of data, availability, and verification as well as privacy consideration whereby under the data credibility frameworks entailed by the concept of embedded supervision the role of regulators is limited to market governance in terms of creating sufficient incentives to guarantee the validity of data in blockchain-based ledger records.

In addition, the BIS noted that the embedded supervision would reduce the administrative burden of regulators by allowing them to harness the trustless nature of distributed ledgers to secure the irreversibility of transactions, thereby ensuring the critical element of finality in the operations of financial networks. From a costs perspective, the BIS gave its thumbs-up to the trustless nature and disintermediation feature of blockchain as this would help reduce the costs of financial services which, as the BIS puts it, "has remained stubbornly high" whereby the role of blockchain in this regard would be to reduce the costs associated with the provision of financial services by dispensing with layers of intermediaries whereby this would help lower the barriers of entry to the financial sector, thereby facilitating the promotion of financial inclusion in line with the agenda of regulators.

In many ways, the BIS' concept of embedded supervision avails itself as a handy tool to regulators. Taking some lessons from the 1MDB scandal, the role of BNM has not gone unnoticed whereby the million-dollar question is as to how it is possible that the financial proceeds of more than USD40 billion were able to be transferred out of Malaysia to more than ten countries around the world, from Asia to the Middle East to North

America (WSJ, 2016). Although BNM had on 23 February 2022 issued a statement which reads: "All investments abroad by resident entities are subject to the requirements under the Exchange Control Act 1953 that was in force prior to 2013 (since replaced by the Financial Services Act 2013). These requirements and criteria governing such investments are transparent and published on BNM's website. All submissions made by 1MDB, including the said application, were subject to the same approval criteria and internal governance process that apply to any submission by other entities to BNM" (BNM, 2022). It has to be said that the sheer scale of the 1MDB scandal which involves the transfers of large amounts of funds out of Malaysia through financial institutions falling under the regulatory supervision of BNM indicates a degree of oversight on the part of the BNM in terms of fulfilling one of its primary functions which is "to regulate and supervise financial institutions which are subject to the laws enforced by the Bank." As for the MAS, it too could only take remedial, as opposed to preventive, measures by closing down two banks, namely, BSI Bank and Falcon Private Bank Ltd, and imposing penalties on eight other banks as well as issuing prohibition orders against a host of individuals implicated by the scandal in addition to facilitating the return by the Singaporean government of USD16.3 million which had been misappropriated from the 1MDB fund (The Business Times, 2021).

In many ways, the 1MDB scandal has made clear the fault lines in the regulation of the conventional financial system and the limitations in the role of the regulators as illustrated by the failure of the BNM to exercise effective supervision of transfers of financial funds out of Malaysia and the extent to which the MAS was merely able to take remedial as opposed to preventive measures by ensuring proper regulatory compliance by financial institutions in Singapore to deter them from being implicated in the scandal. If a scandal of the proportion of the 1MDB saga could happen in the heavily regulated conventional financial system, the pertinent risks of a similar scandal happening in time to come in the DeFi, which is currently mostly unregulated, are much more pertinent. As much as there is a palpable need for regulation of the DeFi domain, the decentralized nature of the domain which operates in a cross-border manner presents a distinct set of challenges to regulators that are unlike those of the conventional financial system. It was in this context that the BIS came up with the concept of embedded supervision which entails shifting the exercise of regulatory oversight by regulators to the financial market players themselves with blockchain as the trust mechanism and economic incentives as the driving factor to secure compliance, thereby allowing regulators such as BNM and the MAS to harness the use of blockchain-based SupTech to facilitate their monitoring and supervision efforts in the DeFi domain.

2.4.2 *Deploying the Embedded Blockchain Regulatory Hand*

For financial institutions and regulators, the use of blockchain as part of the monitoring activities of regulators can fall under three possible categories or boxes. Firstly, for financial institutions, there is the Recycle Box whereby blockchain is used as a tool to improve the existing mechanisms operated by regulators. An example of this is the Ripple network which uses blockchain to improve the existing interbank payment settlement process by leveraging distributed ledgers to facilitate the instant settlement of interbank transactions in a real-time manner. Nonetheless, a pertinent issue in this regard which arises from the enhanced interconnectivity between financial institutions spurred by the ease of data sharing between themselves may increase the risk of collusion between these institutions whereby a prime case example of this, albeit one which occurred before the coming to the fore of blockchain, is the Libor scandal in which 16 banks, including Deutsche Bank, Barclays, UBS, Rabobank, and the Royal Bank of Scotland, attempted to the rig the global financial system by manipulating the London Interbank Offered Rate (LIBOR) (CFR, 2016).

The LIBOR scandal involved collusion between traders and employees of the banks whereby these employees would submit rates that would benefit the traders instead of rates that the employees' banks would pay to borrow money, resulting in a situation under which the fluctuations in LIBOR rates were based "entirely on a trader's position." With the advent of blockchain, scandals such as LIBOR would likely be a thing of the past as the automated nature of the technology means that the all-important element of control no longer lies in the hands of financial institutions, thereby reducing the risks of fraudulent manipulation whereby, if coupled with the use of public ledger records to provide the much-touted element of transparency, it would considerably reduce the risks of fraud undertaken by financial institutions.

This leads us to the second box, i.e., the Dark Box which includes the use of blockchain for the furtherance of illegal activities or to achieve an objective that is deemed by regulators to be illegal. From the perspective of the SupTech initiatives of regulators, notwithstanding the much avowed transparent nature of blockchain, distributed ledgers can be made private whereby when used in tandem with privacy coins such as Monero and Zcoin this poses a big challenge for regulators as the decentralized nature of blockchain coupled with the use of private permissioned distributed ledger records would effectively shield the identity of perpetrators and the details of transactions from the regulators (Sapkota & Grobys, 2019). Additionally, the use of privacy-centric cryptocurrencies such as Monero (XMR), Zcash (ZEC), and Decreed (DCR) would mean that the efforts of regulators to identify the perpetrators and the customers would come to a naught as the cryptographic encryption of privacy coins grant total anonymity to both the sender and the receiver of any transaction undertaken using these coins.

A middle option between the uses of blockchain under the Recycle Box and Dark Box is the sandbox which aim is to provide a conducive regulatory environment for the development of prospective blockchain use cases that are not illegal in themselves but which the regulators nonetheless feel the need to exercise some degree oversight upon, though at the same time the regulators are wary about imposing on such use cases the full extent of the regulatory requirements because to do so would render the use cases to be practically untenable (Wright et al., 2006). In short, the use cases of blockchain that fall under the sandbox are those that are unable to comply with the strict letter of the law but aim to comply with the spirit of the law. In this day and age of digital revolution and internet connectivity, the use of blockchain is likely to transcend across multiple jurisdictions in a cross-sectoral manner whereby for the sandbox option to be viable their development would require the collaboration of regulators on an international level encompassing the different areas which are relevant in this regard, most notably those of capital market, financial services, and consumer protection.

Additionally, the regulatory environment envisaged under the sandbox option needs to consider the reality in the modern-day commercial domain. Unlike conventional businesses, tech startups tend to be small and operate under limited staffing with only a few employees (Miller & Bound, 2011). For many of these startups, their approach is one of experimentation whereby their prototype idea is their main capital and their goal is to transform their prototype ideas into reality before turning them into a commercial success through the large-scale deployment of the relevant system. Accordingly, regulators must keep this in mind when developing sandboxes for blockchain use cases by ensuring that the compliance requirements imposed on the startups under the regulators' sandboxes are not unduly burdened with overly cumbersome obligations. Instead of adopting a one-size-fits-all approach, regulators should adopt a case-by-case tailored approach to ensure that the compliance requirements imposed by their sandboxes on these startups are suited for their size and the scale of their operations.

Embodying this approach through its triple elements of parity, proportionality, and neutrality is BNM's sandbox which was launched in October 2016 to provide "a regulatory environment that is conducive for the deployment of financial technology and facilitate overall innovation in the Malaysian financial sector" whereby the sandbox had received 109 applications as of July 2022. Adopting a similar approach is the MAS which FinTech Regulatory SandBox framework offers three options, i.e., sandbox, sandbox Express, and sandbox Plus to cater to the needs of first movers and early adopters of FinTech solutions through the provision of full-customization facilities, fast-tracked approvals, and financial grants.

The primary regulator for Malaysia's capital markets the SC in its report for Project Castor noted that the notion of "decentralize everything" may not serve as the ultimate solution for capital markets (SC, 2018). Instead, they envisioned a future with a multi-tier market environment where centralized and decentralized markets coexist harmoniously. The report offered general guidance on how the key considerations about the use of blockchain for the unlisted and over-the-counter (OTC) markets should be approached and considered. As a final note, the report suggested a pragmatic approach that takes into account the requirements, risk appetite, and technological capabilities of the respective participants in the decentralized markets.

2.4.3 *Chinks in the Embedded Blockchain Regulatory Hand*

Nonetheless, the use of blockchain brings with it a certain degree of risks whereby the most prevalent risks are those concerning what is generally known as a 51% attack which aims to exploit blockchain's consensus mode of operations to force the network to undergo changes in an unauthorized manner for the benefit of the perpetrators of the attack. Under a 51% attack, the perpetrators would try to obtain control over more than half the network to dictate its mode of operations whereby although this may consume an enormous amount of processing powers, the perpetrators may dispense with this requirement by engaging in tactics such as misleading the members of the network into loading a decoy version of the network's code which shows a false representation of the network's capabilities. Other than that, the perpetrators of a 51% attack may also resort to manipulative tactics such as the prisoner's dilemma strategy by offering compensation to members of the network to upload a false code into the network or turning to the divide-and-conquer strategy by splitting the members into factions and pitting them against one another to create a vacuum for the perpetrators to exploit to take over control of the network (Sayeed & Marco-Gisbert, 2019). Nonetheless, the sheer costs required for the execution of a 51% attack renders the likelihood of such an attack negligible whereby an example of this is the fact that the likelihood of a 51% attack on the Bitcoin network is a mere 0.49% as it is estimated that undertaking a 51% on the Bitcoin network would cost about USD752,000 per hour (UToday, 2022).

It is trite knowledge that the global financial market is one in which financial institutions engage in intense competition to expand their market share to enlarge their profit base whereby given the fact that the use of digital technologies such as blockchain for the operations of these institutions may help enhance their competitiveness, this presents the distinct possibility that in their race to leverage blockchain these institutions may fail to properly safeguard their information and network systems against the risks associated with the use of blockchain (Vovchenko et al., 2017). Notwithstanding the claims that blockchain offers foolproof security, empirical evidence shows that information and network systems that operate using blockchain are not immune to cyberattacks as illustrated by two events in 2016 that seriously challenged the notion of blockchain security, the first of which was the hacking of the Decentralized Autonomous Organization (DAO) network in July which resulted in a loss of USD50 million followed by the theft of more than USD72 million worth of Bitcoins from Hong Kong–based cryptocurrency exchange BitFinex in August (Baldwin, 2016). The fact that these organizations were operating using blockchain but yet still had the security of their networks being compromised by cyber hackers and thieves illustrates the fact that the infallibility of blockchain is very much a myth.

In 2016, a critical event highlighted the issues that may arise from the use of blockchain-based networks whereby the Ethereum platform was hacked, resulting in the unauthorized transfer of USD50 million worth of Ether tokens from a DAO (Dhillon et al., 2017). With the support of 85% of the members on the Ethereum network, the operators of the network did two things that were supposed to be impossible for a blockchain network whereby the first was the making of changes to the ledger records of transactions whereas the second was the execution of human-based intervention to alter the automated process of smart contracts. Although the actions of the operators of the Ethereum network were undertaken with the approval of the majority of the members of the network, the implementation of these actions has raised some significant questions about the much-touted features of blockchain, namely, the immutability of its distributed ledger records, and the self-executing features of smart contracts.

Another risk that arises from the use of blockchain is that in the event of any entry being mistakenly inserted into the ledgers, it may be replicated throughout the entire system given the interconnected nature of the ledgers which automatically reconcile with one another. A factor that may further exacerbate the effects of the mistake is the fact that the immutable nature of the ledgers renders the task of correcting the mistake to be tedious one as any revision can only be undertaken following the underlying consensus mechanism, i.e., with the approval of the participants of the network under the applicable consensus mechanism (Zheng, et al., 2018). Additionally, as with every other digitization process, there is the risk of data that has been uploaded onto the blockchain network being misused because the security of blockchain networks is not infallible whereby in the context of the financial and corporate governance domains the sensitive nature of the data on its blockchain networks would mean that these data can be easily monetized which in turn means that there would be no lack of financial motivation for cyber hackers to target these networks (Li et al., 2020).

Moreover, as blockchain is run using software its network may carry bugs, i.e., defects in the program, and thereby be vulnerable to attacks. In the context of financial transactions, any attack on the software underlying a blockchain network may result in transactions that have been settled on the network being reversed in addition to the completion of the processing of existing and future transactions being unduly held up (Iuon Chang & Tzu-Chun, 2017). Moreover, like other forms of software, the software underlying blockchain networks would require upgrading from time to time whereby, unlike centralized databases which can straightforwardly implement software upgrades, the decentralized nature of blockchain networks means that the consensus of all the participants of the network is required before the implementation of any software updates and the obtaining of this consensus may be anything but straightforward particularly under circumstances where the participants have conflicting interests (Wang et al., 2016).

Lastly, the decentralized feature of blockchain networks which operate without the need for any human intervention places a huge amount of responsibility and power on those who set up these networks whereby if they choose to misuse or abuse their skills, knowledge, and expertise, then the participants of the network would be in a vulnerable position as they may be held to ransom by these people who could use their know-how to usurp the consensus mechanism embedded in the network (Mohanta et al., 2019).

2.4.4 *Final Take on the Use of Blockchain for Financial Regulatory Compliance in Singapore and Malaysia*

In Malaysia, the use of blockchain financial for regulatory compliance has been evolving gradually, with the SC and BNM issuing guidelines and regulations to govern digital assets and FinTech innovations. However, the adoption and utilization of blockchain for regulatory compliance purposes in Malaysia could be stifled by the pace of regulatory development in the country which may be perceived as slower compared to Singapore which has been proactive in embracing blockchain and fostering a conducive environment for its development and adoption. In this regard, the MAS has taken significant steps to regulate and promote blockchain-based innovations, establishing initiatives like Project Ubin, Project Guardian, Project Partior, and Project Harbour, which explore the potential of blockchain and CBDCs in the financial sector. This proactive stance has encouraged the integration of blockchain solutions for regulatory compliance purposes in areas such as KYC/AML processes, trade finance, and securities settlement.

Both Malaysia and Singapore face cross-border regulatory challenges for their use of blockchain for financial regulatory compliance especially for applications that involve international transactions or partnerships. Differences in regulatory requirements between Singapore and Malaysia, as well as other jurisdictions, may complicate compliance efforts and require careful navigation to ensure regulatory alignment.

As the use of blockchain for financial regulatory compliance involves sensitive personal data such as financial information, the use of blockchain particularly public or permissionless blockchains by financial institutions in Malaysia and Singapore entails personal data protection issues under the Personal Data Protection Act 2010 (PDPA) in Malaysia and the PDPA 2012 in Singapore.

References

ABA Banking Journal. (2019, December 1). As synthetic identity fraud rises, so does KYC/CDD compliance cost. *ABA Banking Journal.*

Abdullah, A., Suolong, Z., & Said, R. M. (2014). An analysis on ethical climate and ethical judgment among public sector employees in Malaysia. *Journal of Applied Business and Economics, 16*(2) http://www.na-businesspress.com/JABE/SulongZ_Web16_2_.pdf

Arner, W., Barberis, J., & Buckley, P. (2017). FinTech and RegTech in a nutshell, and the future in a sandbox. *Northwestern Journal of International Law and Business, 37*(3) https://scholarlycommons.law.northwestern.edu/cgi/viewcontent.cgi?article=1817&context=njilb

Association of Banks in Singapore. (2021). Banking trust index for Singapore. https://abs.org.sg/docs/library/btis-2021-report.pdf

Baldwin, C. (2016, August 14). Bitcoin worth $72 million stolen from Bitfinex exchange in Hong Kong. *Reuters.* https://www.reuters.com/article/us-bitfinex-hacked-hongkong-idUSKCN10E0KP

Bank for International Settlements (BIS). (2020). BIS Working Papers No. 811: Embedded supervision: How to build regulation into decentralised finance. https://www.bis.org/publ/work811.pdf

Bank for International Settlements (BIS). (n.d.). Ellipse overview. https://docs.bis.org/ellipse/

Bank Negara Malaysia (BNM). (2019). Annual report 2019. https://www.bnm.gov.my/documents/20124/2724769/ar2019_en_full.pdf

Bank Negara Malaysia (BNM). (2021). Annual report 2021. https://www.bnm.gov.my/documents/20124/6458991/ar2021_en_book.pdf

Bank Negara Malaysia (BNM). (2022). Financial sector blueprint 2022–2026. https://www.bnm.gov.my/documents/20124/5915429/fsb3_en_book.pdf

Bektenova, G. S. (2018). Are RegTech, FinTech, Blockchain the future? In *III Network AML/CFT Institute International Scientific and Research Conference "FinTech and RegTech"* (pp. 61–67). KnE Publishing. https://knepublishing.com/index.php/KnE-Social/article/view/1525/3615

Bloomberg. (2017, November 30). Banks are spending $20 billion on compliance tech ahead of MiFID. *Bloomberg.* https://www.bloomberg.com/news/articles/2017-11-29/banks-are-spending-20-billion-on-compliance-tech-as-mifid-looms

Bloomberg. (2018, March 3). A guide to the worldwide probes of Malaysia's 1MDB fund. https://www.bloomberg.com/news/articles/2018-03-07/malaysia-s-1mdb-fund-spawns-worldwide-probes-quicktake

Butler, T., & O'Brien, L. (2019). Understanding RegTech for digital regulatory compliance. In *Disrupting finance: FinTech and strategy in the 21st century* (Chapter 6). Palgrave Macmillan. https://library.oapen.org/bitstream/handle/20.500.12657/23126/1007030.pdf?sequence=1#page=106

Cai, C. (2019). Triple-entry accounting with blockchain: How far have we come? *Journal of Accounting and Finance, 61*(2) https://www.researchgate.net/publication/336645713_Triple-entry_accounting_with_blockchain_How_far_have_we_come

Capgemini. (2021). World FinTech Report 2021. https://fintechworldreport.com/resources/world-fintech-report-2021/

Chainalysis. (2022). Crypto crime report. https://go.chainalysis.com/rs/503-FAP-074/images/Crypto-Crime-Report-2022.pdf

Chaisse, J., & Kirkwood, J. (2022). Smart courts, smart contracts, and the future of online dispute resolution. *Stanford Journal of Blockchain Law and Policy*. https://stanford-jblp.pubpub.org/pub/future-of-odr/release/1

Chang, V., Baudier, P., Zhang, H., Xu, Q., Zhang, J., & Arami, M. (2020). How blockchain can impact financial services: An overview, challenges, and recommendations from expert interviewees. *Technological Forecasting and Social Change, 158*. 120166. Elsevier.

Charles, A. E. (2008). The regulatory response to the financial crisis. CESifo Working Paper, No. 2257. Center for Economic Studies and Ifo Institute for Economic Research. https://www.econstor.eu/bitstream/10419/26302/1/560533586.PDF

Chen, Y., & Bellavitis, C. (2020). Blockchain disruption and decentralized finance: The rise of decentralized business models. *Journal of Business Venturing Insights, 13*. https://www.researchgate.net/publication/337111343_Blockchain_Disruption_and_Decentralized_Finance_The_Rise_of_Decentralized_Business_Models

Chohan, U. W. (2017). A history of Bitcoin. SSRN Electronic Journal. https://papers.ssrn.com/sol3/papers.cfm?abstract_id=3047875

Chowdhury, N. (2019). An IoT and blockchain-based approach for ensuring transparency and accountability in regulatory compliance. In *UbiComp/ISWC '19 Adjunct: Adjunct proceedings of the 2019 ACM International Joint Conference on Pervasive and Ubiquitous Computing and Proceedings of the 2019 ACM International Symposium on Wearable Computers* (pp. 957–962).

Council on Foreign Relations (CFR). (2016, October 12). Understanding the Libor scandal. https://www.cfr.org/backgrounder/understanding-libor-scandal

Dato' Sri Mohd Najib bin Hj Abd Razak v Public Prosecutor [2021] MLJU 2485.

Dhillon, V., Metcalf, D., & Hooper, M. (2017). The DAO hacked. In *Blockchain enabled applications* (pp. 67–78). Apress.

Federal Reserve History. (2013, November 22). Subprime mortgage crisis. Federal Reserve History. https://www.federalreservehistory.org/essays/subprime-mortgage-crisis

Finance and Economics Club IITG. (2018, August 16). Credit default swap and its role in the 2008 financial crisis. Finance and Economics Club IITG. https://finecoiitg.wordpress.com/2018/08/16/credit-default-swap-and-its-role-in-the-2008-financial-crisis/

Financial Stability Board (FSB). (2020). The use of supervisory and regulatory technology by authorities and regulated institutions. https://www.fsb.org/wp-content/uploads/P091020.pdf

Guo, Y., & Liang, C. (2016). Blockchain application and outlook in the banking industry. *Journal of Financial Innovation, 2*, 1–12. https://doi.org/10.1186/s40854-016-0034-9

Haber, S., & Stornetta, W. S. (1991). How to time-stamp a digital document. *Journal of Cryptography, 3*(1), 99–111. https://link.springer.com/article/10.1007/BF00196791

Halewi, S., & Krawczyk, H. (1999). Public-key cryptography and password protocols. *ACM Transactions on Information and System Security, 2*(3). https://doi.org/10.1145/322510.322520

Hofmann, F., Wurzster, S., Ron, E., & Böhmecke-Schwafert, M. (2017). The immutability concept of blockchains and benefits of early standardization. In 2017 ITU Kaleidoscope: Challenges for a data-driven society (ITU K), Nanjing, China. https://www.inno.tu-berlin.de/fileadmin/a38335100/PDF_Dateien/Publikationen/T-PROC-KALEI-2017-PDF-E-Hofmann.pdf

Hughes, A., Park, A., Kietzmann, J., & Archer-Brown, C. (2019). Beyond Bitcoin: What blockchain and distributed ledger technologies mean for firms. *Business Horizons, 62*(3), 273–281. Elsevier.

Ijiri, Y. (1986). A framework for triple-entry bookkeeping. *Accounting Review, 61*(4), 745–759.

International Banker. (2018, November 7). The cost of compliance. International Banker. https://internationalbanker.com/technology/the-cost-of-compliance/

Investopedia. (2021, August 27). What role did securitization play in the global financial crisis? *Investopedia*. https://www.investopedia.com/ask/answers/041515/what-role-did-securitization-play-us-subprime-mortgage-crisis.asp

Iuon-Chang, L., & Tzu-Chun, L. (2017). A survey of blockchain security issues and challenges. *International Journal of Network Security, 19*(5), 653–659. http://ijns.jalaxy.com.tw/contents/ijns-v19-n5/ijns-2017-v19-n5-p653-659.pdf

Jagannathan, R., Kapoor, M., & Schaumburg, E. (2016). Causes of the great recession of 2007–2009: The financial crisis was the symptom, not the disease! *Journal of Financial Intermediation, 22*(1), 4–29. http://es.saif.sjtu.edu.cn/attachments/publication/2016/01/b08744b0-a2cc-476c-937e-b63d26521c85.pdf

Jarwal, D. (2019). Issue of securities through blockchain technology. *International Journal of Advance and Innovative Research, 6*(3(I)), 19–22. https://papers.ssrn.com/sol3/papers.cfm?abstract_id=3468205

Jett, D. C. (2001). The essential elements of a functioning democracy. *Florida Journal of International Law, 14*(1), 71–78. https://scholarship.law.ufl.edu/cgi/viewcontent.cgi?article=1382&context=fjil

Kinyua, D. (2020). KYC, client onboarding: Leveraging blockchain technology. SSRN Electronic Journal. https://papers.ssrn.com/sol3/papers.cfm?abstract_id=3528323

LexisNexis. (2019a). APAC true cost of AML compliance—Malaysia. LexisNexis. https://risk.lexisnexis.com/global/en/insights-resources/presentation/true-cost-of-aml-compliance-malaysia-snapshot

LexisNexis. (2019b). APAC true cost of AML compliance—Singapore. LexisNexis. https://risk.lexisnexis.com/global/en/insights-resources/presentation/true-cost-of-aml-compliance-singapore-snapshot

Li, K. C., Chen, X., Jiang, H., & Bertino, E. (2019). *Chapter 6: Application of blockchain and smart contracts*. CRC Press.

Li, X., Jiang, P., Chen, T., Luo, X., & Wen, Q. (2020). A survey on the security of blockchain systems. *Journal of Future Generation Computer Systems, 107*, 841–853. https://doi.org/10.1016/j.future.2017.08.020

Lootsma, Y. (2017). Blockchain as the newest RegTech application—The opportunity to reduce the burden of KYC for financial institutions. *Journal of Banking & Financial Services Policy Report, 36*(8) https://static1.squarespace.com/static/567bb0614bf118911ff0bedb/t/59ca5fc4017db2da07ec290c/1506435012176/Article+-+Blockchain+as+the+Newes+Regtech+Application+-+Yvonne+Lootsma+%281%29.pdf

Maxim Integrated. (2019, October 21). Securing electronic transactions using SHA-1 secure hash algorithm (Application Note 1770). https://www.maximintegrated.com/en/design/technical-documents/app-notes/1/1770.html

Meralli, S. (2020). Privacy-preserving analytics for the securitization market: A zero-knowledge distributed ledger technology application. *Journal of Financial Innovation, 6*(7). https://doi.org/10.1186/s40854-020-0172-y

Mignolicio, A. (2020). Automated regulation and supervision: The impact of RegTech on banking compliance. *European Business Law Review, 31*(4), 641–662. https://kluwerlawonline.com/journalarticle/European+Business+Law+Review/31.4/EULR2020025

Miller, P., & Bound, K. (2011). The startup factories: The rise of accelerator programmes to support new technology ventures (NESTA Discussion Paper). https://www.bioin.or.kr/InnoDS/data/upload/policy/1310018323687.PDF

Ministry of Finance. (2022, January 13). Malaysia receives RM340.92 million from KPMG as 1MDB settlement. https://www.mof.gov.my/portal/en/news/press-release/malaysia-receives-rm340-92-million-from-kpmg-as-1mdb-settlement

Mohanta, B. K., Jena, D., Panda, S. S., & Sobhanayak, S. (2019). Blockchain technology: A survey on applications and security privacy challenges. *Journal of Internet of Things, 8*, 100107.

Monetary Authority of Singapore (MAS). (2019, March 30). Response to "Questions for MAS on 1MDB" in The Straits Times, 23 March 2019. https://www.mas.gov.sg/news/letters-to-editor/2019/response-to-questions-for-mas-on-1mdb

Monetary Authority of Singapore (MAS). (2021, April 30). MAS commits $42m to spur adoption of technology solutions for risk management and regulatory compliance. Monetary Authority of Singapore. https://www.mas.gov.sg/news/media-releases/2021/mas-commits-42m-to-spur-adoption-of-technology-solutions

Nabi, A. G. (2017). *Comparative study on identity management methods using blockchain*. University of Zurich. https://files.ifi.uzh.ch/CSG/staff/Rafati/ID%20Management%20using%20BC-Atif-VA.pdf

Organisation for Economic Co-operation and Development (OECD). (2021). OECD Business and finance outlook 2021: AI in business and finance—The use of SupTech to enhance market supervision and integrity. https://www.oecd-ilibrary.org/sites/d478df4c-en/index.html?itemId=/content/component/d478df4c-en

Panisi, F. (2017). Blockchain and 'smart contracts': FinTech innovations to reduce the costs of trust. SSRN Electronic Journal. https://papers.ssrn.com/sol3/papers.cfm?abstract_id=3066543

Pereira, J., Taveleei, M. M., & Ozalp, H. (2019). Blockchain-based platforms: Decentralized infrastructures and its boundary conditions. *Technological Forecasting and Social Change, 146*(3) https://eprints.whiterose.ac.uk/146947/1/Pereira%2C%20Tavalaei%2C%20and%20Ozalp%2C%202018%20Open%20access%20version.pdf

Prewett, K. W., & Prescott, G. L. (2019). Blockchain adoption is inevitable—Barriers and risks remain. *Journal of Corporate Accounting and Finance, 31*(2), 21–28.

RealWire. (2019, September 3). KYC compliance costing banks €50 million a year as financial sanctions soar. RealWire. https://www.realwire.com/releases/KYC-compliance-costing-banks-50-million-a-year-as-financial-sanctions-soar

Reuters. (2016, October 11). Singapore shuts Falcon Bank unit, fines DBS and UBS over 1MDB. https://www.reuters.com/article/us-malaysia-scandal-falcon-idUSKCN12B03Y

Sapkota, N., & Grobys, K. (2019). Asset market equilibria in cryptocurrency markets: Evidence from a study of privacy and non-privacy coins. SSRN Electronic Journal. https://papers.ssrn.com/sol3/papers.cfm?abstract_id=3407300

Sayeed, S., & Marco-Gisbert, H. (2019). Assessing blockchain consensus and security mechanisms against the 51% attack. *Journal of Applied Sciences, 9*(5) https://www.mdpi.com/2076-3417/9/9/1788

Securities Commission Malaysia. (2018). Capital market architecture blueprint in a decentralised world. https://www.sc.com.my/api/documentms/download.ashx?id=a720347d-a637-4652-a393-14d96db91ef5

Sinba, P., & Kaul, A. (2018). Decentralized KYC system. *International Research Journal of Engineering and Technology (IRJET), 5*(8), 1206–1211.

Singhal, N., Sharma, M. H., Samant, S. S., Goswami, P., & Reddy, Y. A. (2020). Smart KYC using blockchain and IPFS. In *Advances in Cybernetics, Cognition, and Machine Learning for Communication Technologies* (pp. 77–84). Springer. https://doi.org/10.1007/978-3-030-43007-2_9

Supriadi, I. (2020). The effect of applying blockchain to accounting and auditing. *Ilomata Journal of Tax and Accounting, 1*(3). https://www.ilomata.org/index.php/ijtc/article/view/101

The Business Times. (2021, November 20). Malaysia says Singapore has returned US$16.3m in 1MDB funds. https://www.businesstimes.com.sg/government-economy/malaysia-says-singapore-has-returned-us163m-in-1mdb-funds

The Edge. (2015, May 7). Tabung Haji admits to land deal with 1MDB. https://www.theedgemarkets.com/article/tabung-haji-admits-land-deal-1mdb

The Wall Street Journal (2016, 26 December). How a Malaysian Scandal Spread Across the World. https://www.wsj.com/graphics/1mdb-how-a-malaysian-scandal-spread-across-the-world/

Thirkell-White, B. (2014). Dealing with the banks: Populism and the public interest in the global financial crisis. *Journal of International Affairs, 85*(4), 689–711.

Transparency International Malaysia. (n.d.). TI-M urges Lembaga Tabung Haji to disclose financial information on the land deal with 1MDB. https://transparency.org.my/pages/news-and-events/press-releases/ti-m-urges-lembaga-tabung-haji-to-disclose-financial-information-on-the-land-deal-with-1mdb

UToday. (2022, September 17). Here's how much it costs to 51% attack Bitcoin (BTC). https://u.today/heres-how-much-it-costs-to-51-attack-Bitcoin-btc

Vovchenko, N. G., Andreeva, A. V., Orobinskiy, A. S., & Filippov, Y. M. (2017). Competitive advantages of financial transactions on the basis of the blockchain technology in digital economy. *European Research Studies Journal, 20*(3B), 193–212. https://www.ersj.eu/dmdocuments/2017-xx-3-b-19.pdf

Wang, H., Chen, K., & Zu, D. (2016). A maturity model for blockchain adoption. *Journal of Financial Innovation, 2*(12) https://link.springer.com/article/10.1186/s40854-016-0031-z

Wang, Y., & Kogan, A. (2018). Designing confidentiality-preserving blockchain-based transaction processing systems. *International Journal of Accounting Information Systems, 30*, 1–18.

World Economic Forum. (2022). Regulatory technology for the 21st century. https://www3.weforum.org/docs/WEF_Regulatory_Tech_for_the_21st_Century_2022.pdf

Wright, W., Schroh, D., Proulx, P., Skaburskis, A., & Cort, B. (2006). The sandbox for analysis: Concepts and methods. In *CHI '06: Proceedings of the SIGCHI Conference on Human Factors in Computing Systems*, 801–810.

Zheng, Z., Xie, S., Dai, H. N., Chen, X., & Wang, H. (2018). Blockchain challenges and opportunities: A survey. *International Journal of Web and Grid Services, 14*(4).

CHAPTER 3

Blockchain Toolkit for Islamic Financial Services

Abstract Blockchain technology, including public ledgers and decentralized identities (DIDs), can ensure *zakat* reaches the rightful recipients while preserving their privacy. In Singapore, the shift to digital cash *waqf* results in a greater need for transparency and accountability through blockchain and smart contracts to ensure the proper use of *waqf* funds. For businesses, blockchain can reduce the issuance costs of micro sukuk, enabling micro, small, and medium enterprises (MSMEs) and small and medium enterprises (SMEs) in Malaysia and Singapore to raise funds. Blockchain also has much to offer to address the operational issues in Islamic financial institutions (IFIs), such as the technical Shariah non-compliance of foreign exchange (FX) spot. For *murabaha* transactions, smart contracts can address the current imbalance where IFIs provide guarantees without charging fees. Blockchain could also help manage IFIs' liquidity risks through decentralized liquidity saving mechanisms (LSMs) particularly when combined with using cryptocurrencies such as stablecoins as Shariah-compliant alternatives to fiat currency.

M. S. Thong, *Blockchain for Financial Governance in Malaysia and Singapore*,
https://doi.org/10.1007/978-981-96-1281-9_3

3.1 Rise of Islamic Financial Services as an Alternative to Conventional Financial Services

The birth of Islamic finance took place sometime in the ninth century when Muslim merchants traveled to distant places by land for trade with Islamic principles and values serving as their guiding compass (Renima et al., 2016). This eventually led to the Islamic Golden Age which was a period of rapid cultural, scientific, political, and economic development in the Islamic world. In line with the growth of commercial activities in that historical period, the needs of the business community for trade financing services also grew in tandem and it was in this context that Islamic trade financing stood out as an alternative to the conventional trade financing framework (Chong et al., 2019).

In contrast with the conventional trade financing framework, which is heavily based on the element of interest, Islamic trade financing prohibits the practice of usury as it considers *riba* (interest) to be *haram* (illegal). In general, Muslims are not allowed to engage in financial transactions that involve the element of interest payment as the focus of Islamic financial services is on the development of the real economy, and in the context of the financial domain, this requires Islamic financial services to be based on the element of participatory finance whereby this requires the transacting parties to be entitled to partake in the profits in an agreed ratio as opposed to the creditor taking advantage of the circumstances of the borrower in a predatory manner (Habib, 2011).

In line with the principles underlying the *Maqasid al-Shariah* (objectives of *Shariah*) which provide for the promotion of the well-being of the people by enabling them to safeguard their *dīn* (faith), *naql* (intellect), *nafs* (lives), *nasl* (posterity), and *mal* (property), the Islamic financial system strives for the promotion of economic growth and social wealth particularly for the benefit of those who are less fortunate whereby this is in stark contrast to the approach of the conventional financial system which tends to leave the poor unbanked, i.e., without access to financial services resulting in the poor being stuck in the vicious cycle of poverty. Unlike the conventional financial system which operates primarily based on profit-making considerations, the Islamic financial system is governed by a host of rules in the form of *Shariah* principles that aim to facilitate the generation of wealth sustainably and the distribution of wealth in a fair manner whereby the primary rules include those which prohibit *haram* activities, *riba* payments as well as any transaction involving the elements of *gharar* (speculation) and *maysir* (uncertainty).

However, putting into practice *Shariah* principles in the context of financial services is certainly no walk in the park. According to a report issued by the International Monetary Fund (IMF) in 2017, there were many gaps in *Shariah* governance frameworks which may affect the stability and development of the Islamic financial system (IMF, 2017). It was in this context that the IMF recommended putting in place a comprehensive legal structure which serves to provide certainty and clarity to the regulation of Islamic financial services to boost the confidence of users who can repose reliance on the established governing standards. From a market perspective, the IMF proposed putting in place proper mechanisms to monitor and manage the liquidity pool and risk exposure of IFIs to ensure that these institutions would not be vulnerable to the volatility of global financial markets. Concerning the internal management of IFIs, the IMF put forth its case for greater clarity and structure in the division of the roles between the different parts of the management system of these institutions whereby this element is highly critical to the implementation of operational policies particularly those about risks management and regulatory compliance.

3.1.1 *The Modern-Day Golden Age of Islamic Finance*

The fundamental objective of Islam is to guide all areas of life for Muslims including commercial matters such as economic and financial activities (Ahmed et al., 2015). In this regard, the primary rule of Islamic laws is that transactions which are undertaken by Muslims have to adhere to *Shariah* principles which strive to ensure that the profits of business transactions would not come at the price of social inclusion or financial sustainability. With the global Muslim population getting close to the 2 billion mark, the use of Islamic financial services has risen considerably, resulting in a more central role for Islam as a guide for the conducting of business transactions (Qardus, 2022).

This is evidenced by the rise in the total assets value of the Islamic financial market which amounted to USD2.2 trillion as of April 2023 led by the growth of the Islamic financial hubs around the world primarily those in countries comprising the Gulf Cooperation Council (GCC), with Malaysia and the UK leading the way for SEA and Europe respectively (Standard Chartered, 2023). In a way, the unbridled capitalism of the conventional financial system framework has facilitated the rise of the Islamic financial services sector as the global population is finding it increasingly difficult to trust traditional financial institutions which in their chase for profits are willing to resort to excessive risk-taking or even outright fraud as exemplified by the 2008 financial crisis and LIBOR scandal respectively.

Unlike the unenviable ways of the conventional financial system, the core theoretical tenet of the Islamic financial framework is based on the principles of fair risk sharing and due transparency as well as proper accountability. Nonetheless, the realization of these principles has proved to be quite a challenge in actual practice leading to criticisms from some parts of the Muslim community that Islamic financial services are not fundamentally different from those offered by the conventional financial system. Critics point to the fact that the balance sheets of most IFIs comprise mainly of *murabaha*, i.e., cost-plus financing, which involves the undertaking of trade financing transactions based on the mark-up value of goods; and *Ijarah*, which involves the undertaking of a lease or rental transaction whereby the ownership of the usufruct of an asset is transferred to another person for a specified period in return for a fee (Sairally, 2002). The critics argue that these instruments which operate based on the concepts of risk transferring and risk shifting have departed from the Islamic principles of risk sharing and are therefore not true embodiments of the underlying objectives of Islamic financial services to promote financial inclusivity and shared prosperity.

It is against such a background that users of Islamic financial services should understand the different categories which these services may fall under. In terms of the general classification of Islamic financial services based on the degree of *Shariah compliance* of these services, the lower levels of the classification structure, i.e., those which have a doubtful degree of *Shariah compliance* are constituted by pseudo-Islamic financial services which amounts to a *hilah*, i.e., legalistic trickery to deceive the public by creating a facade of compliance with Shariah principles but the products violate these principles (Al-Amine, 2015). A word of caution is that although *Shariah* principles do allow the use of Islamic financial services that are not in compliance with these principles where the prevalent circumstances are such that there is no *Shariah*-compliant alternative to fulfill a pressing need, recourse to this exemption would not be available where there are *Shariah*-compliant Islamic financial services available. Accordingly, although the use of pseudo-Islamic financial services which amounts to a *hilah* is generally prohibited, it is permitted under circumstances where there is a valid necessity due to there being no alternative financial services available to meet a pressing need.

Above the category of Islamic-pseudo financial services is the middle category which comprises *Shariah*-compliant financial services that are technically in accordance with Islamic laws but fail to comply with the spirit and objective of these laws, i.e., to help those who are poor and needy. In other words, *Shariah*-compliant Islamic financial services are those which comply with the letter but not the spirit of Islamic laws as expressed through the applicable *Shariah* principles. Lastly, at the top rung of the classification is the category comprising Islamic financial services which truly are *Shariah*-compliant as they adhere to the letter as well the spirit of Islamic laws by properly addressing the needs of the less fortunate sections of society in line with the underlying ideals of Islamic laws which strive for the promotion of financial inclusivity and the furtherance of shared prosperity (Fig. 3.1).

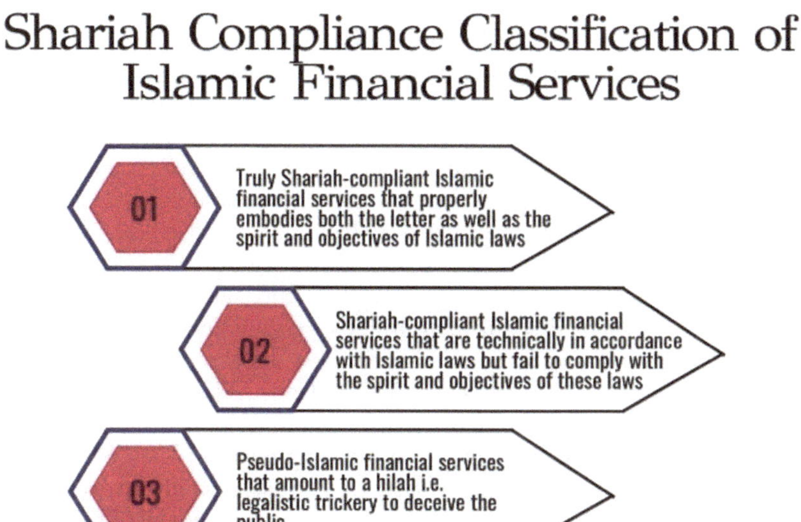

Fig. 3.1 Shariah compliance classification of Islamic Financial Services (Source: Writer's Own)

Given the intricacies of the operations of the *Shariah*-governance frameworks of IFIs which services have to comply with both the spirit and letter of Islamic laws, the use of financial technology supported by technologies such as blockchain would come in handy. The automated and decentralized features of blockchain can help ensure that the integrity and legitimacy of *Shariah* governance frameworks can be maintained effectively and efficiently.

3.1.2 Islamic Financial Services Landscape in Malaysia and Singapore

In the Cambridge Global Islamic Finance Report (GIFR) 2023's Islamic Finance Country Index, Malaysia was ranked second behind Saudi Arabia (Cambridge-IIF, 2023). Globally, Malaysia has an 18.4% share of Islamic financial assets through 16 BNM-licensed Islamic banks, of which 11 are local Islamic banks whereas 5 are foreign Islamic banks currently operating in Malaysia (BNM, 2022). Locally, Islamic banking assets in Malaysia were worth USD264.5 billion in 2022 whereby this constituted about 34.2% of the total banking assets of the country (The Malaysian Reserve, 2022). In terms of Islamic financing, the market share of such services constituted 41% of Malaysia's financing services, meeting the target of 40% set by BNM in its Financial Sector Blueprint 2011–2020 (BNM, 2011).

Moving forward, BNM has set out its plans for Malaysia's Islamic financial services sector through the central bank's fifth strategic thrust under its Financial Sector Blueprint 2022–2026 under which BNM would be looking to leverage the country's position as a global leader in Islamic finance to advance value-based financing through a three-pronged approach which includes financing foundation-building, mainstreaming, as well as driving diversification and innovation to transform Malaysia into a global gateway to enter Asia's and OIC's Islamic finance markets (BNM, 2022). At the same time, BNM would continue to deepen Malaysia's Islamic capital markets domain which made up for more than 60% of the country's capital markets value as of 2022 (The Malaysian Reserve, 2022).

In Malaysia, the regulation of IFIs falls under the purview of the BNM which is tasked with enforcing the Islamic Financial Services Act 2013 (IFSA) which provides, for among other things, the *Shariah* governance of IFIs including the establishment of a *Shariah* committee and the undertaking of *Shariah* audit compliance if instructed to do so by BNM. In addition, BNM has also issued policy documents for specific Islamic financial products and services including *murabaha*, *ijarah*, and *istina* as well as a policy document that provides for the capital adequacy requirements of IFIs offering these Islamic financial products and services. Other than the IFSA and BNM's policy documents, IFIs in Malaysia also have to abide by the resolutions of BNM's Shariah Advisory Council (SAC) whereby these resolutions cover among other things, matters on *ijarah* and *sukuk* based on *bai bithamin ajil* (BBA).

As for Singapore, the MAS' approach to the regulation of Islamic banks in Singapore is not too dissimilar with that for conventional banks. In this regard, the MAS through its Guidelines on the Application of Banking Regulations to Islamic Banking had established a single regulatory framework under which Islamic banks in Singapore are subjected to the same sets of rules and regulations as conventional banks including the Banking Act, Banking Regulations, Notices and Directives as well as the relevant guidelines. Nonetheless, the MAS does recognize the unique features of Islamic financial products and services whereby the approach of the MAS in this regard is to assess the form of such products and services to assess their economic substance and the risks involved, and in circumstances where the economic substance and risks of Islamic financial products and services differ from those of conventional financial products and services, the MAS would specifically cater to these differences.

In particular, the MAS acknowledges the fact that Islamic banks generally face greater reputational risks than conventional banks due to the need on the part of Islamic banks to comply with *Shariah* principles and rules. Accordingly, the MAS' *Guidelines on the Application of Banking Regulations to Islamic Banking* sets out the funding structures for several main Islamic financial products and services including *murabaha*, *ijarah*, *istina*, and *sukuk*.

3.2 Blockchain as a Technological Enforcer of Islamic Financing Ethics

In its report titled "Islamic Financial Services Industry Stability Report 2019," the International Financial Services Board (IFSB) noted the potential offered by the automated feature of smart contracts concerning the execution of *Shariah*-based contracts, though the IFSB noted that there is a need to put in place of appropriate regulatory arrangements to support the use of blockchain in the Islamic financial services sector

(IFSB, 2019). The IFSB also noted that the use of blockchain in the Islamic financial service sector is likely to bring more challenges to *Shariah* experts than the regulators who are tasked with governing the operations of IFIs. This is because the current scope of uses of blockchain in the sector which covers the areas of *zakat* (almsgiving), *sadaqah* (voluntary charity), and *waqf* (charitable endowment) fall within the domain of Islamic Social Finance (ISF) concerning which the *Shariah* principles on financial banking and capital markets only apply partially.

From the outset, given the ethics-based operational modes of IFIs, all dealing on the transactions undertaken by these institutions must be done in a transparent and accountable manner. It is in this context that the automated and immutable features of blockchain-based shared ledgers come in handy as they warrant that the dealings of IFIs are undertaken in a manner that complies with the applicable *Shariah* principles (Mohamed & Ali, 2018). As for the use of smart contracts, the parameters of the relevant *Shariah* principles which are required to be complied with by a particular Islamic financial transaction can be inserted as computer codes into a smart contract whereby this would warrant the due adherence of the transaction with the relevant *Shariah* principles.

The automated implementation of Islamic financial transactions using smart contracts which leverage the neutrality of technology to warrant due *Shariah compliance* stands in stark contrast with conventional paper-based contracts where implementation is dependent on the interpretation of the parties whereby this may lead to any ambiguity being interpreted in a manner which suits the exigencies of the situation potentially leading to *Shariah* non-compliance. In other words, the automated features of smart contracts would ensure that Islamic financial transactions would be undertaken in a *Shariah*-compliant manner regardless of any change in the prevalent circumstances. This helps avert the risks, however minimal, of the parties succumbing to the tendency of interpreting the contractual terms, in light of the changed circumstances after the execution of the contract, in a manner that affects the degree of *Shariah compliance.* The risks in this regard are particularly pertinent where the prevalent circumstances are such that departing from *Shariah compliance* would be in the interests of the parties.

In addition to covering situations whereby there is a failure of an IFI to ensure that the transactions entered into by it are in due compliance with the applicable *Shariah* principles, *Shariah* non-compliance can also arise where there is a failure on the part of an IFI to fulfill its duties and obligations under a transaction. In the context of the highly popular *mudarabah* arrangement, such a failure on the part of an IFI would likely be concerning its fiduciary responsibilities as a *mudarib* (financier) though it should be noted that there appears to be no recorded case of any such failure on the part of a *mudarib*. Through the use of smart contracts, these risks can be reduced considerably as any material non-compliance on the part of an IFI would automatically trigger the appropriate alert whereby the computer code of the smart contract can be programmed in such a manner as to invalidate the underlying contract upon the occurrence of a series of material non-compliance with the applicable *Shariah* principles (Hidajat, 2020).

Given the fact that one of the main objectives of Islamic laws is to promote the welfare of the public, IFIs may have recourse to smart contracts as a technological tool to gauge the impact of Islamic financial services offered by these institutions on their customers. The smart contracts can be programmed in such a manner as to issue a request to the customers upon the completion of an Islamic financial transaction before storing these responses in a blockchain-based ledger which can be reviewed by regulators to assess the extent to which their respective Islamic finance system has been able to meet the objectives of Islamic laws. The process undertaken by the regulators would be similar to the Social Return On Investment (SROI) method generally undertaken by financial institutions operating within the Social and Solidarity Finance (SSF) framework. The common theme is the assessment of the impact of financial services on the general public, albeit for IFIs the assessment would be undertaken in the context of the general mode of operations of these institutions including without limitation the degree of adherence to *Shariah* principles.

3.2.1 *Zakat and* Waqf*: The Twin Pillars of Islamic Social Finance*

The importance of *zakat* collection as part of the Islamic way of life is evidenced by the fact that *zakat* is mentioned 32 times in the Quran and over the years the arrangements for *zakat* collection have been institutionalized in most Muslim countries (Jaelani, 2016). In terms of the operations of *zakat* collection mechanisms, they need to comply with the principles governing *zakat* collection as set out in the Quran to properly fulfill the role of *zakat* as a form of obligatory charity constituting one of the five pillars of Islam in aid of the eight categories of the less fortunate

(Wahab & Rahim, 2011). In terms of the implementation of *zakat* collection, the collection mechanisms must be imbued with the elements of transparency and accountability not only to further the objectives of *zakat* collection but also to boost the confidence of Muslims in the overarching *zakat* framework.

From a macroeconomics perspective, *zakat* brings about the redistribution of social wealth by requiring those whose net wealth is above the prescribed threshold to pay *zakat* on an annual basis in aid of the less fortunate, thereby rendering *zakat* to essentially function as a tool for the promotion of social welfare. In terms of the volume of *zakat* collections, it is estimated that in countries such as Qatar, Malaysia, Indonesia, Saudi Arabia, and Yemen which collectively make up only 17% of the global Muslim population the total annual *zakat* collection amounts to an estimated USD5.7 billion thanks to the institutionalization of *zakat* management frameworks and collection mechanisms (Shaikh, 2016). Globally, the value of *zakat* collection is estimated to be somewhere within the range of USD200 billion and USD1 trillion whereby it has been suggested that the use of technology can significantly increase the value of *zakat* collection (Solferino Academy, 2018). This would go a long way toward furthering the social justice ideals of Islamic social finance by helping to reduce the global humanitarian funding deficit which stood at a worrying USD16.7 billion at the end of 2018 (UNOCHA, 2018).

As for *waqf*, it refers to Islamic charitable endowments which usually take the form of donation of assets such as land and buildings whereby the endowment of a particular asset would be deemed as belonging to Allah (SWT) (Shaikh et al., 2017). Accordingly, assets that are the subject matter of a *waqf* endowment fund must be preserved for the religious or charitable purposes for which they were intended whereby any income generated from these assets must be channeled to socially beneficial causes. From an Islamic perspective of human existence, *waqf* is in line with the teaching that the charitable giving of one's assets for benevolent purposes when one is in *duniya* (worldly life) will lead to a better *akhirah* (afterlife) (Zaman, 2015).

Conventional *waqf* endowment frameworks operate using direct and indirect cash as well as *sukuk* fundraising methods (Kusumaningtias, 2019). The direct cash fundraising method is the most straightforward form of fundraising method whereby monetary contributions are channeled toward the acquisition of *waqf* assets. The indirect cash fundraising method involves the accumulation of cash contributions which are then invested before the revenue generated from the investments is channeled toward the underlying social charitable causes of the *waqf* fund. As for the *sukuk* fundraising method, it involves the issuance of *sukuk* bonds whereby the funds obtained from the sale of these bonds are channeled to the *waqf* endowment fund. In Malaysia, two successful *waqf* use cases in line with the Islamic stipulation of *istibdal* (substitution) are the conversion of two old *waqf* schools into colleges, i.e., the Al-Mashoor Maahad in Penang and the Maahad Tahfiz Mithaful Ulum in Klang (Gazali & Che Ismail, 2019).

The *waqf* domain is increasingly turning to the use of crowdfunding particularly in the form of donation-based crowdfunding by utilizing the direct and indirect *waqf* crowd mechanisms which are respectively the crowdfunding modular representations of the direct and indirect cash fundraising methods (Abdel Mohsin, 2019). The use of the crowdfunding mechanism for *waqf* endowment frameworks has opened the door for the use of blockchain to support the operations of these frameworks.

3.2.1.1 Blockchain as a Technological Remedy for the Trust Deficits of Zakat Mechanisms

The obligation to pay zakat is universally applicable to all Muslims. In Malaysia (MASB, 2006) and Singapore (Zakat Singapore, n.d.), those who possess the required minimum amount (*nisab*) which is equivalent to the prevalent market value of 85g and have held this for a period of 1 Hijri year or 355 days (*haul*) are required to make *zakat* payments at the rate of 2.5% of the amount of wealth above the *nisab* threshold. In the context of *zakat* mechanisms, the main issues are concerning the distribution of funds. As *zakat* is essentially a faith-based contribution, religious commitment is the only power to drive Muslims in Malaysia whose accumulated wealth exceeds the *nisab* to make *zakat* contributions (Migdad, 2019).

A positive development in this regard is the 90% increase in the number of *zakat* payers in the Federal Territory of Malaysia during the period from January to November 2021 as compared to 2019 (The Malaysian Reserve, 2020). In this regard, the availability of various *zakat* digital payment options including FPX, debit card, and Islamic banking credit card facilities, coupled with the rising trend in Malaysia of the use of digital payments, has played a key role in the increase of *zakat* payers in the country. Although there are no available statistics for the number of *zakat* payers in Singapore, it is opined that the availability of digital payment options for *zakat* in Singapore would have a similar effect in terms of boosting the number of *zakat* payers in the country.

Whilst the *zakat* collection mechanisms in Malaysia and Singapore have been digitalized to offer greater convenience to encourage more *zakat* payers to fulfill their religious obligations, the distribution mechanism of *zakat* funds to the rightful beneficiaries (*asnafs*) is plagued by certain fundamental issues. In the context of Malaysia, some local scholars have commented that "in a Muslim majority country such as Malaysia, where not only is zakat collected regularly, with multiple zakat bodies taking on the role of managing zakat, the issue of poverty remains. This indicates a flaw within the existing zakat management system whereby there is either a lag between the funds collected and funds distributed, or the zakat management is inefficient" (Hassan et al., 2021).

Worse still is the issue of a lack of trust in Malaysia's zakat management systems as highlighted by some local scholars who observed that "zakat payers choose not to pay zakat through the Zakat Management System. The reason not to pay zakat through the Zakat Management System is either the zakat payers prefer to directly liaise with the zakat recipients or the zakat payers has some issues with Zakat Management System such as the system itself is claimed are with lack of transparency, storing inaccurate data or the zakat payers have trust issues towards the system" (Aqmal et al., 2021). All in all, the lack of transparency in the management of zakat management organizations (ZMOs) in Malaysia has resulted in a lack of public confidence in these organizations which could negatively affect the utility of *zakat* as an Islamic social finance mechanism in the country.

Blockchain, with its automated and transparency features, could be a technological game-changer to enhance the systemic operations and fund management frameworks of ZMOs which in turn would have a positive effect on strengthening the trust and faith of Muslim donors who can rest assured that their *zakat* payments are put to good use. The use of public-permissioned blockchains, or better yet public-permissionless blockchains, would enable *zakat* donors as well as the general public to track and trace the processing of *zakat* donations from the point of collection up till the distribution stage (Taskinoy, 2019). As for the distribution stage itself, the use of blockchain-based DIDs would warrant that *zakat* donations reach the *asnafs* while maintaining the privacy of these *asnafs* through the securing of the confidentiality of their identities (Dunphy & Peticolas, 2018).

Pioneering the use of blockchain for the collection of *zakat* is Dr. Ziyaad Mahomed, who has developed an application that leverages blockchain for this purpose. The application which was developed with the support of the International Federation of Red Cross and Red Crescent Societies (IFRC) allows users to pay *zakat* in accordance with their Islamic school of thought, i.e., Hambali, Hanafi, Maliki, or Shafi'i before choosing the projects which they wish to support through their *zakat* payment contribution (INCEIF, 2018). Upon the successful completion of *zakat* payment using a secure payment gateway, the details of the transaction will be set out in a public blockchain ledger whereby this not only warrants the transparency and accountability of the process but also addresses one of the main concerns of *zakat* contributors, i.e., the channeling of their *zakat* payment to those who are in need.

Besides that, Indonesia's Blossom Finance has developed a platform, i.e., its Zakat Via Blockchain payment service, which enables users to make *zakat* payments using their cryptocurrency holdings (Blossom Finance, 2018). The operational framework of Blossom Finance's *zakat* platform is such that the cryptocurrencies transferred by *zakat* payers will be deposited in a digital wallet owned by Blossom Finance before being converted to Indonesian Rupiah (Rp) and redistributed to cooperatives as well as non-profit organizations that would use the money to help the less fortunate in the regions of Sumatra and Central Java in Indonesia (Muneeza & Nadwi, 2019). In addition to the convenience offered to *zakat* payers, Blossom Finance's platform *zakat* platform also illustrates the cost reduction potential of the use of blockchain for the management of *zakat* payments as it eliminates the need for processing fees, thereby enabling the services to be offered free of charge.

Although the operations of the platform do incur transaction fees as the conversion of cryptocurrencies to Rp does incur exchange fees, Blossom Finance, after having consulted its *Shariah* advisors, formed the opinion that these fees constitute part of *zakat* payment, thereby enabling the services of the platform to be offered free of charge. The use cases of blockchain for the collection of *zakat* payment aptly illustrate the potential of blockchain to boost the transparency and accountability of *zakat* management frameworks as well as the efficiency that arises from the use of blockchain for cost management. From a spiritual perspective, the benefits arising from the use of blockchain would boost the confidence of Muslims in *zakat* payment systems, which in turn strengthens the faith of *zakat* payers who can rest easy knowing that their *zakat* payments are put to good use for the benefit for the intended recipients.

3.2.1.2 *Blockchain as a Technological Remedy for the Management Gaps of* Waqf *Mechanisms*

One of the main issues facing *waqf* institutions in Malaysia and Singapore is liquidity problems due to the use of immovable assets result in problems arising from difficulties in identifying these assets which in turn results in an over-dependence on the government whereby this has led to some scholars to propose the use of cash *waqf*. A notable suggestion in this regard is that of Sadeq, who has proposed the use of cash *waqf* through the issuance of *waqf* certificates by *waqf* institutions (Sadeq, 2002). The proposed model is such that parties who are looking to undertake socio-economic projects to support poverty eradication efforts would put forward their projects to *waqf* administrative bodies (WABs) who would then promote the projects to the public who would be able to donate cash in return for *waqf* certificates issued by the relevant WAB whereby the certificates would be in different denominations based on the amount of cash contribution.

In 2007, a breakthrough was achieved in this regard when the 77th Fatwa Committee of the National Council for Islamic Religious Affairs Malaysia, which convened on 10–12 April 2007 in Kuala Terengganu, ruled on the permissibility of cash *waqf* (Ali & Markom, 2010). Following thereafter, the fifth Selangor State Fatwa Committee Meeting, which convened on 17 October 2017, stipulated the conditions for the use of cash *waqf* including the growth of the value of the original endowment and the making of purchases in compliance with Islamic laws.

Over in Singapore, cash *waqf* are endowed in the form of compulsory contributions made through the automatic deductions through Central Provident Fund (CPF) accounts based on a tiered rate of USD1–USD7 depending on the monthly gross income of Muslim employees, though they are encouraged to make additional voluntary contributions (Mohsin, 2013). As efficient as Singapore's *waqf* collection is, it lacks the element of perpetuity as it is estimated that 92% of the *waqf* funds collected are disbursed to social development initiatives, thereby leaving little funds left for investment purposes (Pertiwi et al., 2018).

In 2017, a key milestone in the development of the *waqf* framework was achieved in Malaysia through the launch of myWakaf, a digital cash *waqf* which was established through the collaboration of eight State Islamic Religious Councils (SIRCs) and six IFIs, i.e., Affin Islamic Bank Berhad, Bank Islam Malaysia Berhad, Bank Muamalat Malaysia Berhad, Bank Rakyat, Maybank Islamic Berhad, and RHB Islamic Malaysia Berhad.

The immense potential of digital cash *waqf* was aptly illustrated by the success of myWakaf in raising a total of RM7.6 million by the end of 2020 whereby the funds were distributed to various impactful social financing projects in the areas of healthcare, education, and community empowerment (BNM, 2020).

Nonetheless, the use of digital cash may bring about issues of transparency and trust due to their high convertibility and exchangeability as well as the ease of transferability of digital cash whereby these issues may affect the commitment of donors to contribute to *waqf* endowment funds (Masruki & Shafi, 2013). In this regard, the discussions above on the transparency and accountability arising from the use of smart contracts in the context of *zakat* collection are also applicable to *waqf* endowment funds. From the perspective of the trustees of *waqf* endowment funds, they face the challenge of establishing and maintaining the trust and confidence of *waqf* donors whereby the automated feature of smart contracts would warrant the systemic integrity of the operations of the endowment framework as the permitted parameters for the use of the *waqf* funds can be coded into smart contracts, thereby ensuring the proper usage of these funds (Mohsin & Muneeze, 2020). Additionally, the distribution of shared ledger records to the *waqf* donors would enable the donors to be updated about the use of their contributions thereby boosting their trust and confidence in the framework.

Leading the way for the use of blockchain in the *waqf* domain is Finterra which *Waqf*chain leverages the use of smart contracts to unlock the liquidity of *waqf* assets as part of an integrated Islamic philanthropic ecosystem (Finterra, n.d.). In this regard, transactions undertaken through *Waqf*chain are executed using the ERC-777 standardized interface, thereby ensuring that all parties are on the same page when it comes to securing the accessibility of information as well as the making of informed decisions on the management and use of the assets under a *waqf* endowment fund. This effectively addresses any qualms or doubts that the donors may have concerning the transparency or integrity of *waqf* endowment funds managed by *Waqf*chain. Additionally, the fact that the algorithm of *Waqf*chain's smart contracts is encoded with the parameters of socially charitable causes and projects which are financed using the assets of the underlying *waqf* endowment fund means that donors can be rest assured that their digital cash contributions would be properly utilized for the permitted purposes.

As Finterra has operations in both Malaysia and Singapore, *Waqf*chain is an industry case study that illustrates how the use of blockchain could help allay the risks associated with the use of digital cash *waqf* in these two countries by ensuring that the use of digital cash as a form of *waqf* contributions would not bring about any issues on the lack of transparency concerning the management of these contributions. The role of blockchain in enhancing the efficiency of the management of *waqf* endowment funds would go a long way toward supporting the building of a relationship of perpetual trust between the donors and trustees of *waqf* endowment funds in Malaysia and Singapore.

3.2.2 Sukuk Financing for Islamic Social Finance

In line with ideals of Islamic social finance, the *sukuk* mechanism under the guise of green *sukuk* has been deployed to help address global issues on climate change and environmental degradation whereby green *sukuk* is structured based on the parameters of the SRI framework, albeit in the particular context of environmental conservation (Nurain Muhmad & Nasuha Muhmad, 2018). Conceptually, green *sukuk* is similar to Social Impact Bonds (SIB) which form the basis for the funding of environmentally friendly projects through private-public partnerships whereby the focal point is on achieving profits in a manner that does not come at the price of harm to the environment (Ramadahn & Wirdyanigsih, 2019).

In other words, green *sukuk* aims to curtail the social effects of unbridled capitalism using SRI which considers the environmental impact of investment projects by ensuring that these projects are environmentally sustainable from a long-term perspective In this regard, the application of the SRI framework complements the application of *Shariah* principles which already warrant that the underlying projects are of a wholesome nature and bring about beneficial effects to our world. The application of the SRI framework would further enhance the social value of green *sukuk* by providing distinct categorization elements through which the environmental impact values of green *sukuk* can be assessed (Moghul & Safar-Aly, 2015). A subset of green *sukuk* is blue *sukuk* that caters to the sustainability of the marine and sustainable fisheries sector.

The term *sukuk* is based on the Arabic word *sakk* which means certificate (Ahmed et al., 2020). The concept of *sukuk* therefore is very much akin to that of bonds in the conventional financial system whereby the Auditing Organisation for Islamic Financial Institutions (AAOIFI) considers *sukuk* to be a certificate that represents value in equal measure to an underlying asset (Maurer, 2010). As of the end of the second quarter (Q2) of 2024, the global volume of outstanding *sukuk* was estimated to be worth about USD875 billion whereby this illustrates the major role played by *sukuk* in the financing of projects not only in Muslim countries but also in non-Muslim regions as illustrated by the increasing popularity of *sukuk* in European countries such as the UK, England, France, and Germany (Franklin Templeton, 2024).

The investment structure of *sukuk* is very similar to that of conventional bonds whereby the underlying assets and its related financial rights are issued through a special purpose vehicle (SPV) except for a critical difference in that conventional bonds are debt-based instruments operating based on interest whereas *sukuk*, which has to abide by the *Shariah* prohibition against *riba*, operates based on profit and risk sharing (Vishwanath & Azmi, 2009). Although there are debt-based *sukuk*, these are fundamentally different from conventional bonds as debt-based *sukuk* entails the execution of a contract of sale for the underlying assets between the issuer and the seller whereby this gives rise to a repayment obligation on the part of the seller in contrast with conventional bonds which issuance are essentially the sale of debt-based instruments in return for interest payments (RAM Ratings, 2013). How capital is raised under *a sukuk* issuance framework is aptly illustrated by the investment structure of *sukuk al-ijara* which is the most popular form of *sukuk* whereby the underlying assets are securitized, albeit with the absolute ownership being surrendered for only a predefined period.

Under a *sukuk* issuance framework, investors would have a beneficial ownership in the underlying assets whereby during the tenure of the *sukuk* the investors would have beneficial rights over the assets that enable them to exercise their rights over the underlying assets in the event of any failure on the part of the issuer to make payment of the shared profits. The utility value of *sukuk* in facilitating the financing of profitable projects has resulted in it growing into a mainstay of the Islamic financial market, though the growth of the *sukuk* market has been curtailed by the high issuance costs as well as the cumbersome regulatory compliance process arising from the need to comply with the applicable *Shariah* principles in addition to the relevant legal provisions (Abdul Halim et al., 2017).

3.2.2.1 Globalizing Sukuk with Blockchain's Decentralization

In general, from a regulatory compliance perspective, the issuance of micro *sukuk* in the form of digital tokens enables regulatory compliance protocols to be undertaken using the credentials stored in blockchain-based shared ledgers, thereby reducing the complexities of the verification process in addition to saving costs (Khan et al., 2020). Additionally, the automated nature of smart contracts would also warrant the due payment of dividends to the investors, thereby reducing the chances of them having to have recourse to the enforcement of their beneficial rights to the underlying assets which is likely to involve a complex legal process requiring the expenditure of financial costs and valuable time.

From the perspective of the regulators, the transparency brought about using blockchain would make their monitoring, supervisory, and enforcement tasks easier as the shared ledgers serve as a database of self-verified information. Nonetheless, the most crucial benefit is perhaps the possible establishment of a cross-border *sukuk* market whereby the decentralized model of the blockchain-based *sukuk* issuance model can break the existing geographical border limitations, thereby paving the way for Islamic finance investors from all around the globe to participate in the *sukuk* issued in any jurisdiction. Essentially, the blockchain-based *sukuk* issuance model entails the tokenization of the ownership rights of subscribers in the form of cryptocurrencies, i.e., securities tokens which replace conventional *sukuk* paper-based certificates (Malika, 2021). As the blockchain frameworks of *sukuk* tokens are only able to recognize cryptocurrencies, all payment transactions involving these tokens have to be undertaken using cryptocurrencies that operate using a protocol that is compatible with the underlying blockchain framework of the relevant *sukuk* token. Nonetheless, the advent of cross-chain bridges has significantly enhanced the interoperability of different blockchain protocols of cryptocurrencies whereby the frameworks of *sukuk* tokens can harness the use of these bridges to provide support for the use of cryptocurrencies that operate on different blockchain protocols for payment purposes.

From a market perspective, the use of common industry standard protocols such as ERC20 which operates using Ethereum's smart contract architecture, *sukuk* tokens are tradable on cryptocurrency exchanges on which the relevant *sukuk* token is listed, thereby boosting their market liquidity and general appeal as financial investment instruments (Elasrag, 2019). Additionally, the use of smart contracts would facilitate the automation of the governance of the issuer's undertaking to buy back their *sukuk* at par value and to make due payment of the allotted dividends (Mohamed, 2019). However, a pertinent consideration in this regard is the fact that the legal validity of smart contracts is not recognized in most jurisdictions, thereby resulting in the possibility of the arising of contractual enforcement issues in the event a cross-border *sukuk* transaction goes wrong in addition to the issue of a lack of consumer protection due to the absence of regulatory oversight, particularly given the fact that blockchain is generally not considered to be fault-proof which gives rise to the risks of default (Raskin, 2017).

As for *Shariah compliance*, the applicable conditions and stipulations can be encoded into the smart contracts thereby ensuring due compliance with the relevant principles. For green *sukuk,* blockchain's traceability by-design features render it ideal for use for the evaluation of the impact of green *sukuk* as part of efforts to inspire investors' confidence in the use of these bonds for the promotion of environmental conservation efforts. A notable use case in this regard is the Green Assets Wallet which utilizes blockchain for the facilitation of impact communications between the issuers of green securities and investors to enable the investors to be aware of the environmentally friendly achievements of the green securities that they have invested in (Schletz et al., 2020).

Given the benefits arising from Sukukchain, i.e., the use of blockchain for the issuance of *sukuk*, it is unsurprising that there have been some notable developments in this regard. Pioneering the use of blockchain in the *sukuk* domain is Abu Dhabi's Al-Hilal Bank which in November 2018 used blockchain for the settlement of a transaction involving the issuance of *sukuk* worth USD1 million to a private investor (Reuters, 2018). Additionally, Dubai-based FinTech company Wethaq had in November 2019 completed the pilot issuance of its digital *sukuk* using R3's platform whereby the issuance of the blockchain-based *sukuk* was undertaken through its Islamic capital markets platform under the supervision of the Dubai Financial Services Authority (DFSA), though Wethaq has no plans to proceed with the issuance of blockchain-based *sukuk* (Ledger Insights, 2019).

3.2.2.2 Shariah-Compliant Blockchain Bridge for the Financing Gaps of MSMEs and SMEs

With MSMEs and SMEs in Malaysia and Singapore facing financing gaps of RM90 billion and SGD20 billion, the use of blockchain to address the issues of costs and complexities could help open the door for the MSMEs and SMEs in both these countries to address the financing gaps they are facing through the issuance of micro *sukuk* in following the path laid down by Indonesian microfinance institution, BMT Bina Ummah which managed to raise about 710 Million Indonesian Rupiah (IDR) (USD50,000) through the issuance of micro *sukuk* via Blossom Finance's SmartSukuk™ blockchain platform (Blossom, 2019).

The use of blockchain to lower the barriers of entry to the use of *sukuk* would open the door for smaller organizations such as MSMEs and SMEs in Malaysia and Singapore to have recourse to *sukuk* as a financing tool for their projects (Shaikh & Zaka, 2019). Using blockchain, *sukuk* can be issued as digital tokens with smart contracts as the underwriting instruments that govern the rights and obligations of the parties. The digital tokens the investors held would represent the beneficial ownership rights to the underlying assets and payment entitlement.

From a cost perspective, the use of blockchain for the issuance of micro *sukuk* by MSMEs and SMEs in Malaysia and Singapore could help reduce the administrative burden and operational risks of these businesses thereby helping to reduce their back office and operational costs for the issuance of their micro *sukuk* (Jibrel, 2019). Additionally, the dispensation of counterparty risks and removal of redundant intermediaries could potentially reduce settlement risks exposure by up to 99% thereby resulting in dramatic savings on capital costs expenditure by MSMEs and SMEs in Malaysia and Singapore for the issuance of their micro *sukuk* on top of the lower auditing and monitoring risks thanks to the transparent and traceable nature of blockchain records coupled with their faultless automated auditing process.

In the context of the prospects of the use of blockchain-based micro *sukuk* by MSMEs and SMEs in Malaysia and Singapore to bridge the financing gaps they are facing, a positive uptick in this regard is the news that Malaysia's stock exchange, Bursa, had in December 2020 completed the proof-of-concept (POC) phase for the issuance of blockchain-based bonds under Project Harbour which entails collaboration between the exchange with Singapore's Hashtacs (STACS) as well as multiple industry stakeholders including Securities Commission of Malaysia, Labuan Financial Services Authority, CIMB Investment Bank, Maybank Investment Bank, and China Construction Bank Corporation Labuan Branch (iFN Fintech, 2020).

In its statement following the completion of the POC phase for Project Harbour, Bursa stated that although the scope of the POC did not include *sukuk* offerings, "the structuring of Sukuk offerings on a blockchain is an area which both the participants and ourselves would like to explore further." If and when Bursa proceeds with its plans to test the viability of the use of blockchain for the issuance of *sukuk*, the path will be set for MSMEs and SMEs in Malaysia and Singapore to have recourse to the use blockchain-based micro sukuk to bridge the RM90 billion and SGD 20 billion financing gaps they are facing.

3.3 The Operational Challenges of Islamic Finance's Ethical Capitalism

Islamic finance operates under a framework rooted in Shariah law, which emphasizes ethical principles and justice in financial transactions. This approach, often referred to as "ethical capitalism," seeks to balance profit-making with moral and social responsibilities. However, implementing these principles presents various operational challenges.

One of the primary challenges in Islamic finance is ensuring compliance with Shariah law. Islamic financial institutions must avoid activities deemed *haram* (prohibited), such as charging interest (*riba*), engaging in excessive uncertainty (*gharar*), or investing in sectors like alcohol or gambling. This requires robust Shariah governance, which includes boards of Shariah scholars to review and approve financial products. However, interpretations of Shariah can differ between scholars, leading to inconsistencies in compliance across jurisdictions. The operational complexity of ensuring uniform standards of Shariah compliance in a global marketplace can be difficult, particularly for multinational Islamic financial institutions.

Developing innovative financial products that adhere to Islamic principles is another operational challenge. Conventional finance products, like interest-bearing loans or insurance, cannot be replicated directly within Islamic finance. Instead, Islamic financial institutions must create alternatives like profit-sharing (*mudarabah*) or cost-plus financing (*murabaha*). While these products are in line with ethical capitalism, their structuring can be more complex and costly, often leading to higher operational costs. Additionally, the lack of standardized product development frameworks across different regions adds to this complexity.

Islamic finance institutions also face the challenge of balancing profitability with ethical and social objectives. Since the core of Islamic finance revolves around justice, fairness, and avoiding exploitation, institutions must ensure their products and services genuinely promote economic welfare. For instance, profit-sharing arrangements may expose institutions to higher risk, making it difficult to remain competitive with conventional financial systems. In addition, Islamic banks often face liquidity management issues due to restrictions on interest-bearing instruments, limiting their ability to generate returns and compete in global markets.

3.3.1 FX Spot Transactions

FX (foreign exchange) spot transactions are one of the most fundamental and straightforward types of currency trading. In an FX spot transaction, two parties agree to exchange one currency for another at an agreed-upon exchange rate, with the transaction typically settling within two business days. This exchange rate, known as the spot rate, is determined by the supply and demand for the respective currencies in the market at the time of the trade.

When two parties enter into an FX spot transaction, they are agreeing on an immediate exchange of currencies. For instance, a US company needing euros might agree to exchange US dollars for euros at the current market rate. The transaction is usually settled within T+2 days (two business days), meaning the currencies are transferred between the parties' accounts after this period. Some currency pairs, like USD/CAD, settle within one day. The spot rate is influenced by factors such as interest rates, geopolitical stability, economic data, and market speculation.

The simplicity and immediacy of FX spot transactions make them appealing for various purposes. They are commonly used by businesses for hedging short-term currency risk, allowing them to buy or sell foreign currencies at the prevailing market rate to meet their international payment obligations. Investors and traders also use FX spot transactions to speculate on currency movements, aiming to profit from fluctuations in exchange rates over the short term.

3.3.1.1 Technical Shariah Non-compliance of FX Spot Transactions

In line with the prohibition in *riba* under *Shariah* principles, Mishkat al-Masabih 2812 (Book 11, Hadith 51) sets out the rule of *Bay al-Sarf* to govern contractual exchanges of goods and money whereby the rule originates from the well-known hadith that "gold for gold is usury unless both hand over on the spot; silver for silver is usury unless both hand over on the spot; wheat for wheat is usury unless both hand over on the spot; barley for barley is usury unless both hand over on the spot; dates for dates is usury unless both hand over on the spot." According to the hadith, therefore, any exchange transaction must be undertaken using equal counter values whereby the payment is required to be made on the spot, i.e., in an instantaneous manner. With regard to the equal countervalue requirement, the operational mode of the conventional financial system whereby the values of different currencies result in the need for the use of the foreign exchange mechanism to facilitate conversions between different currencies has led to differences of opinion between Islamic scholars with regard to the application of the requirement of equal value under the rule of *Bay al-Sarf*. This highlights the issues which can arise from the application of *Shariah* principles in the context of the conventional financial system which was not built in line with the foundations of Islamic laws.

Against this background, *Shariah* experts have sought to find a way to accommodate the operating mode of the conventional financial system particularly for FX spot transactions. According to the Islamic International Fiqh Academy (IIFA), given the nature of FX spot transactions, the average processing time of two days for these transactions is acceptable for complying with *Shariah* principles particularly the rule of *Bay al-Sarf*. An identical stance is taken by BNM's SAC which, through its 179th meeting dated 22 August 2017, ruled that the delivery of the exchanged currency two days after the transaction date (T+2) is allowed based on established customary business practice (*'urf tijari*) arising from operational constraints (BNM, 2017). Similarly, the Majlis Ugama Islam Singapura (MUIS) also recognized that although FX spot transactions are required by *Shariah* laws to be immediate in nature, it concurs with the views of the IIFA that a two-day delay is acceptable as a grace period is permissible under the Maliki school of thought which holds the opinion that a slight delay does not invalidate the exchange (*sarf*) (MUIS, n.d.).

Notwithstanding the acceptance by both the BNM's SAC and MUIS of the delay in FX spot transactions and the fact that the general Islamic financial community has been able to find a way to accommodate these transactions in a manner that complies with the principle of *Bay al-Sarf*, strictly speaking the delayed settlement period of these transactions departs from the "hand to hand" rule which lays down the on-the-spot requirement for exchange transactions (El-Gamal, 2003). In this regard, it is notable that this Shariah non-compliance may have a material impact under circumstances where there are substantial risks of market changes, i.e., where there is a high degree of volatility during periods of upheaval in the financial markets. The risks of a change in market conditions is precisely the underlying basis for the imposition of the on-the-spot exchange requirement under the principle of *Bay al-Sarf* to ensure fairness for parties to an exchange transaction by mandating payment to be made at the point of exchange as the value of goods or assets may fluctuate in the event of any delay.

With regard to the delay in the settlement period of FX spot transactions under the conventional financial system, this is due to the settlement process of these transactions which entails the undertaking of cross-border remittances. For a start, cross-border remittances undertaken through the conventional financial system must involve SWIFT which would act as an intermediary messenger because banks are unable to agree upon a transaction using their respective ledgers (Wandhofer & Casu, 2018). Besides that, the cross-border remittance process involves a host of correspondent banks which would receive, collate, and net payment instructions before sending out confirmations or denials to the respective parties whereby this not only results in a build-up of transaction costs in the form of the fees payable to the intermediaries but also causes undue delay for the settlement period. In the context of *Shariah compliance*, it is precisely this delay in the settlement period of FX spot transactions that causes technical *Shariah* non-compliance of these transactions as the delay results in the transactions being unable to comply with the principle of "hand-to-hand" under the rule of *Bay al- Sarf* which lays down the on-the-spot requirement for exchanges.

3.3.1.2 Blockchain as a Shariah-Tech Solution for FX Spot Transactions

To secure absolute *Shariah compliance* for the processing of FX spot transactions, recourse can be had to the use of blockchain-based financial networks. The disintermediation feature of blockchain which dispenses with the need for multiple layers of processing intermediaries would pave the way for a reduction in settlement times as it dispenses with the need to wait for the messages containing payment instructions from the multiple intermediaries (Yoo, 2017). In other words, the disintermediation feature of blockchain which dispenses with the need for intermediaries would facilitate the processing of payment transactions in a speedier manner though it has to be conceded that the developmental progress of blockchain in this regard has yet to reach its full potential. Leveraging the disintermediation feature of blockchain to speed up the settlement process of payment transactions is the industry-leading example of the Ripple Transaction Protocol (RTXP) which enables money to be transferred in a direct and almost instant manner, i.e., in just a few seconds (Rosner & Kang, 2016).

The prolonged settlement period of FX spot transactions under the conventional financial system arises primarily due to SWIFT's reliance on a multiple-tiered hierarchy comprising a host of intermediary correspondent banks. In contrast, the RTXP operates using a decentralized P2P framework which enables information to be transmitted simultaneously with the payment settlement process thereby resulting in much time savings for transactions involving both fiat money and digital currencies (Qiu et al., 2019). Additionally, as the whole settlement process is undertaken internally under the RTXP, this removes the element of external risks such as the lack of liquidity of intermediary correspondent banks under SWIFT's framework which may unduly delay the settlement process.

The use of blockchain-based payment networks can help speed up the settlement process for FX spot transactions whereby in the context of Islamic financial services in Malaysia and Singapore this would address the technical *Shariah* non-compliance of these transactions specifically with the hand-to-hand principle under the principle of *Bay-al Sarf* which lays down the "hand to hand" rule that requires exchange transactions to be undertaken in an on-the-spot manner. Leveraging the near-instant settlement periods under blockchain-based payment networks such as RTXP for the settlement of FX spot transactions processed by IFIs in Malaysia and Singapore would enable these transactions to be properly *Shariah*-compliant as the exchange of foreign currencies from account to account can be completed virtually instantly in fulfillment of the "hand to hand" rule under the principle of *Bay-al Sarf/*.

3.3.2 Murabaha *Transactions*

Murabaha is a widely used financing structure in Islamic finance, where a financial institution purchases an asset and then sells it to the client at a marked-up price. Unlike conventional loans that charge interest, which is prohibited in Islamic law (Shariah), *murabaha* allows for profit through the markup on the asset's sale price. The buyer agrees to pay the marked-up price, either in a lump sum or through installments, over an agreed period.

In a typical *murabaha* transaction, the financial institution first purchases the desired asset, such as real estate, machinery, or inventory, on behalf of the client. After acquiring the asset, the institution discloses its cost and adds a fixed profit margin. The client then buys the asset at this agreed-upon price. Although *murabaha* is often compared to interest-bearing loans, the key distinction is that the transaction is based on an asset sale, not the lending of money with interest. The price of the asset, including the markup, is agreed in advance, providing the client with certainty about their payment obligations.

Murabaha financing is beneficial for clients seeking Shariah-compliant financing solutions. It is commonly used for home financing, vehicle purchases, or trade financing in sectors like import-export. One advantage is that *murabaha* offers predictability in payments since the markup is fixed, making it easier for clients to plan their finances. Additionally, *murabaha* is structured to comply with Islamic ethical principles by avoiding uncertainty (*gharar*) and interest (*riba*), making it an attractive alternative for individuals and businesses seeking ethical financing options.

3.3.2.1 Prohibition of Fee Imposition by IFIs for the Provision of Guarantees

In the context of the Islamic trade financing framework, the need to comply with *Shariah* principles raises pertinent issues such as the uncertainties surrounding the imposition of guarantee fees to warrant the existence of the goods financed under a *murabaha* transaction whereby there is a division of opinion among *Shariah* scholars on this issue. The general view, however, is that the imposition of guarantee fees are against *Shariah* principles as the IIFA and the AAOIFI have taken the position that IFIs are not allowed to charge any fee for the provision of guarantee for the goods financed under a *murabaha* transaction whereby only the costs which were incurred for the provision of such a guarantee such as administrative fees and secretarial expenses are allowed to be charged (Noor & Haron, 2016).

In many ways, the need for a guarantee in the Islamic trade financing framework is very much a reflection of the risk element between the transacting parties not unlike the case in the conventional trade financing system. In the context of *murabaha* transactions, this risk element effectively puts IFIs in a difficult position because on the one hand, there is the requirement to provide guarantees to warrant the existence of the underlying goods but at the same time IFIs are not allowed to charge any fees for the provision of the guarantees (Sairally, 2002). In other words, IFIs find themselves having to underwrite the risks of the non-existence of the goods without being entitled to gain any profits from shouldering the risks of liabilities in the event anything goes amiss with the goods.

3.3.2.2 Blockchain as a Shariah-Tech Solution for Murabaha *Transactions*

The use of smart contracts for *murabaha* transactions would dispense with the need for IFIs to provide guarantees for the existence of the underlying goods. At each stage of the Islamic trade financing transaction conducted using a smart contract, the completion of every action by a party would have to be validated by the relevant counterparty using the appropriate private key after which a record of it would be automatically entered into the underlying blockchain network (Saba et al., 2019).

As the first step, the customer initiates a smart contract through a platform containing an expression of interest for Islamic trade settlement after which the smart contract would send an invitation to the relevant IFI. The second step is where the underlying blockchain network generates a unique address which constitutes the programming codes for the smart contract between the parties with a set of public and private keys to facilitate the recording of the parties' input. If the IFI is agreeable to the terms of the offer, it would have to verify the proposed contractual terms using its private keys and this verification would constitute the *majlis al-aqd* (i.e. contractual session) which finalizes the contractual terms.

In this regard, a smart contract would effectively act as the technological intermediary that warrants the existence of the underlying goods by encoding these goods in the form of digital representations that can be automatically detected using a blockchain-based tracing mechanism (Hamilton, 2019). A condition precedent for the formation of a contract as encoded in the smart contract would be the pre-existence of the underlying goods as warranted by the detection by the blockchain-based tracing mechanism of the goods in the form of its digital representation.

In terms of its technological architecture framework, the blockchain-based tracing mechanism would tokenize the underlying goods in the form of non-fungible tokens (NFTs) which can be recognized by the smart contracts program. If at any stage of the transaction, the blockchain-based tracing mechanism detects the absence of the underlying goods as represented by the NFTs ascribed to the program, the smart contract would then automatically invalidate the transaction. In this manner, the use of blockchain and smart contracts to warrant the continued existence of the underlying goods of a murabah transaction would enhance the degree of trust between the parties, thereby dispensing with the need for guarantees and resolving the situation for IFIs under which they find themselves having to underwrite the existence of the underlying goods without being able to gain any profits on it (Mat Rahim et al., 2018).

From a regulatory compliance perspective, the use of blockchain to warrant the existence of the underlying goods to a *murabaha* transaction would help IFIs in Malaysia comply with BNM's policy document titled "Murabaha," paragraph 13.1(b) of which provides that the underlying asset of a *murabaha* transaction is required to be "already in existence and owned by the seller." In addition, the automated and transparent features of smart contracts would warrant the effective transfer of ownership to the underlying assets of a *murabaha* transaction thereby helping Malaysian IFI's comply with paragraph 13.7 of the aforementioned BNM policy document which requires the effective transfer of ownership of the underlying assets of a *murabaha* transaction through "the seller disposing of the right of ownership (takhliyah) resulting in the purchaser having access to the asset (tamkin) and assuming its risk." The immutability of the records of transactions undertaken using smart contracts would enable the transfer of ownership of the underlying assets of a *murabaha* transaction to which a Malaysian IFI is a party to be easily verifiable in a conclusive manner.

As for IFIs in Singapore, the emphasis of the MAS is not so much on the transfer of ownership to the underlying assets of a *murabaha* transaction but more on the pricing mechanisms of such transactions. The MAS in paragraph 4.6 of its *Guidelines on the Application of Banking Regulations to Islamic Banking* made clear that IFIs in Singapore which are parties to *murabaha* transactions are obliged to ensure that "both parties do not derive gains or suffer losses from fluctuations in the price of the assets" whereby to ensure this requirement is met, the relevant IFI "is expected to minimise the holding period of the assets so as to avoid being exposed to the price movements of the assets." In this regard, the high transaction speeds of blockchain networks would enable *murabaha* transactions which are undertaken using smart contracts to be settled almost instantaneously, thereby enabling IFIs in Singapore to minimize the holding periods of the underlying assets in line with the MAS' direction.

In general, the use of smart contracts for *murabaha* transactions would enable blockchain to function as a technological intermediary to warrant the existence of the underlying assets, thereby dispensing with the need for guarantees from IFIs and absolving these institutions from having to underwrite the risks of the non-existence of the goods without being entitled to gain any profits from shouldering the risks of liabilities in the event anything goes amiss with the goods. For IFIs in Malaysia, the use of blockchain to warrant the existence and ownership of the underlying goods to a *murabaha* transaction would help these institutions comply with BNM's policy requirement in this regard. Pioneering the way forward for the use of blockchain in this connection is Finterra which had in November 2020 deployed its blockchain infrastructure to enable over 45,000 SMEs and micro fast-moving consumer goods (FMCG) retail businesses in Kenya to obtain funding using the commodity *murabaha* framework.

Additionally, the use of smart contracts would help IFIs in Malaysia comply with BNM's policy requirement concerning the effective disposition by the seller of the right of ownership (*takhliyah*) to enable the purchaser to have access to the asset (*tamkin*), thereby assuming the risks to the asset. As for IFIs in Singapore, the use of smart contracts would help these institutions comply with the MAS' requirement on negating the effects of fluctuations in the price of the underlying assets of a *murabaha* transaction thanks to the high transaction speeds of blockchain network which allows for the near-instantaneous settlement which would help these IFIs comply with MAS' policy requirement of minimizing the holding periods by IFIs of these assets.

3.4 Liquidity Risks

Liquidity risk refers to the possibility that an entity, such as a financial institution or business, may be unable to meet its short-term financial obligations due to an inability to convert assets into cash quickly or efficiently. This type of risk can occur when assets cannot be sold, or liabilities cannot be met without incurring significant losses. Liquidity risk is a critical concern for banks, businesses, and investors, as a lack of liquidity can lead to financial instability or even bankruptcy.

There are two main types of liquidity risk: funding liquidity risk and market liquidity risk. Funding liquidity risk arises when an entity does not have enough liquid assets or cash to meet its debt obligations or other immediate financial requirements. This can be a significant issue for banks if they are unable to raise sufficient funds to cover withdrawals or other short-term liabilities. Market liquidity risk, on the other hand, occurs when an asset cannot be sold or liquidated without a substantial price discount due to a lack of buyers in the market. This risk is particularly relevant during periods of market stress when liquidity tends to dry up, causing asset prices to plummet and limiting the ability to sell at fair market value.

Liquidity risk is a significant concern for financial institutions, as it represents the potential inability to meet short-term obligations or provide cash to clients on demand. This risk arises when an institution's liquid assets are insufficient to cover sudden withdrawals, loans, or other liabilities. Banks, in particular, face liquidity risk when there is a mismatch between the short-term liabilities they owe (such as customer deposits) and the longer-term, less liquid assets they hold (such as loans or investments). During times of financial stress, institutions may find it difficult to sell assets without incurring substantial losses, or they may be unable to access funding in the market. This can lead to a liquidity crunch, causing significant financial instability or even the collapse of the institution. To manage liquidity risk, financial institutions typically hold a buffer of liquid assets, conduct regular stress tests, and rely on central banks for emergency liquidity when necessary.

3.4.1 Liquidity Risks as an Essential Sacrifice for Shariah Compliance

In the context of Malaysia, the availability of BNM's IIMM has enabled IFIs in the country to develop robust liquidity risk management frameworks for their short-term liquid capital needs whereby the correlations between successful liquidity risk management frameworks and well-functioning Islamic money markets have been well documented. Nonetheless, this does not detract from the fact that IFIs in general are exposed to higher levels of liquidity risks. Although the MAS had in its *Guidelines on the Application of Banking Regulations to Islamic Banking* opined that the liquidity risks of IFIs are not dissimilar to those of conventional financial institutions which prompted the MAS to have a single regulatory framework to govern both IFIs and conventional financial institutions, some scholars beg to differ as they believe that IFIs are exposed to a higher degree of liquidity risks than conventional financial institutions.

One of the reasons why IFIs face higher exposure to liquidity risks than conventional financial institutions is due to the high volume of illiquid assets held by these institutions as they are required to abide by the legal maxim of *Al Ghunm Bil Ghurm* which lays down the *Shariah* principle that one is only entitled to gain from a venture if one agrees to bear the responsibility for any loss arising from the venture. The underlying rationale for this principle is to ensure that any profit-sharing is supported by risk-sharing, thereby legitimizing the profits from an economic perspective as it ensures that any venture undertaken would contribute to the development of the economy (Rosly & Zaini, 2008), though this is subject to the conditions that the risks shall not entail an unacceptable level of uncertainty as this is prohibited because it contradicts the *Shariah* principle which provides for the unacceptability of *gharar* (Waemustafa & Suriani, 2016).

To comply with the principle of *Al Ghunm Bil Ghurm*, IFIs are obliged to ensure that they shoulder a certain degree of risk exposure for Islamic finance transactions undertaken by them to render the profits which they obtain from these transactions to be legitimate from a *Shariah* perspective. As there can only be risk exposure in the presence of capital commitment, IFIs find themselves having to ensure that the Islamic financial transactions undertaken by them entail the making of the requisite capital commitment on their part to ensure that they are exposed to a certain degree of risks to grant *Shariah* legitimacy to the prospective profits from the transaction, though it should be noted that the degree of risks need not be proportionate to the amount of profits.

In other words, the need on the part of IFIs to abide by the principle of *Al Ghunm Bil Ghurm* as part of their operations results in these institutions having to commit a considerable part of their capital to share, i.e., shoulder the risks for the transactions entered into by them whereby this results in these institutions having a high volume of illiquid assets which in turn put them in a position in which they may not be able to fund their liabilities without suffering financial losses if there is a sudden change in the circumstances which require this (Basah et al., 2018). The high volume of illiquid assets of IFIs renders them to be subject to a high level of liquidity risks, i.e., risks that the profit earnings and capital pool of an IFI are insufficient to meet its financial obligations promptly without having to incur unreasonable losses.

Although exposure to liquidity risks may result in operational complexities, this is common to all financial institutions as these risks are an inevitable consequence of the systemic conditions of the macro-financial landscape (Ahmed, 2009). In the context of IFIs, however, their high capital outflow due to the need to comply with the principle of *Al Ghunm Bil Ghurm* as part of the offering of Islamic financial services results in these institutions being subjected to higher liquidity risk exposure levels than conventional financial institutions, which have the liberty of devising their operational frameworks in a manner that minimizes their risk exposure arising from their capital commitment to the lowest possible levels.

Another reason for the high liquidity risks of IFIs is the *Shariah* prohibition of interest (*riba*) which considerably narrows the scope of financing options available to IFIs. In contrast with conventional financial institutions which have a wide array of financing options in the form of the general interbank market, secondary market for debt instruments, and the central bank as a lender of last resort, IFIs do not have access to these options which operate using interest-based instruments (usury) (Sulaiman et al., 2013). Although IFIs in Malaysia have the option of resorting to BNM's Islamic Interbank Money Market (IIMM) for their short-term funding needs, the IIMM is only available to IFIs in Malaysia. As for secondary market instruments, the *Shariah* requirement for financial obligations to be backed by real assets means that the secondary market instrument options for IFIs are quite limited. To make matters worse, IFIs do not have the option of issuing interest-based loans to raise funds to support their operations which render IFIs to have higher liquidity risks than conventional financial institutions which can issue such loans to raise funds for their operations.

All in all, the need for IFIs to comply with the principle of *Al Ghunm Bil Ghurm* coupled with the lack of *Shariah*-compliant financing options for IFIs results in them facing higher levels of liquidity risks than conventional financial institutions. Recognizing this fact, BNM had in December 2020 issued its policy document titled "Capital Adequacy Framework for Islamic Banks" which sets out the capital adequacy ratios and capital buffer requirements that are required to be maintained by IFIs in Malaysia, thereby ensuring that these institutions have sufficient liquid capital to meet their financial liabilities and obligations at all material times. As for Singapore, the MAS had taken a different approach as according to the *Guidelines on the Application of Banking Regulations* to Islamic Banking, IFIs in the country are subjected to the same regulations as conventional financial institutions including the minimum capital requirements as provided for under section 9 of the Banking Act 1970.

Besides the need for IFIs to comply with the principles of *Al Ghunm Bil Ghurm*, the liquidity risks of IFIs also arise from the need for the structure of Islamic financial products and services to be *Shariah*-compliant. In general, Islamic financial services can be categorized into sharing contracts, trade-based contracts, and service-based contracts whereby the provision of each of these categories of services brings about a distinct set of liquidity risks to IFIs. With regard to *murabaha* which involves an IFI buying a commodity on behalf of a client before selling it to the client at a cost-plus price payable at a future date, the operational management frameworks of IFIs for *murabaha* contracts are very much similar to receivables in the form of a debt payable upon maturity which in the context of the conventional financial system would take the form of promissory notes (Paldi, 2014). However, unlike promissory notes which can be sold by conventional financial institutions through a secondary market for a price that is different from its face value, the fact that *murabaha* contracts are not allowed to be resold in such a manner presents distinct liquidity risks to IFIs as they are effectively stuck with the *murabaha* contract without the option of reselling it in the secondary market in the event of non-repayment by the client when the maturity date arrives.

Liquidity risks also similarly arise for IFIs under *salam* contracts which involve the purchase by these institutions of a commodity to be delivered at a future date, albeit with payment being due at the point of contract (Dchieche & Aboulaich, 2016). During the period from the date of the contractual signing and payment to the date of delivery of the commodity, IFIs are effectively stuck in a position whereby they would have expended capital outflow without the receipt of the corresponding asset, i.e., the commodity. The element of liquidity risks arises in this regard because in the event an IFI which is a party to a *salam* contract finds itself in need of liquid capital during the aforementioned period, the IFI will not be able to resell the commodity it is due to receive under the *salam* contract because of the *Shariah* prohibition of *Gharar* which disallows the element of uncertainty arising from the sale of something that is not in one's possession (Udin, 2015).

Additionally, liquidity risks also arise under other contracts entered into by IFIs such as *istisna* contracts which involve the manufacturing of future goods, and *ijarah* contracts which involve the leasing of assets owned by IFIs though the extent of the impact of these risks on IFIs is limited by the particular features of these contracts. With regard to *istina* contracts, the fact that the payments by IFIs under these contracts can be made through installments or in a deferred manner lowers the extent of the liquidity risks exposure for IFIs who are parties to these contracts (Nasucha et al., 2019). This is in contrast with *salam* contracts under which IFIs are obliged to make the full payment in an upfront manner. As for *ijarah* contracts, the fact that IFIs already own the asset leased under these contracts renders the *Shariah* prohibition of *Gharar* which disallows the element of uncertainty arising from the sale of something that is not in one's possession to be inapplicable, thereby allowing the IFIs to resell the assets in the event of any non-repayment by the lessee (Abdul Rahman et al., 2010). This is in contrast with *murabaha* contracts under which IFIs are not allowed to resell in a secondary market at a different price due to the aforementioned *Shariah* principle.

The structure of Islamic financial services due to the need to secure compliance with *Shariah* principles exposes IFIs to levels of liquidity risks that are higher than those faced by conventional financial institutions, though in the context of Malaysian IFIs, the availability of BNM's IIMM as a source of short-term liquid capital financing has enabled these IFIs to manage their liquidity risk exposure. As for Singapore, notwithstanding the MAS' opinion that the liquidity risks exposure of IFs are not dissimilar to those of conventional financial institutions, our discussions have illustrated how the structural framework of Islamic financial services results in IFIs facing a lack of exit opportunities and extensive capital lock-in for prolonged periods whereby both these factors collectively result in the high liquidity risk exposure levels of these institutions. When this is taken into consideration together with another cause of the high liquidity risk exposure of IFIs, i.e., the need for IFIs to comply with the principle of *Al Ghunm Bil Ghurm* coupled with the lack of *Shariah*-compliant financing options for these institutions, it can be safely be surmised that IFIs face higher levels of liquidity risks than conventional financial institutions. It is in this context that the use of blockchain for addressing the liquidity risks exposure of IFIs may be worth exploring for IFIs in Malaysia and Singapore, particularly the latter.

3.4.2 Decentralized LSMs a FinTech Solution for the Liquidity Risks Exposure of IFIs

Given the liquidity risk exposure of IFIs, leveraging the use of blockchain to help reduce locked-in capital may reduce the degree of these risks as well as the potential implications in the event of the materialization of the risks. From the perspective of *Shariah compliance*, the transparency brought about by the use of blockchain would ensure that the sources of liquidity of IFIs would not contravene the applicable *Shariah* principles, thereby ensuring the capital boosting and liquidity enhancing benefits arising from the use of blockchain would not come at the price of *Shariah compliance* (Antova & Tayachi, 2019). The potential arising from the use of blockchain in this regard is illustrated by Project Ubin undertaken by the Monetary Authority of Singapore (MAS, n.d.) and Project Jasper undertaken by the Bank of Canada which explored the decentralization feature of blockchain to facilitate inter-bank payments and settlements (Koumbarakis & Dobrauz-Saldapenna, 2019).

The findings of the projects highlighted the potential of the use of decentralized LSMs to address the liquidity risks of Real Time Gross Settlement (RTGS) systems whereby these risks are quite substantial due to the high transaction volume of these systems which may amount to one-fifth of a country's GDP daily (Chapman et al., 2017). In the context of IFIs, although the underlying causes of the liquidity risks faced by these institutions are different (i.e. the liquidity risks of IFIs are due to a lack of exit opportunities coupled with the extended capital lock-in entailed by the need to structure Islamic financial transactions to comply with *Shariah* principles whereas the liquidity risks of RTGS arise due to the sheer volume of transactions), the utility of decentralized LSMs for RTGSs applies to IFIs as the nature of the underlying issue is the same, i.e., the need to maintain a reasonable level of liquidity to enhance the stability of the operating framework (Byck & Heijmans, 2020).

In this regard, the use of decentralized LSMs leverages distributed ledger records to facilitate the matching of incoming and outgoing payments to enable their simultaneous settlement to leverage the netting effect to allow payment settlements using a minimum amount of liquidity (Fugal et al., 2018). The operations of decentralized LSMs are supported by settlement engines which are continuously searching and matching payment instructions to enable financial transactions to be settled in an almost real-time manner whereby the intraday finality of these transactions helps financial institutions unlock the capital tied down pending the finalization of the transactions whereby the unlocked capital would help lower the liquidity risks faced by these institutions.

The use of decentralized LSMs as part of the operations of blockchain-based payment networks can reduce the post-trade settlement period which refers to the duration between the execution of a transaction and the point of completion by the parties of all the necessary duties and obligations on their part as required to give effect to the transaction. By facilitating the reduction in settlement period, the use of blockchain-based payment networks can help address the liquidity risks of IFIs in Malaysia and Singapore by facilitating access to a wider capital pool at their disposal by ensuring that their liquid assets are not unduly held up during the post-trade settlement process (MAS, 2017).

3.5 Islamic Conception of Money and Currency

Under Islamic laws, for an instrument to qualify as money it must possess three qualities, namely, *Mal* (wealth), *Mutaqawwim* (legal value), and *Thamaniyyah* (currency attributes) (Adam & Barkatulla, 2019). Firstly, *Māl*, which is the primary feature of money under Islamic laws, refers to the element of an exchange of consideration involving something which can be acquired and taken into possession whereby the consideration may take the form of an *ayn* (corporeal) or *manfaah* (usurfuct). Linked to the quality of *Mal* is *Mutaqawwim* which refers to the value of money as recognized under the law whereby this supports the use of money to facilitate an exchange of consideration. The third quality, i.e., *Thamaniyyah*, separates money from other commodities and grants stability to monetary systems as it requires that the value of a currency be independent of any external reference. Further enhancing the stabilizing function of the *Thamaniyyah* is its requirement for money to have the currency attribute of a unit of account to enable it to be used for the valuation of goods and services, thereby facilitating the wide use of money which in turn would help establish a stable monetary system.

Instruments that fulfill the three qualities of money under Islamic laws would qualify as money for Islamic laws. *Shariah* jurists and scholars generally divide money into two categories, i.e., natural money and customary money. In terms of their features and functions, natural money has intrinsic value and was created to function as a medium of exchange whereas customary money lacks intrinsic value but has exchange value due to its wide acceptance and use as a medium of exchange by the general population (Sorenson, 2011). An example of customary money is fiat money which is essentially a piece of paper devoid of intrinsic value but has exchange value due to its designation as a legal tender, and its denomination value as ascribed by the issuing government. In other words, although fiat money in the form of the natural currency of a country has no intrinsic value, it is nevertheless accepted as Islamic money due to its wide acceptance and use as a medium of exchange by the population of the country. For example, the IIFA in its fifth session held in 1982 in the city of Makkah Al-Mukarramah resolved that "the paper currency that exists today has become a store of value and has replaced gold and silver as a means of payment, because the community has accepted it as a store of value and as a means of payment even if its value is not the paper but the trust that is placed in it in commercial dealings."

From a practical perspective, the wide acceptance and use of fiat money is because they are national currencies having denomination value as ascribed to them by the country's central bank and their status as legal tender as decreed by law which means that they must be accepted as a valid instrument for the settlement of a payment or debt (Goldberg, 2009). As for Islamic currency, it is constituted by instruments that have intrinsic value, i.e., commodities. It is against this backdrop of the Islamic concept of money and currency that the evaluation of cryptocurrency will be made.

3.5.1 The Case for the Shariah Permissibility of Cryptocurrency as Islamic Money or Currency

Although Islamic laws have prescribed the qualities of *Mal, Mutaqawwim, and Thamaniyyah* which have to be possessed by an instrument to qualify as money, in practice the designation of money through the application of the prescribed qualities is not a straightforward matter. It is in this context that *Shariah* jurists and scholars have obtained guidance by referring to the concept of money during the time of Prophet Muhammad (p.b.u.h) as illustrated by the features of money in use back then such as gold and silver as well other commodities such as dates, wheat, and barley whereby six notable features of these commodities can serve as reference for the designation of money. The first feature was based on the observation that the commodities in use during the time of Prophet Muhammad (p.b.u.h) generally take the form of precious metal or food, though this requirement has since been dispensed over time (Mydin Meera & Larbani, 2009). The second feature of money is that of abundance and free availability for which cryptocurrency would fit the bill as they are available in large amounts and can be mined by anyone with an Internet connection. Nonetheless, some cryptocurrencies do have supply limits such as Bitcoin which issuance is capped at 21 million though this may be changed when the time comes (Bartos, 2015).

Additionally, the notion that anyone with an Internet connection can mine for cryptocurrencies is no longer entirely accurate as the mining of certain cryptocurrencies, particularly those whose mining process is highly competitive, would require specialized equipment with high computer processing speeds (Ilyasova et al., 2019). Moving on to the third feature of money under Islamic laws, i.e., durability, cryptocurrencies would fulfill this requirement easily as the digital nature of cryptocurrencies renders them to be beyond physical damage or destruction whereby the storage of these currencies using blockchain networks further warrants their security and permanency (Harwick, 2015). As for the last Islamic requirement for money to have utility value as a medium of exchange, payment-based cryptocurrencies which can be exchanged for goods and services would fulfill this requirement, though for other forms of cryptocurrencies, this would depend on their precise features and functions.

Consequently, certain cryptocurrencies do have an arguable case to qualify as Islamic money. For cryptocurrencies that fail to meet the requirements of Islamic money, there is an alternative way through which they can gain legitimacy, i.e., by qualifying as commodities with intrinsic value thereby qualifying as Islamic currency, i.e., legal tender. With regard to cryptocurrencies which are mined using the Proof of Work (PoW) protocol whereby miners are rewarded for resolving complex cryptographic mathematical equations, it is arguable that these currencies do have intrinsic value as they are generated through a mining process that consumes electricity (Muedini, 2018). Cryptocurrencies whose mining process consumes electricity such as those mined using the PoW protocol can qualify as Islamic currency as these currencies have intrinsic value which is derived from electricity as the base underlying asset.

Nonetheless, a counter-argument in this regard is that the nature of electricity which does not have any physical existence but instead is simply a force generated by the flow of electrons leads to doubts as to whether electricity qualifies as an underlying base asset that can be used to grant intrinsic value to cryptocurrencies. In response to this counter-argument, as electricity is a force of nature, albeit one which is harnessed by mankind for the betterment of our lives, it is a creation of God whereby this would not only render electricity to qualify as the underlying base asset which grants intrinsic value to cryptocurrencies but better still the intrinsic value is of such nature that it is granted by God.

As for cryptocurrencies which are generated through a mining process that grants entitlements to rewards based on existing cryptocurrency holdings such as those mined using the Proof of Stake (PoS) protocol, these currencies are lacking in intrinsic value and thereby do not qualify as Islamic currency. Additionally, as the reward entitlements of miners under the PoS protocol depend on the value of their pre-existing cryptocurrency holdings, this goes against the *Shariah* prohibition of *riba* as the newly generated cryptocurrencies are tantamount to interest earned from the miners' pre-existing cryptocurrency holdings though this would only be the case if cryptocurrency amounts to "money" under *Shariah* principles in the first place whereby if cryptocurrency does not so amount, the prohibition of *riba* would not apply to cryptocurrencies mined using the PoS protocol (Saleh, 2020).

The key takeaway is that cryptocurrencies whose mining process consumes electricity such as those mined using the PoW protocol have an arguable case to qualify as Islamic currency whereas those with mining process grant entitlements to rewards based on existing cryptocurrency holdings such as those mined using the PoS protocol would not qualify as Islamic currency, though if cryptocurrencies which are mined using the PoS protocol are widely used and accepted as a medium of exchange, then they may be recognized as Islamic money based on customary practices (*urf*).

Nonetheless, there is a lack of *ijma* (consensus) concerning the *Shariah* permissibility of cryptocurrencies in general. During a two-day conference on cryptocurrency organized by the IIFA in Jeddah, Saudi Arabia, it was concluded that further research and study is required to be conducted for the issue of the *Shariah* permissibility of cryptocurrencies to be decided based on the process of *ijtihad* (legal reasoning) (The Coins Post, 2019). This view is reflected in the World Islamic Economic Forum Foundation (WIEF)'s "Declaration on Bitcoin" which resolved that given the wide use of cryptocurrencies such as Bitcoin, it is not possible to give a definitive view on their *Shariah* permissibility (WIFE, 2018).

Based on the opinion of Islamic scholars such as Shaykh Dr. Ali al-Qurra Dagi, and Dr. Abdus Sattar Abu Ghuddah, the major obstacle that stands in the way of the *Shariah* permissibility of cryptocurrencies is their volatile value which renders these currencies incompatible with the *Shariah* prohibition of *gharar* (Billah, 2019). In this regard, stablecoins, which are asset-backed cryptocurrencies, have better prospects of securing *Shariah* permissibility given the reduced volatility in the market value of stablecoins as compared to other cryptocurrencies. In the following section, we will be exploring the role of stablecoins as a more *Shariah*-compliant alternative to fiat money, particularly from the perspective of their functions as a store of value before looking at some related industry developments and the opinion of Islamic scholars which support the case for the *Shariah* permissibility of stablecoins.

3.5.2 *Stablecoins as a More Shariah-Compliant Alternative to Fiat Money*

From the outset, it is notable that notwithstanding the lack of intrinsic value of fiat money, it is generally accepted as qualifying as Islamic money as set out in resolution 9 D/3/07/86 of the IIFA. However, the acceptance of fiat money as Islamic money is not without its detractors as some Islamic scholars have argued that fiat money does not qualify as Islamic money as it does not have intrinsic value but instead is merely a unit of account which representative value of commodities is dictated by the issuing central bank through its control of the quantity of the relevant currency in circulation as undertaken through the management of its fiscal policy.

A central criticism of fiat money is its "unreal or virtual" feature which renders it to be not conducive to the promotion of economic stability thereby rendering fiat money to be incompatible with the *Shariah* principle of *Maqasid al-Shariah* and the *Thamaniyyah* feature of Islamic money. On the other side, some support the recognition of fiat money as Islamic money based on practical convenience and the fact that fiat money has a relatively stable value due to the fiscal policy management of the issuing central bank which is undertaken to secure economic stability.

Nonetheless, as central banks of most countries operate using a fractional reserve banking framework which is not fully backed by liquid assets, this is tantamount to the *Shariah*-prohibited practice of *usury* as noted by some scholars who observed that "The Fractional Reserve Banking system has a serious impact on the structure of ownership in the economy because this system creates an ownership without any risk taking. As such, it also contains elements of usury which are prohibited in Islam" (Syamlan & Istiana, 2018). In contrast, the conceptual framework of stablecoins, i.e., asset-backed cryptocurrencies, is very much akin to a full-reserve banking framework under which the fiat money issued by these banks would be fully backed by liquid assets (Senner & Sornette, 2018). As no central bank currently operates using the full-reserve banking framework, stablecoins would be heralding a paradigmatic shift in this regard (Dow et al., 2015).

Additionally, how fiat money is issued affects its functions as a store of value as it results in the value of paper currency being subjected to volatile fluctuations which is leveraged by investors for profit-making purposes through the undertaking of FX spot transactions. The speculative nature of FX spot transactions goes against the *Shariah* prohibition of the trading of money for investment and profit-making. As Imam Ibn Taymiyyah puts it, "when currencies and money are inter-traded with the intention of investment and profit, it opposes the very purpose of money" (Yuneline, 2019). The uncertainty arising from the volatile value of fiat money renders them to be in contravention of the *Shariah* prohibition of *gharar*.

Not unlike fiat money, the value of cryptocurrencies is also subjected to volatile fluctuations whereby a notable example is the Great Crypto Crash in 2018 during which the price of Bitcoin fell by a staggering 65% during the one month from 6 January to 6 February (Heaven, 2018). However, a lesson learned from the Crash is that the value of stablecoins such as PAX Coin and Tether Gold (both of which are backed by gold) and CannDollar (backed by silver) is less volatile as compared to non-asset-backed cryptocurrencies as the value of stablecoins is inextricably tied to the underlying basket of assets such as gold and silver which have a relatively stable market value. The less volatile market value of stablecoins as compared to that of fiat money renders the function of stablecoins as a store of value superior to that of fiat money (Melachrinos & Pfister, 2021).

Additionally, the transparency brought about by the distributed nature of blockchain records, which govern the operating framework of stablecoins, allows holders of these coins to ascertain how their holdings are being backed by the relevant basket of assets. This stands in stark contrast to how central banks undertake their fiscal management policies which are shrouded in much secrecy, thereby preventing the ordinary man on the street from knowing the extent to which the paper currency in their possession is backed by the issuing central bank's fractional reserve banking framework whereby this goes against the values transparency and accountability which are very much the central tenets of *Shariah* principles, though not expressly stated as such (Goodfriend, 1995).

Stablecoins more properly accord with the *Shariah* principle of *Hifz al mal* (preservation of wealth) as the volatile nature of the market value of fiat money renders it to be vulnerable to inflation or even hyperinflation, particularly in times of economic uncertainties during which governments have to resort to fiscal policy measures such as quantitative easing to stabilize the economy. The materialization of the risks of dilution in the value of fiat money renders it incompatible with the principle of *Hifz al mal* as this dilution reduces the wealth of the paper currency holders. Given the advantages arising from the use of stablecoins vis-à-vis fiat money, particularly the superior function of stablecoins as a store of value coupled with their less volatile market value, stablecoins have the potential to serve as a more *Shariah*-compliant alternative to fiat money.

From a *fiqh* (Islamic jurisprudence) perspective, the increasing use of stablecoins further strengthens the case for the *Shariah* permissibility of the use of stablecoins as Islamic currency as per the observations of Shaykh Abdullah Al-Mani that "currency is whatever is agreed upon, whether by government authority or public practice." In this regard, it is notable that Imam Ibn Taymiyyah postulated that there is no universal definition of Islamic currency as it is based on the prevalent custom and understanding of the people. In support of the case for the *Shariah* permissibility of the use of stablecoins as Islamic currency is the growing use of these coins as reflected in the fact that as of November 2020, the total market capitalization of stablecoins stood at more than USD23 billion led by Tether with a market capitalization of USD18 billion (CoinGecko, 2020).

As the use of stablecoins continues to grow moving forward, the case for the *Shariah* permissibility of stablecoins and their recognition as Islamic currency would be stronger based on their wide public acceptance as reflected in the custom and understanding of the people. Accordingly, from the perspective of *fiqh*, there is no jurisprudential obstacle that stands in the way of the *Shariah* permissibility of stablecoins and their acceptance as well as use as Islamic currency. Support for the *Shariah* permissibility of stablecoins can be found in the certification issued by the Shariyah Review Bureau (SRB) in November 2018 through which the SRB warranted the *Shariah compliance* of Swiss-based cryptocurrency firm X8 AG's X8X stablecoin which is backed by a basket of eight fiat currencies and gold (MIFC, 2018). Additionally, the Islamic Republic of Iran had in February 2019 launched its Peyman stablecoin which is backed by gold (Bitcoin Exchange Guide, 2019).

In Malaysia, the country's Shariah Advisory Council (SAC) had in June and July 2020 decided through its 233rd and 234th resolutions that stablecoins that are backed by *ribawi* items in the form of gold, silver, or currency are deemed as Islamic currency whereas stablecoins that are backed by *ribawi* items other than gold, silver or currency are deemed as *amwal ribawiyyah* (*ribawi* items). As for cryptocurrencies other than stablecoins, i.e., digital currencies that are not backed by anything, the SAC had through its aforementioned resolutions categorized these currencies as goods (*urudh*) thereby not amounting to currency or *ribawi* items under *Shariah* principles.

As for Singapore, the MUIS has yet to indicate its stance on the permissibility of cryptocurrencies such as stablecoins which means that the *Shariah* permissibility of stablecoins accord with the official position of the MAS which permits the use of stablecoins of payment instruments under the Payment Services Act but is currently studying the introduction of stablecoin regulations following the USD65 billion crash of TerraUSD which was at one time the third largest stablecoin in terms of market capitalization (MAS, 2022). Based on these industry and regulatory developments, it can be surmised that the underlying conceptual frameworks of stablecoins, particularly those which are backed by *ribawi* items, are *Shariah*-compliant, thereby paving the way for the possible use of these cryptocurrencies by IFIs in Malaysia and Singapore as a more *Shariah*-compliant alternative to fiat money.

In line with the global shift toward Industry Revolution 4.0 (IR4.0), IFIs in Malaysia and Singapore can have recourse to stablecoins as part of their business strategies to tap into the digitally savvy millennial generation. Although critics may argue against the use of stablecoins by IFIs due to the general propensity of cryptocurrencies to be used for money laundering and other illicit activities, a report published in February 2020 by SWIFT in collaboration with BAE Systems noted that the risks of money laundering using cryptocurrencies are minimal compared to those involving fiat money undertaken using methods such as cash mules and businesses as well as through the use of deceptive methods such as *hawala* and front companies (SWIFT, 2020). In this regard, it is notable that according to the estimates of the UN, the financial value of money laundering activities undertaken using fiat money amounts to about USD800 billion to USD2 trillion per year (UN, n.d.).

The reduced money laundering risks arising from the use of stablecoins as compared to fiat money render the use of these cryptocurrencies as a more *Shariah*-compliant alternative to fiat money a viable option for IFIs in Malaysia and Singapore. In this regard, the propensity of stablecoins which warrant anonymity to its users to be misused for money laundering and other illicit activities need not hinder the use of these cryptocurrencies by IFIs. This proposition is made based on the *Shariah* principle which provides that the mere fact that an item or instrument can be used for an improper purpose does not stand in the way of its general use for other valid purposes. An analogical example of this can be found in Book 12, Hadith 2302 whereby Prophet Muhammad (p.b.u.h) forbade the selling of grapes to wine merchants but permitted the production and sale of grapes for valid purposes provided the sale is made before the grapes turn dark. With this the path is cleared for the use of stablecoins by IFIs in Malaysia and Singapore as a more *Shariah*-compliant alternative to fiat money.

3.6 Shariah Permissibility of Blockchain Use for Islamic Financing

In general, the use of technologies such as blockchain for Islamic finance is permissible under Shariah principles. In particular, the application of the principle of *fiqh al-mu'āmalāt* is such that technological innovations including blockchain are permissible for the furtherance of a social good unless they are expressly prohibited by certain Shariah principles (Mihajat, 2014). The operational efficiency and cost reduction benefits arising from the use of blockchain for Islamic finance would amount to a social good as it helps reduce the costs of Islamic financial services which would help alleviate the financial burden of its users. According to estimates, the use of blockchain-based smart contracts to warrant the immutability of the ownership records of assets of Islamic banking transactions could result in cost savings of up to 95% (Gassner & Lawrence, 2018).

In addition, the transparency features of blockchain would also come in handy for facilitating the due compliance of Islamic financial institutions with their Environmental, Social and Governance (ESG) goals which is a key pillar of Islamic finance's principles-based investing approach (Irfan & Ahmed, 2018). Given these benefits arising from the use of blockchain, the application of the Shariah principle of ***maqāṣid al-sharīʿah*** in tandem with the doctrine of ***maslahah*** renders the door open to the use of the technology in Islamic finance for the furtherance of public good in line with the objectives of Shariah.

3.6.1 General Challenges of Blockchain Use for Islamic Financing

In a study of 250 respondents on the use of blockchain for Islamic financing, the most commonly cited challenges are as below (Al Dakash & Azrak, 2021).

(a) **Regulatory Uncertainties**
Lack of acceptance by central banks and government regulators which resulted in a lack of regulations on the governance of blockchain use for Islamic finance.

(b) **Illegality Risks**
The propensity of blockchain use for illegal financial activities such as money laundering and terrorism funding entails material risks connected to the Shariah prohibition of *haram* activities which applies to Islamic financial institutions.

(c) **High Costs**
The high costs for improving the security of blockchain networks is a critical factor for Islamic financial institutions considering the relatively smaller customer base of these institutions vis-à-vis conventional financial institutions.

a. **Shariah Permissibility**

The absence of a central Shariah supervisory authority leads to a lack of Shariah standards on the permissibility of blockchain use for Islamic finance which in turn has led to contradictory decisions and fatwas.

3.6.2 Specific Challenges of Blockchain Use for Islamic Social Financing

Although the transparency features of blockchain could boost the trust levels of Islamic social financing institutions, a key challenge that stands in the way for the use of blockchain in this regard is the question of the technical feasibility of the computational encoding of Shariah principles. If it's not technically feasible for Shariah principles to be computationally encoded, this would be an obstacle to the use of blockchain for Islamic financing. In this regard, some authors have noted the challenge of encoding into smart contracts subjective concepts such as good faith and fair dealing which are prevalent in the Shariah principles of Islamic social financing transactions (Koulu, 2016).

In the particular context of the use of blockchain for the issuance of *sukuk*, a case study of two Smart *sukuk* projects found that there is no clear-cut indication that the use of blockchain for the issuance of *sukuk* results in any significant enhancement to the efficiency levels of the process (Busari & Aminu, 2022). The study inferred that this could be because the use of blockchain for the issuance of *sukuk* is still very much in the stage of infancy, and hence there is still much room for development to optimize the use of the technology in this regard.

Shariah experts generally concur that the *akad* requirements for Islamic banking transactions are such that these transactions can be valid if one of the parties to the transaction is represented by a technical device such as a vending machine so long as the other party to the transaction is a human who can find out the identity of the seller from the device (Bintang et al., 2022). In the case of blockchain-based smart contracts, however, where the identities of both parties to the transaction may be hidden behind a code, it is an open question as to whether such a transaction would be recognized as a valid *akad* under Shariah principles.

On the assumption that blockchain-based Islamic banking transactions amount to *akad* under Shariah principles, the propensity of cryptocurrencies to be misused for illegal financial activities such as money laundering and terrorism financing as well as the security risks of blockchain networks would be the next challenge for the use of blockchain for Islamic banking. In this regard, the Shariah principle of *Sadd al-Dhari'ah*, which provides for the requirement to close off any means that can be used for evil, may be applicable. The application of this principle in the context of the use of blockchain and cryptocurrencies by Islamic financial institutions may require the application of a strict liability regime to Islamic financial institutions to safeguard *maslahah* (public interest) by requiring these institutions to ensure that cryptocurrencies and blockchain networks under their purview are not misused for the commissioning of activities that are *haram* (forbidden) under *Shariah* principles or illegal under conventional laws (Oseni & Ali, 2018).

References

Abdel Mohsin, M. I., & Muneeza, A. (2020). Integrating waqf crowdfunding into the blockchain. In *Fintech in Islamic finance: Theory and practice* (Chapter 17, pp. 266–280). Routledge. http://www.iefpedia.com/english/wp-content/uploads/2019/12/EBOOK9250.pdf

Abdel Mohsin, M. M. (2019). Waqfintech and sustainable socio-economic development. *International Journal of Management and Applied Research, 6*(3), 130–141. http://ijmar.org/v6n3/19-009.html

Abdul Halim, Z., How, J., & Verhoeven, P. (2017). Agency costs and corporate sukuk issuance. *Pacific-Basin Finance Journal, 42*, 83–95. https://eprints.qut.edu.au/95982/1/__qut.edu.au_Documents_StaffHome_StaffGroupR%24_robinsm2_Desktop_Eprints_Janice%20How_2016_Agency%20Costs%20and%20Corporate%20Sukuk%20Issuance

Abdul Rahman, R., Tafr, F. H., & Al Janadi, Y. (2010). Instruments and risks in Islamic financial institutions. *Malaysian Accounting Review, 9*(2), 11–21. http://arionline.uitm.edu.my/ojs/index.php/MAR/article/view/244

Adam, F., & Barkatulla, A. K. (2019). Currency in Islamic law. In *Fintech in Islamic Finance* (Chapter 9). Routledge. http://www.iefpedia.com/english/wp-content/uploads/2019/12/EBOOK9250.pdf#page=145

Affin Islamic Bank Berhad, Bank Islam Malaysia Berhad, Bank Muamalat Malaysia Berhad, Bank Rakyat, Maybank Islamic Berhad, & RHB Islamic Malaysia Berhad. (n.d.). BNM, Annual report 2020. https://www.bnm.gov.my/documents/20124/3026128/ar2020_en_book.pdf

Ahmed, H. (2009). Financial crisis: Risks and lessons for Islamic finance. *ISRA International Journal of Islamic Finance, 1*(1), 7–32. https://www.researchgate.net/publication/228337197_Financial_crisis_risks_and_lessons_for_Islamic_finance

Ahmed, E. R., Islam, M. A., & Hashim, F. (2020). Sukuk history and development. In *Handbook of research on theory and practice of global Islamic finance* (Chapter 36, pp. 704–731). IGI Global. https://www.researchgate.net/publication/338778041_Sukuk_-History-and-Development_chapter

Ahmed, H., Mohieldin, M., Verbeek, J., & Aboulmagd, F. (2015). On the sustainable development goals and the role of Islamic finance (Policy Research Working Paper 7266). World Bank Group. https://openknowledge.worldbank.org/bitstream/handle/10986/22000/on0the0sustain0e0of0islamic0finance.pdf?sequence=1

Al Dakash, M., & Azrak, T. (2021). Implementing blockchain technology in Islamic financial industry: Opportunities and challenges. *Journal of Information Technology Management, 13*(3), 99–117. https://jitm.ut.ac.ir/article_83116_d3fcd59cdcaa586536fd9ba2f700410d.pdf

Al-Amine, M. A. (2015). Product development and maqaṣid in Islamic finance: Towards a balanced methodology. *Islamic Economic Studies, 23*(1), 33–71. http://iesjournal.org/english/Docs/175.pdf

El-Gamal, M. A. (2003). "Interest" and the paradox of contemporary Islamic law and finance. *Fordham International Law Journal, 27*(1), Article 6. https://ir.lawnet.fordham.edu/cgi/viewcontent.cgi?article=1915&context=ilj

Ali, N. A., & Markom, R. (2010). The challenges of implementing cash waqf in Malaysia. *Journal of Contemporary Islamic Studies, 6*(2) https://ir.uitm.edu.my/id/eprint/42984/1/42984.pdf

Antova, I., & Tayachi, T. (2019). Blockchain and smart contracts: A risk management tool for Islamic finance. *Journal of Islamic Financial Studies, 5*(1), 29–42. https://journal.uob.edu.bh/bitstream/handle/123456789/3564/3.pdf

Aqmal, M. N., Salikin, M., & Yahya, N. (2021). Blockchain-based zakat collection to overcome the trust issues of zakat payers. *International Journal on Perceptive and Cognitive Computing (IJPCC), 7*(1), 5.

Bank Negara Malaysia. (BNM). (2011). Financial sector blueprint 2011–2020. https://www.bnm.gov.my/documents/20124/5800313/FSB_2011_en.pdf

Bank Negara Malaysia. (BNM). (2017). The 179th meeting of the Shariah Advisory Council (SAC) of Bank Negara Malaysia. https://www.bnm.gov.my/documents/20124/1085561/SAC+179th+Meeting+Statement+EN.pdf

Bank Negara Malaysia. (BNM). (2020). Annual report. https://www.bnm.gov.my/documents/20124/6458991/ar2021_en_book.pdf

Bank Negara Malaysia. (BNM). (2022). Financial sector blueprint 2022–2026. https://www.bnm.gov.my/documents/20124/5915429/fsb3_en_book.pdf

Bartos, J. (2015). Does Bitcoin follow the hypothesis of efficient market? *International Journal of Economic Sciences, 4*(2) http://citeseerx.ist.psu.edu/viewdoc/download?doi=10.1.1.902.3664&rep=rep1&type=pdf

Basah, Y. A., Mohamad, S. N. A., Aziz, M. R. A., & Khairi, K. F. (2018). Risks in Islamic banks: Challenges and management. *Journal of Engineering and Applied Sciences, 3*(8), 2081–2085. https://www.researchgate.net/publication/326057369_Risks_in_Islamic_Banks_Challenges_and_management

Billah, M. M. (2019). *Halal cryptocurrency management.* Springer.

Bintang, S., Haflisyah, T., & Fikr, F. (2022). A study on the conformity of Sharia bank financing Akad to Sharia principles, national laws, and contract drafting techniques. *Syiah Kuala Lumpur Journal, 6*(1), 40–52. https://jurnal.usk.ac.id/SKLJ/article/download/28108/16383

Bitcoin Exchange Guide. (2019, February 1). Iran has launched a gold-backed cryptocurrency 'Peyman' in effort to avoid US sanctions. https://Bitcoinexchangeguide.com/iran-has-launched-a-gold-backed-cryptocurrency-peyman-in-effort-to-avoid-us-sanctions/

Blossom. (2019, October 16). World's first primary sukuk issuance on blockchain closes. https://blossomfinance.com/posts/worlds-first-primary-sukuk-issuance-on-blockchain-closes

Blossom Finance. (2018, May 23). Muslims can now pay zakat in cryptocurrency. https://blossomfinance.com/posts/muslims-can-now-pay-zakat-in-cryptocurrency

Busari, S. A., & Aminu, S. O. (2022). Application of blockchain information technology in Sukūk trade. *Journal of Islamic Accounting and Business Research, 13*(1), 1–15. http://irep.iium.edu.my/92097/1/10-1108_JIABR-10-2019-0197.pdf

Byck, S., & Heijmans, R. (2020). How much liquidity would a liquidity-saving mechanism save if a liquidity-saving mechanism could save liquidity? A simulation approach for Canada's large-value payment system. De Nederlandsche Bank Working Paper, 682. https://www.dnb.nl/en/binaries/Working%20paper%20No.%20682_tcm47-388290.pdf

Cambridge Institute of Islamic Finance (Cambridge-IIF) & Ajman University Center for Excellence in Islamic Finance (AU-CEIF). (2023). Global Islamic Finance Report 2023.

Chapman, J., Garatt, R., Hendry, S., McCormack, A., & McMahon, W. (2017). Project Jasper: Are distributed wholesale payment systems feasible yet? *Bank of Canada, Financial System Review*. https://www.bankofcanada.ca/wp-content/uploads/2017/05/fsr-june-2017-chapman.pdf

Chong, R., Abdullah, R. F. S., Anderson, A., & Amin, H. (2019). Economics of Islamic trade financing instruments. *International Review of Business Research Papers, 5*(1), 230–241.

CoinGecko. (2020, November 14). Stablecoins by market capitalization. https://www.coingecko.com/en/stablecoins

Dchieche, A., & Aboulaich, R. (2016). Pricing bounded value-based Salam. *Journal of Applied Economic Sciences, 11*(3, No. 41). https://www.researchgate.net/publication/306208986_Pricing_bounded_value_based_salam

Dow, S., Johnsen, G., & Montagnoli, A. (2015). A critique of full reserve banking. Sheffield Economic Research Paper Series (No. 2015008). https://www.sheffield.ac.uk/polopoly_fs/1.448817!/file/paper_2015008.pdf

Dunphy, P., & Peticolas, F. A. P. (2018). A first look at identity management schemes on the blockchain. *IEEE Security and Privacy Magazine*, Special issue on "Blockchain Security and Privacy." https://arxiv.org/ftp/arxiv/papers/1801/1801.03294.pdf

Elasrag, H. (2019). Blockchains for Islamic finance: Obstacles & challenges. Munich Personal RePEc Archive (MPRA Paper No. 92676). https://mpra.ub.uni-muenchen.de/92676/1/MPRA_paper_92676.pdf

Finterra. (n.d.). About us. https://finterra.org/about-us/

Franklin Templeton. (2024, June 26). Global sukuk market on the rise. https://www.franklintempleton.lu/articles/2024/western-asset/global-sukuk-market-on-the-rise

Fugal, A., Garratt, R., Guo, Z., & Hudson, D. (2018). A proposal for a decentralized liquidity savings mechanism with side payments. *Research Collection School of Information Systems.* https://ink.library.smu.edu.sg/cgi/viewcontent.cgi?article=5111&context=sis_research

Gassner, M., & Lawrence, J. (2018). Fintech in Islamic finance: Business models and the need for legal solutions. In *Fintech in Islamic Finance: Theory and practice* (Chapter 12, pp. 174–182). Routledge. http://www.iefpedia.com/english/wp-content/uploads/2019/12/EBOOK9250.pdf

Gazali, H. M., & Che Ismail, C. M. H. (2019). A conceptual framework for cash waqf with blockchain in financing education for the Islamic religious school in Malaysia. *Journal of Islamic Sciences and Comparative Studies, 3*(1), 73–88. https://journals.iium.edu.my/al-itqan/index.php/al-itqan/article/download/110/43

Goldberg, D. (2009). Legal tender. Bar-Ilan University Working Paper (No. 2009-04). https://www.econstor.eu/bitstream/10419/96051/1/599987200.pdf

Goodfriend, M. (1995). Monetary mystique: Secrecy and central banking. Centre for the Study of International Economic Relations Working Papers (No. 8527C). https://ir.lib.uwo.ca/cgi/viewcontent.cgi?article=1156&context=economicscsier_wp

Habib, A. (2011). Maqasid al-Shariah and Islamic financial products: A framework for assessment. *ISRA International Journal of Islamic Finance, 3*(1), 149–160. http://dro.dur.ac.uk/9775/1/9775.pdf

Hamilton, M. (2019). Blockchain distributed ledger technology: An introduction and focus on smart contracts. *Journal of Corporate Accounting and Finance, 31*(2), 7–12.

Harwick, C. (2015). Cryptocurrency and the problem of intermediation. *Independent Review, 20*(4) https://papers.ssrn.com/sol3/papers.cfm?abstract_id=2523771

Hassan, R., Ismail, W., Naimah, W. A., & Samah, Z. A. (2021). The centralized zakat management system in solving zakat management issues in Malaysia: The proposed framework. In *Handbook of research on Islamic social finance and economic recovery after a global health crisis* (pp. 107–125). IGI Global.

Heaven, D. (2018). The great Bitcoin crash. *NewScientist, 240*(3208), 24–25. https://www.sciencedirect.com/science/article/pii/S0262407918323054

Hidajat, T. (2020). Financial technology in Islamic view. *Islamic Banking and Finance Journal, 4*(2) https://journal.umsida.ac.id/index.php/perisai/article/download/465/973

iFN Fintech. (2020, December 15). Bursa Malaysia keen to explore blockchain sukuk. https://ifnfintech.com/bursa-malaysia-keen-to-explore-blockchain-sukuk/

Ilyasova, G. B., Bekmukhametova, A. F., & Farooq, A. J. (2019). Cryptocurrency: A new phenomenon in monetary circulation. *Central Asian Journal of Social Sciences and Humanities, 4*(1), 39–46. https://jhumansoc-sc.kaznu.kz/index.php/1-eurasian/article/view/287/244

International Centre for Education in Islamic Finance (INCEIF). (2018). Classical zakat modelling for the blockchain age inspiration (Issue 11, Fourth Edition). https://www.inceif.org/wp-content/uploads/2019/02/IFHUB-11th-Edition_reduce-size-compressed.pdf

International Monetary Fund (IMF). (2017). Ensuring financial stability in countries with Islamic banking. https://www.imf.org/~/media/Files/Publications/CR/2017/cr17145.ashx

Irfan, H., & Ahmed, D. (2018). Fintech: The opportunity for Islamic finance. In *Fintech in Islamic finance: Theory and practice* (Chapter 12, pp. 174–182). Routledge. http://www.iefpedia.com/english/wp-content/uploads/2019/12/EBOOK9250.pdf

Islamic Financial Services Board (IFSB). (2019). Islamic financial services industry stability report 2019. https://www.ifsb.org/download.php?id=5231&lang=English&pg=/sec03.php

Jaelani, A. (2016). Zakat accounting: Metaphor and accounting treatment for business organization (MPRA Paper No. 74782). In *4th International Conference on Islamic Economics and Business (ICONIES)*. https://papers.ssrn.com/sol3/papers.cfm?abstract_id=2843071

Jibrel. (2019, January 22). Sukuk bonds on the blockchain. https://medium.com/jibrel-network/sukukbonds-on-the-blockchain-9b5bf02778d0

Khan, N., Kchouri, B., Yatoo, N. A., Kraussl, Z., Patel, A., & State, R. (2020). Tokenization of sukuk: Ethereum case study. *Global Finance Journal*. https://doi.org/10.1016/j.gfj.2020.100539

Koulu, A. (2016). Blockchains and online dispute resolution: Smart contracts as an alternative to enforcement. *Journal of Law, Technology & Society, 13*(1), 40–69.

Koumbarakis, A., & Dobrauz-Saldapenna, G. (2019). Central bank digital currency: Benefits and drawbacks. *PricewaterhouseCoopers*. https://papers.ssrn.com/sol3/papers.cfm?abstract_id=3429037

Kusumaningtias, R. (2019). The role of waqf in social development. In *International Conference on Economics, Education, Business and Accounting* (Conference Paper). https://www.knepublishing.com/index.php/KnE-Social/article/view/4018/8273

Ledger Insights. (2019, November). R3's partner Wethaq issues its first blockchain sukuk. https://www.ledgerinsights.com/wethaq-blockchain-sukuk/

Malaysia International Islamic Financial Centre (MIFC). (2018, November 18). A stablecoin gets Sharia certified, the IMF considers central bank digital currencies. http://www.mifc.com/index.php?ch=ch_contents_capital_markets&pg=pg_cm_global&ac=26842

Malika, B. (2021). Sukuk tokenization: Successful experiences. *Journal of Studies in Economics and Management, 4*(1). https://www.asjp.cerist.dz/en/downArticle/635/4/1/155687

MAS. (2017). Project Ubin Phase 2: Re-imagining interbank real-time gross settlement system using distributed ledger technologies. https://www.mas.gov.sg/-/media/MAS/ProjectUbin/Project-Ubin-Phase-2-Reimagining-RTGS.pdf

Masruki, R., & Shafi, Z. (2013). The development of waqf accounting in enhancing accountability. *Middle-East Journal of Scientific Research, 13*, 1–6. https://www.researchgate.net/publication/288972132_The_development_of_Waqf_accounting_in_enhancing_accountability

Mat Rahim, S. R., Mohamad, Z. Z., Abu Bakar, J., Mohsin, F. H., & Isa, N. M. (2018). Artificial intelligence, smart contract, and Islamic finance. *Asian Social Science, 14*(2), 145–154. https://pdfs.semanticscholar.org/ebb7/b64cee7a139198c6259bedd8c95e865dfa88.pdf

Maurer, B. (2010). Form versus substance: AAOIFI projects and Islamic fundamentals in the case of sukuk. *Journal of Islamic Accounting and Business Research, 1*(1), 32–41. https://escholarship.org/content/qt97b714d5/qt97b714d5.pdf

Melachrinos, A., & Pfister, C. (2021). Stablecoins: A brave new world? Stanford Journal of Blockchain Law and Policy. https://stanford-jblp.pubpub.org/pub/stablecoins-brave-new-world/release/1

Migdad, A. (2019). Managing zakat through institutions: Case of Malaysia (Vol. 3, pp. 28–44). Derive Park. https://dergipark.org.tr/en/download/article-file/868357

Mihajat, M. I. S. (2014). Hybrid contract in Islamic banking and finance: A proposed Shariah principles and parameters for product development. *EJBM-Special Issue: Islamic Management and Business, 2*(2) https://www.researchgate.net/profile/Mohammad-Bhuiyan-31/publication/335961824_Professional_Ethics_Under_Islamic_Perspective/links/5d85fc7c299bf1996f8516f8/Professional-Ethics-Under-Islamic-Perspective.pdf#page=92

Moghul, U. F., & Safar-Aly, S. (2015). Green sukuk: The introduction of Islam's environmental ethics to contemporary Islamic finance. *Georgetown International Environmental Law Review, 27*(1). https://papers.ssrn.com/sol3/papers.cfm?abstract_id=2580864

Mohamed, H. (2019). Blending Islamic finance and impact investing for the sustainable development goals. *4th Annual Islamic Finance Conference, JW Marriott Surabaya, 24–25 July*. https://www.academia.edu/41300047/Blending_Islamic_Finance_and_Impact_Investing_for_the_Sustainable_Development_Goals

Mohamed, H., & Ali, H. (2018). Blockchain, fintech, and Islamic finance. Walter de Gruyter. http://dln.jaipuria.ac.in:8080/jspui/bitstream/123456789/8274/1/Blockchain%2C%20Fintech%2C%20and%20Islamic%20Finance.%20Building%20the%20Future%20in%20the%20New%20Islamic%20Digital%20Economy.pdf

Mohsin, M. I. A. (2013). Financing through cash-waqf: A revitalization to finance different needs. *International Journal of Islamic and Middle Eastern Finance and Management, 6*(4) https://www.inceif.org/wp-content/themes/inceif/images/ISF/financing_through_cash_waqf_revitalization_finance_different_needs_magda.pdf

Monetary Authority of Singapore (MAS, n.d.). Guidelines on the application of banking regulations to Islamic banking. https://www.mas.gov.sg/-/media/MAS-Media-Library/regulation/guidelines/BD/guidelines-on-application-of-banking-regulations-to-islamic-banking/Guidelines-on-the-Application-of-Banking-Regulations-to-Islamic-Banking.pdf

Monetary Authority of Singapore (MAS, 2022). (2022, August 1). Reply to parliamentary question on extent of Singaporeans' exposure to recent collapse in value of TerraUSD stablecoin and Luna token. https://www.mas.gov.sg/news/parliamentary-replies/2022/reply-to-parliamentary-question-on-extent-of-singaporeans-exposure-to-recent-collapse-in-value-of-terrausd-stablecoin-and-luna-token

Muedini, F. (2018). The compatibility of cryptocurrencies and Islamic finance. *European Journal of Islamic Finance* (No. 10). http://www.ojs.unito.it/index.php/EJIF/article/download/2569/pdf

MUIS. (n.d.). FAQs. https://eservices.muis.gov.sg/ifaq/apps/fcd_faqmain.aspx#FAQ_156341

Muneeza, A., & Nadwi, S. (2019). The potential of application of technology-based innovations for zakat administration in India. In *International Conference of Zakat 2019 Proceedings*. https://www.researchgate.net/publication/342431437_The_Potential_of_Application_of_Technology_Based_Innovations_for_Zakat_Administration_in_India

Mydin Meera, A. K., & Larbani, M. (2009). Seigniorage of fiat money and the Maqasid al-Shariah: The compatibility of the gold dinar with the Maqasid. Jurnal Muamalat (No. 2, pp. 93–116). https://www.researchgate.net/profile/Moussa_Larbani/publication/46545900_Seigniorage_of_fiat_money_and_the_Maqasid_al-Shari%27ah_The_compatibility_of_the_gold_dinar_with_the_Maqasid/links/00b7d51918c80d6300000000.pdf

Nasucha, M. N., Ahmed, R., & Barre, G. M. (2019). Examining the viability of Istisna for project financing: An economic perspective. *International Journal of Management and Applied Research, 6*(4), 259–270. http://ijmar.org/v6n4/19-019.pdf

Noor, A. M., & Haron, M. N. (2016). A framework for determination of actual costs in Islamic financing products. *Journal of Islamic Finance, 5*(2), 37–52. https://www.researchgate.net/publication/312946226_Determination_of_Actual_Cost_Framework_in_Islamic_Financial_Product

Nurain Muhmand, S., & Nasuha Muhmad, S. (2018). Potential development of sukuk in competitive market. *International Journal of Business and Management, 2*(2), 26–29. https://www.researchgate.net/profile/Siti_Muhmad/publication/326675959_Potential_Development_of_Sukuk_in_Competitive_Market/links/5b5d7b43458515c4b2507eeb/Potential-Development-of-Sukuk-in-Competitive-Market.pdf

Oseni, U. A., & Ali, S. N. (2018). Fintech in Islamic finance: Business models and the need for legal solutions. In *Fintech in Islamic Finance: Theory and practice* (Chapter 1, pp. 3–16). Routledge. http://www.iefpedia.com/english/wp-content/uploads/

Paldi, C. (2014). Capital adequacy, liquidity, and risk: Is Islamic banking too expensive? *Journal of Business and Economics, 5*(11), 2169–2172. http://jibf-net.com/journals/jibf/Vol_2_No_1_March_2014/23.pdf

Pertiwi, R. S., Ryandono, M. N. H., & Anita, K. R. (2018). Regulations and management of waqf institutions in Indonesia and Singapore: A comparative study. In *The 2nd International Conference on Islamic Economics, Business, and Philanthropy* (2nd ICIEBP), 766–783. https://knepublishing.com/index.php/KnE-Social/article/view/4246/8722

Qardus. (2022, January 5). The Islamic financial services industry statistics. https://www.qardus.com/news/the-islamic-financial-services-industry-statistics

Qiu, T., Zhang, R., & Gao, Y. (2019). Ripple vs. SWIFT: Transforming cross-border remittance using blockchain technology. *Journal of Procedia Computer Science, 147*, 428–434. https://www.researchgate.net/publication/331006094_Ripple_vs_SWIFT_Transforming_Cross_Border_Remittance_Using_Blockchain_Technology

RAM Ratings. (2013). Sukuk contracts: The evolution. http://www.mifc.com/?ch=28&pg=72&ac=33&bb=uploadpdf

Ramadhan, I. A., & Wirdyanigsih. (2019). Green sukuk issuance as an investment instrument for sustainable development. *Journal of Advances in Social Science, Education and Humanities Research, 413*, 95–98. https://download.atlantis-press.com/article/125936124.pdf

Raskin, M. (2017). The law and legality of smart contracts. *Georgetown Law Technology Review, 1*(2), 305–341. https://georgetownlawtechreview.org/wp-content/uploads/2017/04/Raskin-1-GEO.-L.-TECH.-REV.-305-.pdf

Renima, A., Tiliouine, H., & Estes, R. J. (2016). The Islamic Golden Age: A story of the triumph of the Islamic civilization. In *The state of social progress of Islamic societies* (pp. 25–25). Springer.

Reuters. (2018, November 26). Abu Dhabi's Al Hilal Bank uses blockchain to sell sukuk in secondary market. https://www.reuters.com/article/al-hilal-sukuk-blockchain-idUSL8N1Y11PH

Rosly, S. A., & Zaini, M. A. M. (2008). Risk-return analysis of Islamic banks' investment deposits and shareholders' fund. *Managerial Finance, 34*(10), 695–707. https://www.researchgate.net/publication/228848052_Risk-return_analysis_of_Islamic_banks'_investment_deposits_and_shareholders'_fund

Rosner, M. T., & Kang, A. (2016). Understanding and regulating twenty-first century payment systems: *The Ripple case study. Michigan Law Review, 114*(4). https://repository.law.umich.edu/cgi/viewcontent.cgi?article=1239&context=mlr

Saba, I., Kouser, R., & Chaundhry, I. S. (2019). FinTech and Islamic finance: Challenges and opportunities. *Review of Economics and Development Studies, 5*(4), 581–590. https://www.researchgate.net/publication/338342216_Fintech_and_Islamic_Finance-challenges_and_Opportunities

Sadeq, A. M. (2002). Waqf, perpetual charity and poverty alleviation. *International Journal of Social Economics, 29*(1/2), 135–151.

Sairally, B. S. (2002). Murabaha financing: Some controversial issues. *Review of Islamic Economics, 12*, 73–86. http://www.iaif.ir/images/khareji/articles/finance/64.pdf

Saleh, F. (2020). Blockchain without waste: Proof-of-Stake. *SSRN Electronic Journal*. https://papers.ssrn.com/sol3/papers.cfm?abstract_id=3183935

Schletz, M., Nassiry, D., & Lee, M. K. (2020). Blockchain and tokenized securities: The potential for green finance. Asian Development Bank Working Paper Series (No. 1079). https://www.think-asia.org/bitstream/handle/11540/11466/adbi-wp1079.pdf?sequence=1

Senner, R., & Sornette, D. (2018). The holy grail of cryptocurrencies: Ready to replace fiat money? *Journal of Economic Issues, 53*(4), 966–1000. https://papers.ssrn.com/sol3/papers.cfm?abstract_id=3192924

Shaikh, S. A. (2016). Zakat collectible in OIC countries for poverty alleviation: A primer on empirical estimation. *International Journal of Zakat, 1*(1), 17–35. http://ijazbaznas.com/index.php/journal/article/download/4/2

Shaikh, S., & Zaka, F. (2019). Blockchained sukuk-financing. In *Lecture Notes in Business Information Processing Book Series* (Vol. 345).

Shaikh, S. A., Ismail, A. G., & Shafiai, M. H. M. (2017). Application of waqf for social and development finance. *ISRA International Journal of Islamic Finance, 9*(1) https://www.emerald.com/insight/content/doi/10.1108/IJIF-07-2017-002/full/html

Solferino Academy. (2018, May 15). Catalyzing sustainable financing with duty and dignity. http://media.ifrc.org/innovation/2018/05/15/catalyzing-sustainable-financing-with-duty-and-dignity/

Sorenson, B. (2011). Ethical money: Financial growth in the Muslim world. *American University International Law Review, 23*(4), 647–659. https://digitalcommons.wcl.american.edu/cgi/viewcontent.cgi?article=1029&context=auilr

Standard Chartered. (2023, April 17). Islamic finance and the securities market outlook for 2023. https://www.sc.com/en/news/financial-institutions-investor-groups/islamic-finance-securities-market-outlook-2023/

Sulaiman, A. A., Mohamad, M. T., & Samsudin, M. L. (2013). How Islamic banks of Malaysia manage liquidity: An emphasis on confronting economic cycles. *International Journal of Business and Social Science, 4*(7). https://ijbssnet.com/journals/Vol_4_No_7_July_2013/28.pdf

SWIFT. (2020). Follow the money. https://www.swift.com/sites/default/files/files/swift_bae_report_Follow-The%20Money.pdf

Syamlan, Y. T., & Istiana, N. (2018). Does fractional reserve banking system exist in Indonesian Islamic banking? *Journal of Islamic Monetary Economics and Finance, 4*(1), 369–400. http://jimf-bi.org/index.php/JIMF/article/download/1009/738

Taskinoy, J. (2019). Blockchain: A misunderstood digital revolution. In Things you need to know about blockchain. SSRN. https://papers.ssrn.com/sol3/papers.cfm?abstract_id=3466480

The Malaysian Reserve. (2020, December 18). Number of zakat payers jumps 90% this year. https://themalaysianreserve.com/2020/12/18/number-of-zakat-payers-jumps-90-this-year/

The Malaysian Reserve. (2022, July 27). Malaysia's Islamic capital market remains dominant. https://themalaysianreserve.com/2022/07/27/malaysias-islamic-capital-market-remains-dominant/

TheCoinsPost. (2019, September 15). International Fiqh Academy: Dealing with cryptocurrencies is risky. https://www.thecoinspost.com/international-fiqh-academy-dealing-with-cryptocurrencies-is-risky/

Udin, M. A. (2015). Principles of Islamic finance: Prohibition of riba, gharar, and mays. Munich Personal RePEc Archive (MPRA Paper No. 67711). https://mpra.ub.uni-muenchen.de/67711/1/MPRA_paper_67711.pdf

United Nations (UN). Money-laundering and globalization. https://www.unodc.org/unodc/en/money-laundering/globalization.html

United Nations Office for the Coordination of Humanitarian Affairs (OCHA). (2018). Global humanitarian overview 2018. https://reliefweb.int/sites/reliefweb.int/files/resources/GHO2018.PDF

Vishwanath, S. R., & Azmi, S. (2009). An overview of Islamic sukuk bonds. *Journal of Structured Finance, 14*(4), 58–67.

Waemustafa, W., & Suriani, S. (2016). Theory of gharar and its interpretation of risk and uncertainty from the perspectives of authentic Hadith and the Holy Quran: Review of literatures. *Journal of Islamic Economics, Banking and Finance, 12*, 100–126. http://repo.uum.edu.my/18860/1/Wae_gharar.pdf

Wahab, N. A., & Rahim, A. R. A. (2011). A framework to analyse the efficiency and governance of zakat institutions. *Journal of Islamic Accounting and Business Research, 2*(1), 43–62. https://www.researchgate.net/profile/Norazlina_Abd_Wahab/publication/254192398_A_framework_to_analyse_the_efficiency_and_governance_of_zakat_institutions/links/57450ad408ae9f741b40857d/A-framework-to-analyse-the-efficiency-and-governance-of-zakat-institutions.pdf

Wandhofer, R., & Casu, B. (2018). The future of correspondent banking cross-border payments. SWIFT Institute Working Paper (No. 2017-001). https://swiftinstitute.org/wp-content/uploads/2018/10/SIWP-2017-001-The-Future-of-Correspondent-Banking_FINAL.pdf

World Islamic Economic Forum (WIEF). (2018). Islamic Economic Forum's declaration on Bitcoin (No. 1/2018). http://www.iefpedia.com/english/wp-content/uploads/2018/12/Islamic-Economic-Forum%E2%80%99s-Declaration-on-Bitcoin.pdf

Yoo, S. (2017). Blockchain-based financial case analysis and its implications. *Asia Pacific Journal of Innovation and Entrepreneurship, 11*(3). https://www.emerald.com/insight/content/doi/10.1108/APJIE-12-2017-036/full/html

Yuneline, M. H. (2019). Analysis of cryptocurrency's characteristics in four perspectives. *Journal of Asian Business and Economic Studies, 26*(2). https://www.emerald.com/insight/content/doi/10.1108/JABES-12-2018-0107/full/html

Zakat Singapore. (n.d.). Zakat on savings. https://www.zakat.sg/types-of-zakat/zakat-on-savings/

Zaman, A. (2015). Building genuine Islamic financial institutions. *Journal of Islamic Economics, Banking and Finance, 11*(2), 13–32. https://papers.ssrn.com/sol3/papers.cfm?abstract_id=2478277

CHAPTER 4

Blockchain Drive for Financial Inclusion

Abstract The philosophical value of financial inclusion is rooted in Adam Smith's moral philosophy. Financial inclusion efforts in Malaysia and Singapore are focused on the issues faced by BNM and MAS in banking the unbanked. Malaysia struggles with limited physical access to financial services, while Singapore's challenge is the low financial and digital literacy among migrant workers. Blockchain-based mobile banking is a potential solution to improve access to financial services for individuals. For businesses, the financing gaps for MSMEs and SMEs in both countries point to the ineffectiveness of traditional crowdfunding. Crypto crowdfunding via initial decentralized offerings (IDOs) could help businesses leverage DeFi to access global fundraising networks. On the international level, projects such as the BIS' Project Dunbar and the MAS' Project Partior are exploring blockchain solutions to improve speed and reduce costs for cross-border remittance, resulting in multipartisan debates around the use of central bank digital currencies (CBDCs) that could disrupt global financial monopolies and promote greater individual autonomy.

M. S. Thong, *Blockchain for Financial Governance in Malaysia and Singapore*,
https://doi.org/10.1007/978-981-96-1281-9_4

4.1 The Philosophical Foundations of Financial Inclusion

Adam Smith, who is widely regarded as the father of modern economics as well as the father of capitalism, envisaged the idea of an economic framework that is located within a macro scheme of moral philosophy whereby this in itself set forth the need for the application of principles of morality within the overall economic framework in general and that of capitalism in particular (Smith, 1776). The need for Adam Smith's moral philosophy to buttress the effects of unbridled capitalism is aptly illustrated by the grossly unbalanced distribution of global wealth whereby according to the World Inequality Lab's "World Inequality Report 2022," 0.01% of the richest individuals in the world, i.e., about 520,000 people own at least 11% of the world's wealth (World Inequality Labs, 2022). In many ways, the issue of global wealth inequality has been made worse by the Covid-19 pandemic whereby according to Oxfam's report titled "Inequality Kills," since the onset of the pandemic, the world's ten richest men have more than doubled their collective net worth from USD700 billion to USD1.5 trillion whereas 99% of the global population have had their income reduced and more than 160 million people from around the world were pushed into poverty (Oxfam, 2022).

The global patterns of wealth distribution resulted in the global phenomenon of the rich getting richer and the poor getting poorer in response to which the UN has set up its UN Inter-Agency Task Force on Social and Solidarity Economy (UNTFSSE) to harness the concept of social solidarity economy (SSE) for the attainment of its 2030 Agenda for Sustainable Development and Sustainable Development Goals (SDGs) (UNTFSSE, 2016). In its position paper titled "Realizing the 2030 Agenda through Social and Solidarity Economy," the UNTFSSE noted that "SSE can play a crucial role in the realization of the 2030 Agenda and the SDGs by promoting inclusive and sustainable development through concrete social, institutional and technological innovations and practices" (UNTFSSE, 2016).

The concept of SSE has a central role to play in the attainment of both the UN's 2030 Agenda as well as its SDGs. However, there remains the issue of the business-as-usual profit-oriented nature of modern-day financial institutions have led some economists such as David Kreps to question whether the underlying ideals of capitalism have departed from principles of morality to become one of pure greed in which each party strives to further nothing else but their interests (Kreps, 1997). In this regard, the issue of financial exclusion is very much a reflection of unbridled financial capitalism which has prompted some experts such as Polychroniou to put forth the idea for the development of an alternative financial system whose principal driver is for long-term public good instead of short-term profit-making (Polychroniou, 2012).

4.2 Standing in Solidarity in Finance and Economics

In the financial domain, the concept of SSE is manifested in the form of social and solidarity finance (SSF). The microfinance industry developed SSF principles to support the needs of SSE (i.e. in response to the relationships of interdependence between the social and financing institutions comprising the SSE framework) whereby the objective of the SSF domain is to facilitate the implementation of its principles to address the long-term needs of the collective enterprises constituted by these institutions (ILO, 2019). If these principles are properly implemented with the support of technologies such as blockchain, SSF principles could go a long way toward supporting SSE specifically for remedying the effects of unbridled capitalism particularly that of financial exclusion.

The promotion of financial inclusion is very much in line with the ideals of SSF which, unlike the capitalistic roots of the conventional financial system that focuses on profit-seeking, emphasizes on the element of mutual dependency between individuals as the basis for socio-economic relationships which means that no one should be left out (Artis, 2017). In terms of its practical implementation, SSF postulates that the underlying objective of socio-economic transactions is for the generation of profits sustainably while at the same time facilitating the formation of meaningful relationships between the stakeholders. In the context of the promotion of financial inclusion, SSF aims to help the unbanked who are unable to obtain access to financial services through the provision of financial services which are offered through a network of solidarity-financing relationships under which productive and sustainable financing are made available through mutual trust relationships that are reinforced by socialization forums (UNRISD, 2015).

The core basis of SSF, i.e., solidarity-financing relationships which are based on mutual trust and productive financing, renders transactions undertaken under the SSF framework to be unlike those in the conventional financial system as SSF transactions are not merely commercial but serves to establish trust-enhancing financial relationships between the stakeholders whereby the formation of social links between these stakeholders is the objective of SSF, unlike conventional financial systems which objective is primarily for profit-making (Mendell & Nogales, 2011). The application of SSF principles would open up a whole new dimension when it comes to efforts to promote financial inclusion as the existing barriers that prevent financial institutions from making available their services to the unbanked, i.e., tight profit margins would be thrown out of the window as the central tenet of SSF revolves around social considerations as opposed to financial calculations.

Unlike the conventional financial system which focuses on the immediacy of profits whereby this results in financial institutions being unwilling to offer their services to unbanked due to tight profit margins, the application of SSF principles would bring about a paradigmatic shift of sorts in this regard. This is because the application of SSF principles would change the focal point of financial institutions to that of a long-term perspective whereby the establishment of solidarity-finance relationships would translate into profits for these institutions not in the immediate or short-term future but at a point of time that lies much further down the road.

In terms of its ideals, the use of SSF is very much in line with the democratization ideals of blockchain as manifested in the financial domain through the decentralized finance (DeFi) framework which aims to promote the decentralization of financial services through the establishment of an alternative financial system to the conventional one (Scott, 2016). In this regard, it is notable that SSF transactions that take place in the context of solidarity-finance relationships are not commercial market transactions with a view of profit but are instead very much social transactions based on the element of trust built on the distribution of shared information among the stakeholders.

4.3 Blockchain as a Technological Foundation for Social Solidarity Finance

It is in this connection that blockchain comes into the picture to offer a technological mechanism for the verification and sharing of information among the stakeholders. Information sharing is a critical component of

SSF as the very basis of SSF transactions is centered around solidarity-finance relationships which in turn are based on the underlying mutual trust between the stakeholders for which the sharing of accurate information plays a crucial role in the establishing and maintenance of. Given the trustless nature of blockchain-based shared ledger records, the use of the technology would help maintain the structural integrity of the internal information system of SSF transactions as well as warrant the efficiency of the monitoring and supervision mechanisms of such transactions.

In terms of its deployment, SSF endeavors to complement the conventional financial system whereby the focal point of SSF is on those who have been left out of the conventional financial services framework, i.e., the unbanked which large numbers spanning across the globe renders this issue to be a major systemic weakness of the conventional financial system as it constitutes a major aberrant from the basic principle of universal accessibility to financial services (UN, 2016). Besides that, the systemic weaknesses of the conventional financial system also extend to the uneven balance of powers between financial institutions and their customers particularly in the context of loan transactions whereby financial institutions as creditors would inevitably have a superior bargaining position over their debtor customers and this unequal balance of negotiation powers may be to the detriment of the latter (Machauer, 1998). In this connection, financial institutions operating under conventional financing principles tend to set their interest rates based on the risk portfolio of the debtor customers in addition to requiring higher levels of security in the form of guarantors and collaterals for borrowers whose portfolios have a higher level of risk exposure whereby this as a whole reflects on the low level of trusts between the transacting parties.

SSF aims to remedy the systemic weakness of a lack of universal accessibility under the conventional financial system by transforming the underlying ideals and operational objectives of financial institutions from one that aims to make short-term profits through commercial transactions into one that has its eyes on long-term projections of mutual growth undertaken through solidarity-finance relationships which goes beyond the commercial sphere to cover social connections as well. As the element of trust forms the basis for all relationships, particularly for social ones, blockchain with its trustless and automated system which allows it to operate in a manner free from centralized control without the need for human intervention would come in handy for the establishment and maintenance of trust-based relationships between stakeholders forming the SSF framework.

Moreover, the use of blockchain-based share ledger records coupled with automated smart contracts can help promote a more neutral negotiation process as the parties can put their cards on the table with the self-verifying ledger records functioning as reliable information databases. The automation of smart contracts provides the essential features of autonomy to the transaction, thereby acting as a neutral and impartial third party albeit a technological one (Almakhour et al., 2020).

4.4 Financial Inclusivity as an Antidote to Financial Capitalism

In this day and age of capitalism of which financial services are a central part, it is only natural that the business strategies of financial institutions are devised and implemented based on profit-oriented considerations (Elsner, 2012). In line with their profit-seeking agenda, as a general rule, financial institutions tend to set up branches at locations where the profile of the population renders it commercially viable to expend investment costs that are required to set up the branches whereby these costs include staffing and equipment costs, regulatory compliance costs as well as the costs of rental or purchase of the physical office among others. As financial institutions operate based on a profit-oriented business model, the costs expended by these institutions would have to be recovered from their customers who are required to pay for using the services offered by the institutions whereby the financial services sector is very much a profitable one, particularly for 4,500+ banks in the United States which collectively made a total profit of USD71.5 billion in the second quarter (Q2) of 2024 alone (FDIC, 2024).

However, the profits made by financial institutions come at a cost to the general public as the profit-seeking agenda of these institutions has resulted in a social issue in the form of financial exclusion. This is because the capitalist mode of operations of financial institutions tends to leave out those who lack the requisite financial standing to fulfill the eligibility criteria of these institutions which had been devised to maintain their profit margins. Research indicates that access to financial services is particularly critical for developing economies in terms of boosting the income of the population in such economies. The beneficial effects of financial inclusion are notably pertinent in the population sector which is at the lower end of the income scale whereby this is very much in line with the poverty reduction agenda of governments as part of their economic development policies (Honohan et al., 2009).

4.4.1 *State of Financial Inclusion in Malaysia*

In the context of Malaysia whose latest data indicates that the national poverty rate stood at 8.4% as of 2019 (World Bank, n.d.), the country can leverage its financial inclusion rate of 80.7% (World Bank, n.d.-a) which is one of the highest in Southeast Asia to reduce its poverty rate (World Bank, n.d.-c). In this regard, the World Bank has observed that Malaysia's success in promoting financial inclusivity lies in its policies which capitalize on the country's high mobile penetration rate and wide networks of banking agents to expand access to financial services for the country's population but the World Bank was unable to single out any particular factor which resulted in Malaysia's success in banking the unbanked. In its Working Paper titled "Financial inclusion in Malaysia: Distilling Lessons for Other Countries," the World Bank went on to highlight the fact that now that Malaysia has attained such a high financial inclusion rate, the country would be facing another challenge in that it would now have to find a way to ensure that those who have access financial services can make active use of such services (World Bank, 2017).

Picking up on the World Bank's observations, Bank Negara Malaysia (BNM), in its Financial Blueprint 2022–2026, has set as one its main priorities the undertaking of efforts to further the promotion of financial inclusion by "focusing on take-up and meaningful usage of financial services" (BNM, 2022). In other words, moving forward BNM would be aiming to improve the quality of access to financial services to encourage sustained and meaningful use of such services by Malaysians to elevate their financial standings while at the same time BNM would also be working on expanding the coverage of Malaysia's financial services network to include the "last mile" unbanked population whereby blockchain could come in as a handy technological tool to support the central bank's efforts in this regard.

4.4.2 *State of Financial Inclusion in Singapore*

When it comes to financial inclusion, Singapore is the undoubted leader in SEA with a financial inclusion rate of 96.4% of the adult population (World Bank, n.d.-b) thanks to the country's world-leading financial system which has incorporated the concept of open banking through the MAS' Financial Industry API Register that aims to facilitate the transfer of information between financial institutions operating in the country (MAS, n.d.). Nonetheless, this is not to say that Singapore does not face any issues concerning access to financial services as there is a particular group in the country that for one reason or another may be unable to access the country's sophisticated financial services network.

It is estimated that only about one in two migrant workers in Singapore has access to financial services, i.e., the rate of financial inclusion among migrant workers in Singapore stood at a mere 49% (Experian, 2019). Recognizing the issue of financial exclusion among migrant workers in Singapore and the negative effects this issue is having on these workers, the country's Ministry of Manpower (MOM) had in September 2018 issued new work permit conditions under which employers are encouraged to pay the salaries of their migrant workers electronically and to help their migrant workers open a POSB payroll account which is designed to meet the needs of migrant workers in the country (MOM, 2018). However, this does not address the underlying issue of the financial exclusion of migrant workers in Singapore, i.e., the lack of financial and digital literacy of these workers which may prevent them from properly utilizing the services which are available through their POSB payroll account.

4.5 Fundamentals of Financial Inclusion

Referring to Sarma's three-pronged classification of the features of financial inclusion, namely, accessibility, suitability, and affordability, the first feature of access to financial services is generally defined by geographical limitations whereby remote areas tend to be left out by financial institutions in terms of their services outreach, resulting in the population of these areas not having access to financial services (Sarma, 2008). Although it may be possible for regulators to put in place requirements that mandate financial institutions to ensure that the outreach of their services covers remote areas, the availability of services tends to be limited in terms of their quality due to the costs associated with the provision of financial services in these areas.

The feature of suitability refers to the extent to which financial services can meet the needs of the market by covering large parts of the population and businesses whereby the limiting factors resulting in financial exclusion tend to be the terms and conditions associated with financial services which more often than not are framed by financial institutions in such a manner as to maintain their profit margins as opposed to meeting the needs of the market. As for the cost factor, the key consideration would be that of affordability whereby the issue of the profit margins of financial institutions once again comes into play as the tight profit margins of financial services offered to low-income households and small businesses result in very little financial incentives for these institutions to do so which inevitably results in the financial exclusion of such households and businesses.

Most economists and financial experts concur with the fact that financial inclusion is most needed by those who are living in poverty, yet at the same time it is precisely their lack of money that stands in the way of the poor breaking the barriers of entry which stand in their way of accessing financial services (Chitranjan, 2020). Although the United States is the leading global economy, it is interesting to note that about one in ten, i.e., 10.5% of its population, is living in a state of poverty based on the estimates of the country's Census Bureau as of 2019 (University of California Davies, 2020). In this regard, it is notable that in the US Federal Deposit Insurance Corporation's (FDIC) National Survey of Unbanked Households carried out in 2019 it was found that of the 5.7% of unbanked households in the country, a staggering 29% stated the reason for their lack of access to financial services was due to not having enough money to meet the minimum balance requirements (FDIC, 2018). It is in this context that we shall explore the various factors of financial exclusion in Malaysia and Singapore and the manner in which blockchain can help address these factors.

4.5.1 Improving Accessibility to Financial Services with Blockchain-Secured Mobile Banking

In BNM's "Overview of Financial inclusion in Malaysia" which was published in July 2021, the central bank identified sub-optimal physical access as one of the key challenges to attaining full financial inclusion in Malaysia (BNM, 2021a). In the Overview, BNM noted that Malaysia has a lower physical outreach compared to high-income countries whereby although 100% of districts in the country have financial institutions access points, 449 out of 837 sub-districts in which 17% of the country's adult population reside are uncovered. Given the fact that Malaysia has a high mobile phone penetration rate of 89.6%, the use of mobile banking could help drive the nation toward the attainment of full financial inclusion by covering the "last mile" of the unbanked population in the country, i.e., those from low-income households (Data Reportal, 2022).

It is a well-known fact that Singapore is a global financial hub with well-developed financial networks, but this does not do much to facilitate the promotion of financial inclusion among migrant workers in the country as 24% of these workers cited their lack of financial literacy as the reason for not having a bank account (Shimanuki, 2021). In addition, the lack of digital literacy among migrant workers in Singapore further worsens the issue of financial exclusion among these workers as, notwithstanding the wide availability of digital financial services in the country, these workers are unable to utilize such services. Although most migrant workers own POSB accounts and POSB's services are available through mobile, access to these services is only available through POSB's Digibank mobile app which means that only migrant workers who own a smartphone and have adequate digital literacy to use the app would be able to access POSB's services through mobile

In this regard Singapore can learn about the simplification of mobile banking services through the notable use case example of BNM's MyMobile program which was launched in 2013 through the central bank's wholly owned subsidiary Malaysian Electronic Clearing Corporation Sdn Bhd (MyClear) in partnership with the country's three largest banks, i.e., telco operators, i.e., CIMB, Maybank, and Public Bank as well as the country's three largest three telco operators, i.e., Maxis, Celcom, and DiGi (PayNet, n.d.). In the context of our discussions on the use of mobile banking for the promotion of financial inclusion in Malaysia, MyMobile's effectiveness lies in the fact that it can facilitate mobile-to-mobile payment services without the need for smartphones or mobile apps, i.e., it can work with any mobile phone, thereby enabling it to be used by those from low-income households who may not have the financial means to own a smartphone. In this regard, it is notable that BNM has identified that low-income households have considerably lower take-up rates of financial services as compared to general households. For example, the take-up rates of low-income households for savings accounts, credit card, and insurance services are respectively 14%, 22%, and 31% lower than those of general households.

Another simple-to-use mobile banking platform is that of M-Pesa which is a joint project between Kenyan telecommunications company Safaricom and its UK counterpart Vodafone Group to develop a mobile banking platform through which Kenyans can obtain financial services using text messages using short messaging service (SMS) (Communications Authority of Kenya, 2020). Among the financial services that can be undertaken by Kenyans through the M-Pesa platform include the sending, receiving, and withdrawal of money, purchase of goods and services, the payment of utility bills, as well as cryptocurrency transactions whereby the accessibility of these services from any mobile phone provided it has Global System for Mobile Communications (GSM), which enables it to send and receive SMS text messages, has resulted in the platform having a market share of almost 99% of the mobile banking market in Kenya, with the number of subscribers totaling up to 29 million in 2020. Nonetheless, the convenience brought about by mobile banking comes at a price as mobile banking service providers do impose service fees of up to 10% depending on the value of funds transferred (Conley, 2019). Besides that, users of mobile banking services also face certain limitations such as the inability to transfer funds between countries or to transfer funds using different currencies in addition to facing security issues arising from having to rely on their mobile phones as their point of access to financial services.

For those living in countries that are equipped with internet connectivity, mobile banking users would generally access financial services through smartphone-based applications whereas for those living in countries that are lacking in internet connectivity mobile banking access would generally be undertaken through SMS sent via GSM networks (Donner & Tellez, 2008). With regard to mobile banking services which are accessed through smartphone applications, there is a myriad of malware that are devised to attack the devices running these applications whereby these malwares include Trojans, rootkits, and other viruses. A common malware in the form of ransomware that targets smartphone devices is one known as Svpeng which upon entering a device would start to search for mobile banking applications on the device before activating a programming code to encrypt the files stored in the device after which the perpetrator will blackmail the owner of the device for money in return for decrypting the owner's files in the device (Wazid et al., 2019). In this regard, it is notable that Svpeng is just one of a host of malware targeted at smartphone devices whereby another notable malware is Zeus-in-the-mobile (ZitMo) which infiltrates smartphone mobile banking applications to intercept transaction authorization codes (TAC) sent by financial institutions to their customers.

As for GSM-based mobile banking services, security issues arise due to the use of the "store and forward" data communication technique whereby SMS messages sent by users containing the details of financial transactions are not directly sent to the receiving financial institutions but instead is first sent to an intermediate station, i.e., the SMS Center (SMSC), which would collect and store the message before delivering it to the financial institutions (Sharma & Muharrami, 2018). Additionally, critical security issues arise due to the lack of encryption for SMS whereby although telecommunication networks would generally use the A5 encryption method for SMS messages, the short key length of this encryption method renders it relatively prone to being deciphered in the event of a security breach (Paik, 2010). In general, the lack of an end-to-end encryption (E2EE) method for SMS messages renders them vulnerable to hackers, which renders this form of communication unsuited for sending sensitive information such as those involving financial transactions.

Although the use of mobile banking has brought about dual-pronged benefits for both the banked who can access financial services more conveniently and the unbanked who benefit from the wider outreach of the conventional financial system, the massive rise in hacking attacks on mobile banking applications coupled with the systemic vulnerabilities arising from the use of SMS for financial transactions renders the benefits of mobile banking to come at a price that is possibly too high to pay. This is illustrated by the fact that from 2015 to 2020, the number of hacking attacks involving mobile banking networks has increased by more than 600% whereby these attacks have resulted in a loss of more than USD40 million in 2019 alone (DataProt, 2023).

It is in this context that blockchain steps in to provide a more secure mobile banking platform to leverage the benefits of mobile banking, particularly for the promotion of financial inclusion minus the prevalent risks arising under the existing operating framework. In a survey conducted by data analytics firm Greenwich Associates, 85% of respondents expressed their concerns that centralized networks are putting themselves up as targets for hackers (Johnson, 2018). In this connection, the decentralized nature of blockchain networks can reduce the risks of hackings as it results in the absence of any single point of target for hackers to aim at whereby the disintermediation feature of these networks which effectively dispenses with the need for intermediaries results in a reduction in the risks of information breaches in addition to facilitating the functioning of E2EE which further reduces the risks of such breaches (Mattila, 2016).

Additionally, the use of cryptographic encryption in the form of private keys provides a further layer of security as it is mathematically impossible to hack this form of encryption but this does not mean that blockchain networks are foolproof as, although private keys are virtually hack-proof, they are nevertheless vulnerable to being stolen (Steger et al., 2017). In the event of the theft of a private key, the security of a blockchain network goes out the window as anyone with the key would be recognized by the network as a legitimate user and thereby would have authorized access to the data secured using the key as well as being granted with autonomy to carry out transactions bestowed on the actual owner of the key. To make matters worse, transactions that have been undertaken on a blockchain network are generally irreversible due to the immutable nature of the distributed ledger records (Lemieux, 2017).

Given the pertinent risks associated with the theft of private keys, a solution has been developed in the form of hardware security modules (HSMs) which can be used to secure private keys through industry-grade control systems. HSMs are mainly used in institutional settings, though these modules are slowly shifting toward public use as they have been incorporated into personal computers, which reflects on the modules' increasing affordability and user-friendliness (Wired, 2017).

Notwithstanding the security vulnerabilities of blockchain networks arising from the theft of private keys, as long as users keep their private keys safe, the security offered by blockchain networks is almost impenetrable by hackers which renders the use of blockchain to be much suited for mobile banking transactions as these transactions entail the transmission of a large amount of sensitive financial information. In time to come as HSMs grow into mainstream use, the security of blockchain networks would move up another notch whereby the case for the use of blockchain for mobile banking transactions would be even stronger given the enhanced level of security offered by the technology in contrast with those of GSM networks which rely on SMS messages and smartphone-based applications which face systemic vulnerabilities.

As the unbanked as well as those who rely on mobile banking as their sole channel of access to financial services are generally from the lower-income group of underdeveloped and developing countries, the security risks of mobile banking may inhibit the use of this mode of banking by those who need it the most, i.e., those who are in the lower-income group (Medhi et al., 2009). With regard to the unbanked from the lower-income group, a prevalent concern among them is that the use of mobile banking may result in them falling victim to hackers, resulting in them losing their scarce financial resources whereby this concern prompts them to refrain from using mobile banking services resulting in them remaining unbanked (Kabir, 2013). As those from the lower-income group constitute a majority of the unbanked, the security enhancements brought about by the use of blockchain for the operations of mobile banking networks could have a significant impact on the role of mobile banking in the promotion of financial inclusion. This is because the security enhancements brought about by the use of blockchain would address a major inhibiting factor which prevents the unbanked from the lower-income group from subscribing to mobile banking services, i.e., the fear of suffering financial losses as a result of falling victim to hackers.

The reduced security risks brought about by the use of blockchain to safeguard the operations of mobile banking networks would allay the concerns of the unbanked from the lower-income group, thereby encouraging them to subscribe for mobile banking services. As for those from the lower-income group who rely on mobile banking as their sole channel of access to financial services, the security enhancements brought about by the use of blockchain could improve the degree and extent of their financial inclusivity as these enhancements would pave the way for mobile banking service providers to make available a wider range of financial services due to the lower security risks affecting the operations of their networks (Shaikh et al., 2017).

Mobile banking has much to offer to both Malaysia and Singapore, particularly for their respective financial inclusion agenda whereby for Malaysia the use of mobile banking can help address the issue of suboptimal physical access to cover the "last mile" of the unbanked population whereas for Singapore the use of a simpler form of mobile banking can help address the issue of lack of financial and digital literacy among its migrant workers population whose financial inclusion rate stands at a mere 50%. Through the use of blockchain for strengthening the security frameworks of mobile banking networks in Malaysia and Singapore, the technology would pave the way for the wide use of mobile banking in these countries to enable them to achieve their respective financial inclusion agenda.

As an archipelago comprising about 7641 islands, ensuring financial inclusion in the Philippines is a logistical nightmare (World Atlas, 2018). The paradoxical thing in the Philippines is that the 492 rural banks in the country are themselves effectively unbanked as these banks are disconnected from the national financial network which is a major limitation on the suite of financial services that they can offer to their customers, i.e., the rural population which makes up 56% of the national population (UnionBank, 2019). It is in this context that UnionBank, which is one of the Philippines' leading banks, has launched Project i2i (which refers to island-to-island, individual-to-individual, and institution-to-institution) to leverage blockchain to connect rural banks in the country with the national financial network.

Under Project i2i, UnionBank has partnered with global blockchain platform developer Consensys to develop an Ethereum-based platform that connects rural banks with other banks within the national financial network to expand the scope of financial services that the rural banks could offer whereby these include payment remittances, credit financing as well as capital investment facilities. Launched in April 2019, project i2i, which is supported by the Philippines' central bank, i.e., the Bangko Sentral ng Pilipinas (BSP), has already onboarded 130 rural banks as of January 2019, with the BSP set to mandate the participation of the remaining rural banks as part of its efforts to promote the digital transformation of the country's financial framework (ConsenSys, 2019).

In terms of its blockchain infrastructure, the platform of Project i2i is made up of a web application programming interface (API) which is connected with an Ethereum blockchain-back-end whereby this connection is responsible for the handling of key management protocols by allowing participating banks to construct and send signed transactions to smart contracts. Upon receipt of a signed transaction, the web API triggers the operation of the automated smart contracts which initiate a three-step transaction whereby firstly digital tokens would be pledged in a manner that corresponds to the Pesos deposited in a bank account outside the network followed by the redemption of the pledged digital tokens before culminating in the transfer of tokens between the customers of the participating banks.

As for the different phases of its development, Project i2i started with Phase 1 which entailed the tokenization of cash in the form of cryptocurrencies which is processed by commercial banks to execute payment transactions among their customers, i.e., for intra-bank transactions before proceeding to Phase 2 which involve the use of cryptocurrencies for the settlement of inter-bank payment transactions. The final phase, i.e., Phase 3 involves the development of a CBDC to be issued by the BSP under the guise of a crypto Peso. How Project i2i had been able to use blockchain to overcome the issue of physical accessibility highlights the potential for the use of the technology by BNM to address the issue of sub-optimal physical access identified by BNM as resulting in Malaysia's financial services having a lower physical outreach as compared to high-income nations which stand as an impediment to expanding the country's financial services network to cover the last mile of the unbanked population.

4.5.2 *Enhancing the Suitability of Financial Services for Businesses with Crypto Crowdfunding*

The concept of alternative lending came about in response to the shortcomings of the credit facilities of conventional financial institutions which entail cumbersome requirements such as minimum borrowing amounts and high interest repayment rates. For business loans, the market response to the shortcomings of the credit mechanisms of conventional financial institutions is the inception of crowdfunding which is an umbrella term that refers to the various types of capital financing mechanisms undertaken through the solicitation of investment funds via online platforms which may be accessible using mobile phones whereby the underlying idea of the concept is that a small amount of contributions, albeit with a high market capture, is an effective way to tap into the power of the crowd for capital funding purposes (Hemer, 2011). As crowdfunding lies within the sphere of the shadow financial system, i.e., outside the scope of conventional financial frameworks, it is undertaken mainly through the Internet whereby individual investors have the option of choosing which project they wish to invest in and after they have deposited their investment funds these funds will be transferred from the platform to the relevant fundraiser as capital investments in the underlying project (Kshetri, 2018).

The genesis of crowdfunding started in the UK back in 2007 followed by the United States and the rest of Europe thereafter whereby the crowdfunding boom has been supported by a host of factors primarily the digital revolution which is taking the world by storm, resulting in the high penetration rates of Internet connectivity as well as digital device ownership, all of which has contributed to the establishment of a digital landscape that has allowed crowdfunding to be practicable in reality (Bannerman, 2012). Another factor in the rise of crowdfunding as a capital raising tool is the limitations and restrictions of conventional financial systems in a departure from the deregulation trend for financial institutions after the 2008 financial crisis which has resulted in these institutions imposing more stringent credit requirements as part of the terms and conditions of their services. The imposition of stricter requirements for credit services offered by financial institutions effectively resulted in the door to access such services being closed to a large pool of the commercial market, particularly start-ups whose strength lies not in their financial standing but instead in the degree of innovation of the underlying ideas for their project which they wish to showcase to the world (Kim et al., 2013).

It is in this context that crowdfunding comes in to help promote financial inclusion by providing an alternative channel for smaller businesses, particularly SMEs and startups, to raise capital from the general public in a way which is cost-efficient for transaction fees which they have to expend and to comply in a hassle-free manner in adhering to regulatory compliance obligations (Faisal, 2018). With regard to the promotion of financial inclusion, crowdfunding platforms allow smaller companies such as SMEs and startups which are unable to meet the credit financing requirements imposed by financial institutions under the conventional financial system to resort to the integrity of their business structure and the innovation of their project ideas to obtain funds from the public for the development of their business and projects.

Nonetheless, there is a degree of interconnection between crowdfunding platforms and the conventional financial system as the operational frameworks of crowdfunding platforms require fundraisers to have access to basic financial services in the form of a bank account which is equipped with electronic money capabilities (Jenik et al., 2017). In other words, the users of crowdfunding platforms are likely to have a certain degree of access to financial services offered under the conventional financial system, i.e., they are not unbanked, albeit they are unable to obtain access to a more comprehensive portfolio of financial services, specifically those related to credit financing to meet their business needs, i.e., they are underserved by the conventional financial system.

Accordingly, crowdfunding plays an important role in deepening the foundations of financial markets by helping to bridge the financing gaps that arose due to the stringent qualification requirements imposed by financial institutions for their credit financing services whereby these gaps tend to affect the development of capital markets particularly those in developing economies (Leboeuf & Schwienbacher, 2018). By providing an alternative investment channel for investors and venture capitalists, crowdfunding platforms help rebalance the unequal bargaining positions between creditors and lenders by addressing the issue of information asymmetries between the parties to a credit transaction, thereby helping to reduce the transaction costs between the parties which in turn help promote financial inclusion primarily among the underserved (Agrawal et al., 2014).

In Malaysia, equity crowdfunding platform operators are regulated as RMOs and thereby required to comply with the relevant provisions in the Capital Markets and Services Act 2007 (CMSA) and the Guidelines on Recognized Markets issued by the Securities Commission (SC) (SC, 2019). In its Annual Report 2021, the SC noted that ECFs in Malaysia raised a total of RM221.63 million in 2021 whereby this was a 74% year-on-year (YoY) increase over the RM127.73 million raised through ECFs in Malaysia in 2020 (SC, 2021a). Notwithstanding the rising prominence of ECF services in Malaysia, the SC had in its Capital Market Masterplan 2021–2025 noted that it is estimated that MSMEs in the country are facing a RM90 billion financing gap (SC, 2021b). Considering the fact that MSMEs are the growth engine of the Malaysian economy as they contribute about 60% of the country's GDP, efforts must be undertaken to bridge the RM90 billion financing gap affecting these businesses, failing which the development of the national economy may be hampered.

In Singapore, equity crowdfunding is referred to as securities-based crowdfunding (SCF) whereby SCF platform operators are required to comply with the relevant provisions in the Securities and Futures Act 2001 and the Financial Advisers Act 2001. Thanks to its innovative regulations and strong currency, the crowdfunding segment in Singapore was estimated to be worth USD8.22 million in 2021 and is projected to be worth USD13.27 million by 2026 (Statista, 2022). Notwithstanding the high market value of Singapore's crowdfunding segment, SMEs in the country still face barriers when it comes to access to credit facilities, with only 49% of these SMEs being of the opinion that securing funding is easy and a staggering 97% of them expressing their willingness to switch to their credit facilities if they are able to find a better option (MAMBU, 2021).

The extent of the difficulties faced by Singapore SMEs to secure the necessary funding for the needs of their businesses is aptly illustrated by the fact that in the course of the last five years leading up to 2022, 86% of these SMEs were unable to secure sufficient funding to cover the needs of their businesses. Cumulatively, these factors have resulted in Singapore SMEs facing a financing gap that is estimated to be around SGD20 billion a year (CNA, 2021). Considering the fact that Singapore SMEs are the backbone of the nation's economy as they contribute about half (48%) to the country's GDP and employ about 70% of the country's workforce, efforts must be undertaken to bridge the estimated SGD20 billion financing gaps affecting these businesses, failing which the development of the national economy may be hampered (UOB, 2016).

The shortcomings of the credit facilities offered by conventional financial institutions gave rise to the advent of alternative lending mechanisms, with crowdfunding being the most popular of these mechanisms. Notwithstanding the rising prominence of crowdfunding in Malaysia and Singapore, the fact that MSMEs and SMEs in both these countries are still facing wide financing gaps of RM90 billion and SGD20 billion respectively gives rise to a need to look outside the box which is why we would proceed to explore the advantages and benefits of crypto crowdfunding frameworks over conventional crowdfunding and how these frameworks may be able to help fill the financing gaps of MSMEs and SMEs in Malaysia and Singapore.

The genesis of crypto crowdfunding dates back to the first initial coin offering (ICO) conducted by Mastercoin (now rebranded as Omni) in 2010 (Medium, 2019). From a conceptual point of view, ICO is a more democratized mode of financing as it entails the distribution of decision-making powers among a wide group of investors, i.e., the subscribers to the ICO tokens as opposed to the arrangement of conventional financing whereby decision-making powers are singularly held by the financing institution. Due to the wider distribution of decision-making powers, the risks entailed by the financing of an ICO project are also distributed across the investors, i.e., the subscribers to the ICO tokens whose risk exposure is less due to their large numbers in contrast with conventional financing whereby the risks are shouldered by a single or a few financial institutions. Although IPO financing is also imbued with the element of wide risk distribution, the cumbersome regulatory compliance requirements of IPO which result in high legal compliance costs render this mode of financing to be unavailable to MSMEs and SMEs.

In addition to the lower risk exposure, some ICO projects further the promotion of democratization by harnessing the concept of decentralized autonomous organization (DAO) through DAICO frameworks by leveraging smart contracts to allow token holders to vote on the direction of the project whereby this right to vote fosters a feeling of belonging and inclusivity among the token holders which bode well for the long-term prospects of the project. The only alternative lending mechanism that comes close to DAICOs with regard to the promotion of inclusivity among investors is that of conventional crowdfunding as some crowdfunded projects do allow their investors the right to vote though DAICOs take this one step further through the use of smart contracts under the DAO framework.

Thanks to its advantages and benefits over conventional financing and alternative lending mechanisms such as conventional crowdfunding, ICO grew increasingly prominent until it became a victim of its success as it was hijacked by scammers so much so that about 80% of ICO projects in 2017 were found to be scams (Investopedia, 2018). This led to the advent of another form of crypto crowdfunding, i.e., initial exchange offering (IEO) through which crypto crowdfundings are carried out through reputable exchanges which provides an element of trust anchor by acting as guardian watchdogs through their responsibilities of vetting and undertaking due diligence on the IEOs carried out through their exchange. The viability of IEO over ICO prompted the SC to come up with regulations for IEO operators in October 2020 in the form of the "Guidelines on Digital Assets" which provides for the registration requirements and operational responsibilities of IEO platform operators in Malaysia (SC, 2018).

In many ways, IEOs are conceptually similar to ICOs except for the fact that IEOs entail the element of due diligence vetting by reputable exchanges who would host IEO projects which pass their vetting. In this manner, IEO can address a particularly thorny issue of ICO which is that of a lack of credibility as anyone can launch an ICO project without having their background checked or the contents of their whitepaper being subjected to scrutiny. IEO addresses ICO's issue of a lack of credibility by subjecting exchanges to the responsibility of undertaking due diligence vetting on the proprietor and the whitepaper contents of IEO projects which are hosted on their exchanges, thereby putting the reputation of these host exchanges on the line if anything goes wrong with the IEO projects hosted on their exchanges. In other words, IEO host exchanges are subject to reputational risks in return for the fees they receive from hosting IEOs on their exchanges whereby these fees can reach up to 10 Bitcoins or 10% cut from the sale proceeds of the IEO tokens, depending on the reputation of the relevant exchange (Concise Software, 2020).

Against this backdrop, IEOs are not too unlike conventional crowdfunding whereby the reputational risks exposure of IEO host exchanges are similar to the reputational risks exposure of conventional crowdfunding platforms are obliged to ensure the credibility of campaigns that are hosted on their platforms including by vetting the background of the proprietors and the contents of the disclosure documents failing which they could be risking damage to their reputation. Additionally, with IEOs involving digital tokens amounting to securities now being subjected to regulatory oversight in both Malaysia and Singapore through the SC's *Guidelines on Digital Assets* and the MAS' *A Guide to Digital Token Offerings* respectively, the element of consumer protection is warranted for IEOs in both these countries in much the same way as conventional crowdfunding. Yet another similarity between IEO and conventional crowdfunding is that both dispense with the need for underwriters which are replaced using the wisdom of the crowd.

Nonetheless, there are certain differences between IEO and conventional crowdfunding which may help MSMEs and SMEs in Malaysia and Singapore address their financing gaps. A key difference that sets IEO apart from conventional crowdfunding is the fact that since IEOs are carried out on blockchain networks that operate in an automated manner without the need for an intermediary thereby resulting in cost efficiency gains though similar to conventional crowdfunding platforms that charge a fee for the listing of campaigns, IEOs projects are required to pay fees to the host exchange. Additionally, the fact that IEOs entail the issuance of tokens that do not necessarily need to be imbued with equity rights which stands in contrast with conventional crowdfunding which entails the distribution of equity ownership could prove to be a critical factor in terms of encouraging the use of IEO as a fundraising mechanism by MSMEs and SMEs in Malaysia and Singapore who may before the advent of IEO be reluctant to use conventional crowdfunding for fear of losing control over their businesses whereby this fear has been identified as a key factor in the reluctance of SMEs in general to resort to the use of public equity funding for their fundraising (Nassr & Wehinger, 2015).

Another key difference between IEO and conventional crowdfunding is that whereas IEO projects are usually at the stages of conceptual development and thereby looking for seed or early-stage financing, conventional crowdfunding is geared toward fundraising for projects that are at a later stage, i.e., prototype development financing phase. With 29% of SMEs in Singapore citing a lack of a business plan as the reason for their inability to obtain financing, the use of IEOs may come in handy for SMEs in the country as a lack of a business plan may be acceptable in the context of IEO given the fact that it caters to projects in the early stages when a business plan is still in the process being concretized but this may not be acceptable for conventional crowdfunding which cater to projects in the later stages and thereby requires a concrete business plan.

A last key difference between IEO and conventional crowdfunding is that IEO, if undertaken through a decentralized exchange (DEX), would become an IDO (Lin, 2019). Unlike IEOs which require the approval of the host exchange, no such approval is required for IDOs which are instead vetted by members of the DeFi community themselves (Gemini, 2021). In an IDO, whitelisted investors would subscribe for the tokens in advance in return for an acknowledgment of debt whereby the investors would only be receiving their tokens upon the inception of the Token Generation Event (TGE) which usually takes place after the launching of the IDO (CoinMarketCap, n.d.). The crux of the IDO model is that it is based on the pricing mechanism of the DeFi market whereby IDO tokens are listed on DEXs that function as automated market makers (AMMs) by calibrating the exchange prices of the tokens in their liquidity pools using the Bonding Curves algorithm which allows the price of IDO tokens to be determined exclusively by the prevalent supply and demand market forces (Token Minds, 2021).

As DEXs are effectively peer-to-peer (P2P) crypto marketplaces that operate in geographically boundless manner without the need for any centralized entity, the use of IDOs by MSMEs and SMEs in Malaysia and Singapore would allow these businesses to tap into the global interconnectivity of IDOs with the multibillion-dollar DeFi market, thereby enabling these businesses to harness the greater network effects arising from the connection with the DeFi market which would not have been possible through the use of conventional crowdfunding. In essence, the principle of network effects posits that the value or utility of a good and service would increase in tandem with the rise in the number of users of compatible products. To sum up, in contrast with conventional crowdfunding campaigns which generally stand on their own in silo, the use of IDO as a fundraising mechanism would allow projects to tap into the liquidity pools of the host DEX and thereby access the DeFi ecosystem, giving rise to significant network effects because of the size of the user base of the ecosystem as well as the scope and scale of the services in the ecosystem which include yield farming, liquidity mining, crypto staking as well as lending and borrowing.

In the context of Malaysia, MSMEs can resort to IDOs and potentially harness network effects through the first offering of DeFi services in Malaysia by MyEG, the flagship electronic government (e-government) solutions and services provider which had on 6 August 2021 announced that it would be introducing DeFi services to the Malaysian public by offering its DeFi products to users of licensed DAXs in Malaysia or DAXs which have obtained similar licenses in other jurisdictions. In essence MyEG's Lock-Earn wallet enables owners of digital assets to lock their assets in return for Annualized Rental Fees (ARF) as high as 6% (MyEG, 2021). Conceptually, MyEG's Lock-Earn program which takes the form of crypto staking could be a channel for MSMEs in Malaysia which uses the IDO framework for their fundraising to connect with the DeFi ecosystem, thereby tapping into the network effects of IDO. As for SMEs in Singapore, they too could have a channel through which they can connect with the DeFi ecosystem to tap into the network efforts arising from the use of IDOs as the MAS had on 31 May 2022 announced the launch of its Project Guardian through which the MAS in partnership with DBS Bank, JP Morgan, and Marketnode would be exploring the use of assets tokenization to facilitate DeFi lending using smart contracts on public blockchain networks (MAS, 2022b).

The shortcomings of the credit facilities mechanisms offered by conventional financial institutions have led to the advent of alternative lending mechanisms, primarily of which is that of conventional crowdfunding, though this was unable to prevent the arising of RM90 billion and SGD20 billion financing gaps for MSMEs and SMEs in Malaysia and Singapore. Using conventional crowdfunding as a prime example of alternative lending to compare with crypto crowdfunding frameworks in particular that of IEO, although there are some notable similarities between conventional crowdfunding and IEO, there are also certain key differences between the two which could render IEO to be able to help address the financing gaps of MSMEs and SMEs in Malaysia and Singapore. A last point of discussion is that the conducting of IEOs using DEXs, i.e., through IDOs, could further boost the role of crypto crowdfunding in bridging the financing gaps for MSMEs and SMEs in Malaysia and Singapore as this would enable these businesses to tap into the network effects arising from the connectivity with the DeFi ecosystem.

4.5.3 *Lowering the Costs of Financial Services with Blockchain-Based CBDCs*

In BNM's Annual Report 2023, the central bank highlighted that cross-border remittance made via non-bank channels throughout the year recorded an average cost of 2.2% of transaction value whereas those that used electronic platforms, i.e., electronic remittance (e-remittance), recorded an average cost of 1.9% transaction value (BNM, 2023). As for Singapore, although there are no available statistics on its cross-border remittance costs, the MAS has noted the issue of end-users of cross-border remittance not having clarity with regard to the time required and charges imposed for such transactions (MAS, 2018). The importance of addressing the issue of speed and costs of cross-border remittance was aptly pointed out by BNM's Governor Tan Sri Nor Shamsiah Mohd Yunus who had during the Digital Economy and Finance Festival in July 2022 reiterated the need for Malaysia as a member of ASEAN to "*make cross-border payments cheaper, faster, more transparent and accessible to all 600 million plus of us in the region*" (The Edge, 2022b). In this connection, BNM had already made headways in this direction through its participation in the BIS' Project Nexus which adopted the Proof-of-Concept (PoC) module to facilitate the interoperability of instant payment systems (IPS) of different countries starting with those of the participating nations, i.e., Malaysia, Singapore, and Italy (BIS, 2021).

Besides facilitating the interoperability of IPS, another possible solution to increase the speed and lower the costs of cross-border remittance in Malaysia is the use of digital assets particularly those that are decentralized and tokenized. In its Annual Report 2023, BNM highlighted the issues with the existing arrangement for the processing of cross-border remittance whereby a single transaction needs to pass through multiple layers of intermediaries, resulting in not only higher costs but lower speeds as well (BNM, 2023). In this connection, BNM noted that decentralized and tokenized digital assets allow for the instant transfer of value without the need for intermediaries, thereby resulting in efficiency gains in addition to facilitating the promotion of financial inclusion as these assets are universally accessible using only a smartphone with internet connectivity.

Nonetheless, the BNM cautioned that the use of decentralized and tokenized digital assets through currency substitution under the banner of digital dollarization is fraught with macro-financial risks as they affect the ability of central banks to manage inflation and implement effective countercyclical policies to warrant the economic and financial stability of the nation. These risks are inherently connected with the fragile and unstable nature of the digital assets market as illustrated by the crypto meltdown which was triggered by the USD65 billion collapse of TerraUSD which was once the third largest stablecoin in terms of market capitalization. The collapse of TerraUSD triggered panic selling among crypto investors which led to a fallout in the crypto market that was made worse by the high leverage ratio in the market resulting in leverage-induced fire-sales which led to a snowballing effect that culminated in the crypto meltdown. Accordingly, notwithstanding the potential for the use of tokenized digital assets to lower cross-border remittance fees, the current state of development of the digital assets market renders it overly systemically risky to resort to the use of these assets for the lowering of cross-border remittance fees.

A more promising solution to speed up the processing time and lower the transaction fees for cross-border remittance is the use of blockchain for the processing of these transactions as explored by the BIS' Project Dunbar which involved the participation of both BNM and MAS as well as the central banks of Australia and South Africa. The objective of Project Dunbar was to explore the use of multi-CBDC (m-CBDC) to facilitate the processing of cross-border remittance through the establishment of a m-CBDC platform which would allow participating banks to undertake cross-border remittance transactions with correspondent banks in jurisdictions for which they do not have a presence using the correspondent bank's m-CBDC which are denominated in the currency of the correspondent bank. The main premise of Project Dunbar is its use of smart contracts which are deployed on a blockchain platform, thereby automating the verification of the relevant parameters such as liquidity levels, technical validation, and business requirements in addition to automating the confirmation process for the due compliance of the relevant parties with their respective obligations.

The disintermediation of cross-border remittance transactions through the use of smart contracts deployed on a blockchain platform stands in contrast with the conventional framework for the processing of such transactions using the correspondent banking module that involves multiple layers of intermediaries comprised of a network of financial institutions handling the transactions on behalf of each other under the bilateral agreements between these institutions (BIS, 2016). In its report on Project Dunbar titled "International Settlements Using Multi-CBDCs" published in March 2022, the BIS noted that there is a potential for system-level efficiency gains from use of a shared multi-CBDC platform which operates through smart contracts deployed on a blockchain platform to enable the reduction of duplicative processes but the realization of this potential requires the element of mutual reliance and shared reliability which in turn requires further technological development to allow for improved visibility and traceability (BIS, 2022).

In 2018, Christine Lagarde, who was the then head of the International Monetary Fund (IMF), put forth the case for CBDC as a tool for the promotion of financial inclusion whereby she highlighted the possible role of CBDC as a backup solution that can facilitate regulatory compliance, monitoring, and investigation in an increasingly cashless global financial domain in addition to preventing private payment providers from garnering too much power which may end up destabilizing the global financial system in the event of the occurrence of any untoward incident (Lagarde, 2018). Among the countries that have taken up Lagarde's suggestion for the use of CBDC as a tool to promote financial inclusion are Bahamas, Uruguay, Ecuador, and Tunisia, whose central banks have issued CBDCs as part of their efforts to bank the unbanked in their respective population (Kiff, 2019).

For both developed and developing economies, CBDC does have a role to play in facilitating and speeding up the transformation of the population of these economies into cashless societies whereas for developing economies the reduction in transaction costs brought about by the use of CBDC may promote financial inclusion among the population of such economies (Gopane, 2019). However, similar to the general trend in the digital payment domain, the outlook for the use and adoption of CBDC in both developing and developed economies is affected by a common factor, i.e., the size of the informal economy which is generally larger in developing economies than in developed ones (Capasso & Jappelli, 2013).

How the size of the informal economy affects the rate of use and adoption of CBDC lies in the fact that those working in the informal economy prefer to rely on cash transactions for tax evasion whereby this would mean that regardless of the cost-effectiveness and convenience brought about by the use of digital payment instruments such as the CBDC, workers in the informal economy would prefer to stick to the use of cash transactions as the use of digital payment would leave a paper trail which can be tracked by tax authorities (Auer et al., 2020). Accordingly, the rate of adoption and use of CBDC in any jurisdiction would be dependent on the size of its informal economy whereby if central banks were to remove this limiting factor, they would need to leverage the cost reduction features of CBDC to an extent which renders it to be financially viable for workers in the informal economy to use CBDC. If this can be achieved, it would be a win-win solution for both the informal workers and the government as represented by the central bank and tax authorities who would benefit from this in the form of increased use of CBDC and additional tax receipts respectively.

Without the intervention of central banks, the existing hegemony as manifested in the monopolistic nature of national financial systems whereby major industry players can leverage their place in the hierarchy to further strengthen their market position by increasing their market share would likely to continue unabated (Mintz & Schwartz, 1986). Under the existing state of monopoly common in the financial systems of most countries, the process of "crypto-secession," which refers to the abandonment of the existing operational arrangements to blockchain-based frameworks with cryptocurrency as the underlying instrument, is unlikely to take place except where the use of blockchain would fit in with the profit-making agendas of the dominant financial institutions (Allen, 2017).

The intervention of central banks in the form of the issuance of CBDCs would pave the way for a top-down intervention to curtail the abilities of dominant financial institutions to maintain their stronghold on the national financial system whereby central banks can lead the way for the use of blockchain to promote financial inclusion. In turn, this would pave the way for the notion of the use of blockchain to buttress the sense of social responsibility in the national financial system as financial inclusion represents the central tenet of individual freedom and autonomy as having access to financial services is a basic prerequisite for the participation by members of the public in the economic system through the acquisition and disposal of resources (Engert & Fung, 2017).

In the absence of any intervention by central banks through the issuance of CBDCs, the use of blockchain in national financial systems is likely to be dictated by the whims and fancies of dominant financial institutions whereby even where blockchain is used the objective would likely be for the furtherance of the profit-making agenda of these institutions as opposed to being based on the notion of social responsibility, i.e., for the promotion of financial inclusion. In the context of SSF, the issuance of CBDCs by central banks is very much in line with

In the context of Malaysia and Singapore, the high volume of cross-border remittances between the two countries amounted to USD96 million in 2021 (PYMNTS.com, 2021). However, the total average remittance costs from Singapore to Malaysia in Q4 2022 was 4.68%, which is 1.68% higher than the target of 3% by 2030 set by the United Nations under Target 10.c of its Sustainable Development Goal (SDG); this prompted

BNM and MAS to join forces for the establishment of a phased linkage between Malaysia's DuitNow and Singapore's PayNow which is set to commence operations by the fourth quarter of 2022 whereby through the linkage that would be progressively expanded to cover more features and participants, users would be able to make cross-border remittance between Malaysia and Singapore in a real-time manner by scanning DuitNow or NETS QR codes using their smartphones (BNM, 2021b). Sopnendu Mohanty, Chief FinTech Officer of MAS, was quoted as saying that "The linkage also offers BNM and MAS a valuable opportunity to incorporate the use of distributed ledger and smart contract technologies in the wholesale cross border payments space." With this, the stage is set for the development of a blockchain-based remittance corridor between the two countries.

Nonetheless, although BNM is a part of Project Dunbar, the central bank currently has no plans to develop its own CBDC at the moment but is looking to further explore the use of a shared common platform with other central banks to facilitate cross-border payment (BNM, 2022). With the BIS having identified "digitalisation of international remittances as an unexploited opportunity to increase financial inclusion," the use of an m-CBDC platform could be the key to furthering BNM's agenda of taking financial inclusion to another level by encouraging the sustained and meaningful use of financial services as well as extending the reach of Malaysia's financial network to cover the "last mile" of the unbanked population. It is notable in this regard that BNM has not closed the door to developing its own CBDC as it is open to the possibility of doing so in time to come as it continues to explore the benefits of m-CBDCs through Project Dunbar (The Edge, 2022a).

As for the MAS, although it has already set afoot plans to develop its own retail CBDC including the publication of a report titled "A Retail Central Bank Digital Currency: Economic Considerations in the Singapore Context" in November 2021 which assessed the case for Singapore to have its own retail CBDC and the possible implications for the country's financial and monetary stability as well as having launched its Global CBDC Challenge 2021 to search for innovative retail CBDC solutions to boost the efficiency of its payment networks whilst promoting financial inclusion, Lawrence Wong, who was then the country's Finance Minister and the MAS' Deputy Chairman, had in a reply to a Parliamentary question in March 2022 said that there is "no pressing need" for the issuance of CBDC by Singapore, though he stressed that "this does not mean that MAS has ruled out introducing a retail CBDC at some stage" (MAS,

2022a). A case in point is the fact that the MAS is currently embarking on Project Orchid to prepare for the building of the requisite technology infrastructure and technical competencies in close partnership with the private sector in preparation for the development of a retail CBDC by Singapore if such a need arises in time to come (MAS, 2021).

Nonetheless, the seeds for the use of blockchain for the processing of cross-border remittance in Singapore have already been planted by Project Ubin which has led to the establishment by the MAS of its Partior platform which uses blockchain to help banks transcend the conventional "hub and spoke" model that relies on a centralized hub. Instead with its open-industry model, Partior would allow banks from around the world to join the platform's blockchain network which is interoperable with the existing real-time gross settlement (RTGS) network to process cross-border remittance transactions using blockchain's programmable value transfer mechanism that relies on atomic settlement to warrant that the completion of an exchange transaction would only occur upon the fulfillment by the counterpart of its obligations under the transaction.

With Partior having illustrated the benefits arising from the use of blockchain for cross-border remittance and Project Dunbar having illustrated the benefits of using a common blockchain-based m-CBDC platform for cross-border remittance, it is not too far-fetched to envisage that there will come a day when a Malaysian bank which is not holding any Singapore Dollar (SGD) would be able to process cross-border remittance with a correspondent Singaporean bank using a m-CBDC denominated in SGD or vice versa, thereby enabling better management of liquidity positions in reliance on the automated market-making capabilities arising from the programmable value of the basket of m-CBDCs underlying the network. Not only would this open the door for the participation of more banks in the Malaysia-Singapore cross-border remittance corridor but, in line with the previously discussed positive correlations between the wide availability of cross-border remittance services and higher levels of financial inclusion, uplift the scale and scope of financial inclusivity in both Malaysia and Singapore particularly for migrant workers in the latter.

Practical considerations aside, the development and use of CBDCs also entail some philosophical aspects in terms of breaking the existing financial hegemony by ensuring equal access to financial services for all citizens, though the effectiveness of CBDC with regard to the promotion of financial inclusion would depend on the nature of the existing barriers to entry for the unbanked among the country's population

(Ward & Rochemont, 2019). In the context of China, for example, which is leading the way with the development of its CBDC by the People's Bank of China (PBoC), the promotion of financial inclusion does not appear to be the main objective of PBoC's CBDC project because with more than 90% of the Chinese population having access to financial services this renders China's rate of financial inclusion to be on par with those of high-income Group of 20 (G20) member states (World Bank Group, 2018). Instead, the PBoC's CBDC project seemed to be undertaken to rebalance the private-public dynamics of the country's retail payment system that is mostly controlled by the duopoly of Alipay and WeChat Pay which collectively holds 93% of the local mobile payment market, with Alipay standing at the top with 54.5% and WeChat Pay coming second with 38.8% (FinTech News Hong Kong, 2020).

For example, if the reason for the unbanked in the country not having access to financial services is because of an idiosyncratic aversion to financial services presumably due to cultural issues such as embedded distrust in the formalized institutions, then CBDC may not be able to offer much in terms of promoting financial inclusion among this category of the unbanked population. However, if the underlying reason for the unbanked among the general population not having access to financial services is because of the failure or reluctance on the part of financial institutions to offer their services to the unbanked presumably comprising of those who live in rural areas or who are unable to afford the costs of these services, then CBDC can step in as a form of governmental intervention to remedy the shortcomings on the part of the private financial sector.

References

Agrawal, A., Catalini, C., & Goldfarb, A. (2014). Some simple economics of crowdfunding. *Journal of Innovation Policy and the Economy, 14*, 63–97. https://www.journals.uchicago.edu/doi/abs/10.1086/674021

Allen, D. (2017). Discovering and developing the blockchain cryptoeconomy. SSRN Electronic Journal. https://papers.ssrn.com/sol3/papers.cfm?abstract_id=2815255

Almakhour, M., Sliman, L., Samhat, A. E., & Mellouk, A. (2020). On the verification of smart contracts: A systematic review. In *Proceedings of the International Conference on Blockchain and Cryptocurrency* (pp. 95–107).

Artis, A. (2017). Social and solidarity finance: A conceptual approach. Journal of. *Research in International Business and Finance, 39*(B), 737–749.

Auer, A., Cornelli, G., & Frost, J. (2020). Rise of the central bank digital currencies: Drivers, approaches and technologies (BIS Working Papers No 880). https://www.bis.org/publ/work880.pdf?utm_campaign=BitDigest&utm_medium=email&utm_source=Revue+newsletter

Bank Negara Malaysia (BNM). (2021a, July). Overview of financial inclusion in Malaysia. https://www.comcec.org/wp-content/uploads/2021/07/3-1-Malaysia.pdf

Bank Negara Malaysia (BNM). (2021b, September 27). Malaysia's DuitNow and Singapore's PayNow to link in 2022. https://www.bnm.gov.my/documents/20124/3026128/ar2020_en_box2_digitalcurrency.pdf

Bank Negara Malaysia (BNM). (2022, January 24). Financial sector blueprint 2022–2026. https://www.bnm.gov.my/documents/20124/5915429/fsb3_en_book.pdf

Bank Negara Malaysia (BNM). (2023). Annual report 2023. https://www.bnm.gov.my/documents/20124/6458991/ar2021_en_book.pdf

Bannerman, S. (2012). Crowdfunding culture. Wi: *Journal of Mobile Culture, 6*(4). http://wi.mobilities.ca/wp-content/uploads/2012/12/sbannermanwi_2012_06_04.pdf

BIS. (2016, July). Correspondent banking. https://www.bis.org/cpmi/publ/d147.pdf

BIS. (2021, July). Nexus: A blueprint for instant cross-border payments. https://www.bis.org/publ/othp39.pdf

BIS. (2022, March). Project Dunbar: International settlements using multi-CBDCs. https://www.bis.org/publ/othp47.pdf

Capasso, S., & Jappelli, T. (2013). Financial development and the underground economy. *Journal of Development Economics, 101*, 167–178.

Channel News Asia (CNA). (2021, September 30). How alternative lenders are helping to plug the SME funding gap. https://www.channelnewsasia.com/business/how-alternative-lenders-are-helping-plug-sme-funding-gap-2211961

Chitranjan, J. (2020). A critical assessment of microfinance as a poverty alleviation tool. *Asian Journal of Research in Banking and Finance, 10*(1), 1–15.

CoinMarketCap. Token generation event (TGE). https://coinmarketcap.com/alexandria/glossary/token-generation-event

Communications Authority of Kenya. (2020). Third quarter sector statistics report for the financial year 2019/2020. https://ca.go.ke/wp-content/uploads/2020/07/Sector-Statistics-Report-Q3-2019-2020-.pdf

ConciseSoftware. (2020, February 13). What is an initial exchange offering (IEO) and how to participate in it?. https://concisesoftware.com/blog/what-is-ieo-how-to-participate/

Conley, J. P. (2019). Blockchain as a decentralized mechanism for financial inclusion and economic mobility. Vanderbilt University Department of Economics Working Papers (No. 19-00012). https://johnpconley.com/wp-content/uploads/2019/11/VUECON-19-00012.pdf

ConsenSys. (2019). Project i2i: Blockchain case study for payments in the Philippines. https://consensys.net/blockchain-use-cases/finance/project-i2i/
DataProt. (2023, July 14). Mobile banking statistics: The future of money is in the palm of your hand. https://dataprot.net/statistics/mobile-banking-statistics/
DataReportal. (2022, February 15). Digital 2022: Malaysia. https://datareportal.com/reports/digital-2022-malaysia
Donner, J., & Tellez, C. A. (2008). Mobile banking and economic development: Linking adoption, impact, and use. *Asian Journal of Communication, 18*(4), 318–332.
Elsner, W. (2012). Financial capitalism—at odds with democracy: The trap of an "impossible" profit rate. *Real-World Economics Review, 62*. Post-Autistic Economics Network. http://citeseerx.ist.psu.edu/viewdoc/download?doi=10.1.1.474.3762&rep=rep1&type=pdf
Engert, W., & Fung, S. C. (2017). Central bank digital currency: Motivations and implications (Bank of Canada Staff Discussion Paper 2017-16). https://www.econstor.eu/handle/10419/200452
Experian. (2019, June 13). Migrant domestic workers in Singapore contribute almost 2.4% of GDP but face challenges in managing their finances. https://www.experian.com.sg/migrant-domestic-workers-in-singapore-contribute-almost-2-4-of-gdp-but-face-challenges-in-managing-their-finances
Faisal, S. (2018). Crowdfunding as a potential avenue for mitigating MSME funding issues. *International Journal of Research in Management & Social Science, 6*(1), V. https://www.researchgate.net/profile/Shaha_Faisal/publication/323935047_CROWDFUNDING_AS_A_POTENTIAL_AVENUE_FOR_MITIGATING_MSME_FUNDING_ISSUES/links/5ab379c1a6fdcc1bc0c289df/CROWDFUNDING-AS-A-POTENTIAL-AVENUE-FOR-MITIGATING-MSME-FUNDING-ISSUES.pdf
Federal Deposit Insurance Corporation (FDIC). (2018). 2017 FDIC national survey of unbanked and underbanked households. https://www.fdic.gov/analysis/household-survey/2019report.pdf
Federal Deposit Insurance Corporation (FDIC). (2024). FDIC-insured institutions reported net income of $71.5 billion. https://www.fdic.gov/news/press-releases/2024/fdic-insured-institutions-reported-net-income-715-billion
FinTech News Hong Kong. (2020, July 9). Alipay maintains dominance in China over Tencent's WeChat Pay and QQ Wallet. https://fintechnews.hk/12618/mobilepayment/alipay-maintains-dominance-in-china-over-tencents-wechat-pay-and-qq-wallet/
Gemini. (2021, October 21). IEOs and IDOs: An evolution in crypto fundraising. https://www.gemini.com/cryptopedia/ieo-crypto-ido-crypto-initial-exchange-offering

Gopane, T. J. (2019). An enquiry into digital inequality implications for central bank digital currency. 2019 IST-Africa Week Conference (IST-Africa), IEEE.
Hemer, J. (2011). A snapshot on crowdfunding (Working Papers "Firms and Region"). https://www.econstor.eu/handle/10419/52302
Honohan, P., Beck, T., & Demirgüç-Kunt, A. (2009). Access to financial services: Measurement, impact, and policies. *World Bank Research Observer, 24*(1). https://www.researchgate.net/publication/46513296_Access_to_Financial_Services_Measurement_Impact_and_Policies
International Labour Organization (ILO). (2019). Financial mechanisms for innovative social and solidarity economy ecosystems. https://www.ilo.org/wcmsp5/groups/public/%2D%2D-ed_emp/%2D%2D-emp_ent/%2D%2D-coop/documents/publication/wcms_728367.pdf
Investopedia. (2018, April 24). 80% of ICOs are scams: Report. https://www.investopedia.com/news/80-icos-are-scams-report/
Jenik, I., Lymand, T., & Nava, A. (2017). Crowdfunding and financial inclusion (Consultative Group to Assist the Poor (CGAP) Working Paper). https://www.cgap.org/sites/default/files/Working-Paper-Crowdfunding-and-Financial-Inclusion-Mar-2017.pdf
Johnson, R. (2018). *Blockchain adoption in capital markets - 2018.* Greenwich Associates.
Kabir, M. R. (2013). Factors influencing the usage of mobile banking: Incident from a developing country. *World Review of Business Research, 3*(3), 96–114. https://www.researchgate.net/publication/316582190_Factors_Influencing_the_Usage_of_Mobile_Banking_Incident_from_a_Developing_Country
Kiff, J. (2019). Central bank digital currency: A global outlook. International Monetary Fund (IMF). https://cbcs.spin-cdn.com/media/event_past/20190619_13_cbdc_recent_developments_john_kiff.pdf
Kim, T., Koo, B., & Park, M. (2013). Role of financial regulation and innovation in the financial crisis. *Journal of Financial Stability, 9*(4), 667–672. https://www.sciencedirect.com/science/article/pii/S1572308912000472
Kreps, D. M. (1997). Economics—the current position. *Daedalus, 126*(1), 59–85.
Kshetri, N. (2018). Informal institutions and internet-based equity crowdfunding. *Journal of International Management, 24*(1), 33–51. https://www.sciencedirect.com/science/article/pii/S1075425316301181
Lagarde, C. (2018, November). Winds of change: The case for new digital currency [Speech presented at the Singapore Fintech Festival]. https://www.imf.org/en/News/Articles/2018/11/13/sp111418-winds-of-change-thecase-for-new-digital-currency
Leboeuf, G., & Schwienbacher, A. (2018). Crowdfunding as a new financing tool. In A. Schwienbacher (Ed.), *The economics of crowdfunding* (pp. 11–28). Springer.

Lemieux, V. (2017). Blockchain and distributed ledgers as trusted recordkeeping systems: An archival theoretic evaluation framework. Conference Paper for Future Technologies Conference 2017. https://www.researchgate.net/profile/Victoria_Lemieux/publication/317433591_Blockchain_and_Distributed_Ledgers_as_Trusted_Recordkeeping_Systems_An_Archival_Theoretic_Evaluation_Framework/links/593aa6450f7e9b3317f4d860/Blockchain-and-Distributed-Ledgers-as-Trusted-Recordkeeping-Systems-An-Archival-Theoretic-Evaluation-Framework.pdf

Lin, L. X. (2019). Deconstructing decentralized exchanges. *Stanford Journal of Blockchain Law and Policy*. https://stanford-jblp.pubpub.org/pub/deconstructing-dex/release/1

Machauer, A. (1998). Bank behavior based on internal credit ratings of borrowers. *Journal of Banking and Finance, 22*(10–11), 1355–1383.

Mambu. (2021). Disruption diaries: SME banking and lending. https://cdn.sanity.io/files/0k2k2bbv/redesign_21/49e77dca09c8bb4ee7d95cf317367fa98305l2fa.pdf

Mattila, J. (2016). The blockchain phenomenon. Berkeley Roundtable on the International Economy (BRIE) (Working Paper 2016-1). https://brie.berkeley.edu/sites/default/files/juri-mattila-.pdf

Medhi, I., Ratan, A., & Toyama, K. (2009). Mobile-banking adoption and usage by low-literate, low-income users in the developing world. In *Internationalization, design and global development: Third international conference, San Diego, U.S.* (Lecture Notes in Computer Science, Vol. 5623, pp. 485–494). https://www.researchgate.net/publication/221099347_Mobile-Banking_Adoption_and_Usage_by_Low-Literate_Low-Income_Users_in_the_Developing_World

Medium. (2019, May 23). ICO 101 — History of initial coin offerings (ICOs). https://medium.com/hackernoon/ico-101-history-of-initial-coin-offerings-icos-part-1-from-mastercoin-to-ethereum-4689b7c2326b

Mendell, M., & Nogales, R. (2011). Solidarity finance (International Forum on the Social Solidarity Economy). https://idl-bnc-idrc.dspacedirect.org/bitstream/handle/10625/47358/133709.pdf?sequence=1&isAllowed=y

Ministry of Manpower (MOM). (2018, October 7). New work permit condition to protect both employers and foreign domestic workers from money-related disputes. https://www.mom.gov.sg/newsroom/press-releases/2018/1007-new-work-permit-condition-to-protect-both-employers-and-foreign-domestic-workers-from-money-related-disputes

Mintz, B., & Schwartz, M. (1986). Capital flows and the process of financial hegemony. *Theory and Society, 15*, 77–101.

Monetary Authority of Singapore (MAS). (2020, May 26). A guide to digital token offerings. https://www.mas.gov.sg/-/media/MAS/Sectors/Guidance/Guide-to-Digital-Token-Offerings-26-May-2020.pdf

Monetary Authority of Singapore (MAS). (2021a, November 9). "The future of money, finance and the internet" [Speech by Mr. Ravi Menon, Managing Director, Monetary Authority of Singapore, at Singapore FinTech Festival]. https://www.mas.gov.sg/news/speeches/2021/the-future-of-money-finance-and-the-internet

Monetary Authority of Singapore (MAS). (2021b, November). A retail central bank digital currency: Economic considerations in the Singapore context. https://www.mas.gov.sg/-/media/MAS/EPG/Monographs-or-Information-Paper/A-retail-CBDC%2D%2D-Economic-Considerations-in-the-Singapore-Context.pdf

Monetary Authority of Singapore (MAS). (2022a, March 2). Reply to COS cut on digital Sing dollar. https://www.mas.gov.sg/news/parliamentary-replies/2022/reply-to-cos-cut-on-digital-sing-dollar

Monetary Authority of Singapore (MAS). (2022b, May 31). MAS partners the industry to pilot use cases in digital assets. https://www.mas.gov.sg/news/media-releases/2022/mas-partners-the-industry-to-pilot-use-cases-in-digital-assets

Monetary Authority of Singapore (MAS). Global CBDC challenge 2021. https://www.mas.gov.sg/-/media/MAS-Media-Library/development/fintech/CBDC/Global-CBDC-Challenge-Report-2021.pdf

Monetary Authority of Singapore (MAS). (n.d.). Financial industry API register. https://www.mas.gov.sg/development/fintech/financial-industry-api-register

Monetary Authority of Singapore (MAS), Bank of Canada, & Bank of England. (2018, November). Cross-border, interbank payments and settlements: Emerging opportunities for digital transformation. https://www.mas.gov.sg/-/media/MAS/ProjectUbin/Cross-Border-Interbank-Payments-and-Settlements.pdf

MyEG. (2021). MyEG lock and earn. https://www.myeg.com.my/services/defi

Nassr, I. K., & Wehinger, G. (2015). Unlocking SME finance through market-based debt: Securitisation, private placements, and bonds. *OECD Journal: Financial Market Trends, 2*(2014), 89–112. https://www.oecd.org/finance/Unlocking-SME-finance-through-market-based-debt.pdf

Oxfam. (2022, January). Inequality kills. https://oxfamilibrary.openrepository.com/bitstream/handle/10546/621341/bp-inequality-kills-170122-en.pdf

Paik, M. (2010). Stragglers of the herd get eaten: Security concerns for GSM mobile banking applications. In *HotMobile 2010: Proceedings of the Eleventh Workshop on Mobile Computing Systems and Applications* (pp. 54–59).

PayNet. (n.d.). Bank Negara's MyClear rolls out MyMobile, tapping on 38 million mobile phones to boost e-payments. https://paynet.my/press-release/Archive/BNM-MyClear-rolls-out-MyMobile.html

Polychroniou, C. J. (2012). Reconceiving change in the age of parasitic capitalism: Writing down debt, returning to democratic governance, and setting up alternative financial systems-now (Policy Note No. 3 of 2012). Levy Economics Institute of Bard College. http://www.levyinstitute.org/pubs/pn_12_03.pdf

PYMNTS.com. (2021, October 1). Singapore, Malaysia to test cross-border payments. https://www.pymnts.com/news/international/2021/singapore-malaysia-to-test-cross-border-payments/

Sarma, M. (2008). Index of financial inclusion (Working Paper No. 215). Indian Council for Research on International Economic Relations. http://www.icrier.org/pdf/Working_Paper_215.pdf

Scott, B. (2016). How can cryptocurrency and blockchain technology play a role in building social and solidarity finance? (UNRISD Working Paper 2016, No. 1). https://www.econstor.eu/handle/10419/148750

Securities Commission Malaysia (SC). (2018, October 20). Guidelines on digital assets. https://www.sc.com.my/api/documentms/download.ashx?id=aeb10f62-944b-4d83-8aa0-4ed492dc1109

Securities Commission Malaysia (SC). (2019, May 17). Guidelines on recognized market. https://www.sc.com.my/api/documentms/download.ashx?id=eb8f1b04-d744-4f9a-a6b6-ff8f6fee8701

Securities Commission Malaysia (SC). (2021a). Annual report 2021. https://www.sc.com.my/api/documentms/download.ashx?id=9d3e461f-7fff-47bf-84cf-7fefb4c42881

Securities Commission Malaysia (SC). (2021b). Capital market masterplan 3. https://www.sc.com.my/api/documentms/download.ashx?id=99798151-53e6-4809-b9de-6e2f094202b9

Securities Commission Malaysia (SC). Digital initiatives. https://www.sc.com.my/development/digital/digital-initiatives#id-fintech

Shaikh, A. A., Hanafizadeh, P., & Karjaluoto, J. (2017). Mobile banking and payment system: A conceptual standpoint. *International Journal of e-Business Research, 13*(2), 14–27. https://jyx.jyu.fi/bitstream/handle/123456789/55987/shaikh%20ijebr%20132%20article.pdf?sequence=1

Sharma, S. K., & Muharrami, S. L. (2018). Mobile banking adoption: Key challenges and opportunities and implications for a developing country. In *Emerging markets from a multidisciplinary perspective* (pp. 75–86). Springer.

Shimanuki, S. (2021). Financial inclusion of migrant workers in Singapore. Social Impact Research Experience (SIRE), 90. https://repository.upenn.edu/cgi/viewcontent.cgi?article=1092&context=sire

Smith, A. (1776). *The wealth of nations*. W. Strahan and T. Cadell. https://www.ibiblio.org/ml/libri/s/SmithA_WealthNations_p.pdf

Statista. (2022, April 28). Transaction value of crowdfunding in Singapore from 2017 to 2026. https://www.statista.com/forecasts/1304657/crowd-funding-transaction-value-singapore

Steger, M., Kanhere, S. S., & Jurdak, R. (2017). Blockchain: A distributed solution to automotive security and privacy. *IEEE Communications Magazine, 55*(12), 119–125.

The Edge. (2022a, January 24). BNM remains 'very open' to innovation amid digital finance shift, says assistant governor. https://www.theedgemarkets.com/article/bnm-remains-very-open-innovation-amid-digital-finance-shift-says-assistant-governor%C2%A0

The Edge. (2022b, July 14). Critical for Malaysia to have efficient cross-border payment to support trade, says BNM governor. https://www.theedgemarkets.com/article/critical-malaysia-have-efficient-crossborder-payment-support-trade-says-bnm-governor

TokenMinds. (2021). A comprehensive guide for initial dex offering (IDO) marketing 2021. https://tokenminds.co/blog/knowledge-base/a-comprehensive-guide-for-initial-dex-offering-ido-marketing-2021/

UnionBank. (2019). Project i2i case study. https://content.consensys.net/wp-content/uploads/Project-i2i-Case-Study-Client-Ready-JAN2019.pdf

United Nations. (2016). Shaping the future of social protection: Access, financing and solidarity. https://repositorio.cepal.org/bitstream/handle/11362/2807/S2006001_en.pdf?sequence=1&isAllowed=y

United Nations (UN). International day of family remittances - SDGs. https://www.un.org/en/observances/remittances-day/SDGs

United Nations Inter-Agency Task Force on Social and Solidarity Economy (UNTFSSE). (2016). Realizing the 2030 agenda through social and solidarity economy. https://knowledgehub.unsse.org/wp-content/uploads/2019/12/Final_Position-Paper-SSE-and-SDGs_UNTFSSE.pdf

United Nations Research Institute for Social Development (UNRISD). (2015). Social and solidarity finance in between the failure of the microfinance paradigm and the emergence of the universal financial inclusion paradigm. https://www.unrisd.org/ssfworkshop-morvant

United Overseas Bank (UOB). (2016, November 29). Singapore SMEs: Emerging signs of stress. https://www.uobgroup.com/assets/pdfs/research/SME_1q17.pdf

University of California Davis. (2020). What is the current poverty rate in the United States? https://poverty.ucdavis.edu/faq/what-current-poverty-rate-united-states

Ward, O., & Rochemont, S. (2019). Understanding central bank digital currencies (CBDC). Institute and Faculty of Actuaries. https://www.researchgate.net/profile/Sabrina_Rochemont/publication/338792619_Understanding_Central_Bank_Digital_Currencies_CBDC/links/5e2ac22b92851c3aadd5418b/Understanding-Central-Bank-Digital-Currencies-CBDC.pdf

Wazid, M., Zeadally, S., & Das, A. K. (2019). Mobile banking and economic development: Linking adoption, impact, and use. *IEEE Consumer Electronics Magazine, 8*(2), 56–60.

Wired. (2017, July 23). This ultra-secure PC self-destructs if someone messes with it. https://www.wired.com/2017/06/orwl-secure-desktop-computer/

World Atlas. (2018, October 19). How many islands are there in the Philippines? https://www.worldatlas.com/articles/how-many-islands-are-there-in-the-philippines.html

World Bank. (2017, May). Financial inclusion in Malaysia: Distilling lessons for other countries. https://openknowledge.worldbank.org/handle/10986/27543

World Bank. Remittance prices worldwide. https://remittanceprices.worldbank.org/corridor/Singapore/Malaysia

World Bank. (n.d.-a). Financial inclusion data: Malaysia. https://datatopics.worldbank.org/financialinclusion/country/malaysia

World Bank. (n.d.-b). Financial inclusion data: Singapore. https://datatopics.worldbank.org/financialinclusion/country/singapore

World Bank. (n.d.-c). Poverty headcount ratio of Malaysia. https://data.worldbank.org/indicator/SI.POV.NAHC?locations=MY

World Bank Group. (2018). Toward universal financial inclusion in China: Models, challenges, and global lessons. https://openknowledge.worldbank.org/bitstream/handle/10986/29336/FinancialInclusionChinaP158554.pdf?sequence=9&isAllowed=y

World Inequality Labs. (2022). World inequality report 2022. https://wir2022.wid.world/www-site/uploads/2022/03/0098-21_WIL_RIM_RAPPORT_A4.pdf

Index

M. S. Thong, *Blockchain for Financial Governance in Malaysia and Singapore*,
https://doi.org/10.1007/978-981-96-1281-9

FSC
www.fsc.org
MIX
Papier | Fördert
gute Waldnutzung
FSC® C083411

Kolibri 360 GmbH
Ferdinand-Jühlke-Straße 7
99095 Erfurt, Deutschland
produktsicherheit@kolibri360.de